Neuro-Linguistic Programming

Neuro-Linguistic Programming

A Critical Appreciation for Managers and Developers

Paul Tosey
Senior Lecturer, University of Surrey

Jane Mathison
Visiting Fellow, School of Management, University of Surrey

palgrave
macmillan

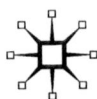

First published 2009 by
PALGRAVE MACMILLAN

Palgrave Macmillan in the UK is an imprint of Macmillan Publishers Limited, registered in England, company number 785998, of Houndmills, Basingstoke, Hampshire RG21 6XS.

Palgrave Macmillan in the US is a division of St Martin's Press LLC, 175 Fifth Avenue, New York, NY 10010.

Palgrave Macmillan is the global academic imprint of the above companies and has companies and representatives throughout the world.

Palgrave® and Macmillan® are registered trademarks in the United States, the United Kingdom, Europe and other countries

ISBN-13: 978-0-230-51603-8   hardback

This book is printed on paper suitable for recycling and made from fully managed and sustained forest sources. Logging, pulping and manufacturing processes are expected to conform to the environmental regulations of the country of origin.

A catalogue record for this book is available from the British Library.

A catalogue record for this book is available from the Library of Congress.

10   9   8   7   6   5   4   3   2   1
18   17   16   15   14   13   12   11   10   09

Printed and bound in Great Britain by
CPI Antony Rowe, Chippenham and Eastbourne

To Sarah, Ellie, Gus, Ailsa and Catriona.

Contents

List of Figures

Acknowledgements

We wish to thank the following people for their help in supplying documents and responding to queries:

Mary Catherine Bateson; Tony Clarkson; Judith DeLozier; Christina Hall; Michael Hall; David Lipset; Isabel Losada; Robert Spitzer; the Bateson archive, University of Santa Cruz; University of Santa Cruz Registry.

Thanks

To Richard Bandler and John Grinder – without your efforts we would have no subject to write about. To Judith DeLozier, who epitomises for us the heart of NLP, and Christina Hall, whose teaching and understanding of language have been inspirational.

Our grateful thanks to the following people, and to anyone else we have neglected to mention who has helped us on this journey:

Suzanne Henwood, Richard Churches, Karen Moxom, Judith Lowe, Charles Faulkner, John Seymour, Judy Rees, Bruce Grimley, Lisa Wake, Trevor Day, Martin Weaver, Christine Miller, Frank Bourke, Susie Linder-Pelz, John Martin, Monique Esser, Dave Allaway, Ranjit Sidhu, Sue White, Josie Gregory, Eugene Sadler-Smith, John Wilson, Chris Rodgers.

The University of Surrey and the Higher Education Academy have both contributed funding that has helped to support this work.

Part I

1
Introduction

Welcome to this critical appreciation of Neuro-Linguistic Programming (NLP). In this first chapter we describe the aims of this book; who is it for, what can you learn from it, where are we coming from as authors, and what you will find when you venture further inside it.

The answer to the question, 'What is NLP?', is in some respects simple. It is an internationally prominent practice in business, management development and professional education, a method used by facilitators of various kinds – coaches, trainers and consultants – who claim to offer some innovative and highly effective approaches to people development. It has been used to train top athletes, salespeople and police forces among others, and it features in a well-known airline's 'flying without fear' course.[1] As Neurolinguistic Psychotherapy (Wake 2008) it is a recognised mode of psychotherapy in the UK. It is used in education (Churches & Terry 2007), healthcare (Henwood & Lister 2007), policing, community work, the arts and more.

In other respects, NLP resembles more of a mystery story.[2] The nature of the field, its origins and its beliefs, can be difficult to pin down. As a movement NLP, which dates back to the 1970s, is seen by some as a relatively young field. Its founders,[3] John Grinder and Richard Bandler, who went their separate ways in 1978 (McLendon 1989), are still alive and active in the field; in 2001, Bostic St. Clair and Grinder (2001:7) spoke of the need for NLP to 'survive its adolescence', and the website of 'NLP Comprehensive'[4] suggests that 'NLP is still in its infancy.' Others see it already dated and passé. It has been said that NLP used to be at least 10 years ahead of its time, but is now more like 20 years behind its time;[5] a colleague even commented, 'I didn't know it was still around'. NLP is also a contested field, one that sometimes draws extreme comment. Critics assert that NLP has been disproven, or that it is 'pseudoscience' (see Chapter 10). An article published in a UK newspaper in 2008 even accused NLP of being the refuge of the 'socially inadequate' (Beadle 2008b).[6]

This book explores both the simplicity and the complexity of NLP.

What are the aims of this book?

Many of the books written about NLP rely on either the marketing hype of those with commercial interests in its promulgation, on the insistence of practitioners that it works because 'they know it works', or upon the polemics of its fiercest critics. While both defence and diatribe are rife, constructive criticism that would help people understand the middle ground and debate the issues in the field is sadly lacking. Yet this is what many existing and potential users say they want and need. Equally, many NLP practitioners express a desire for NLP to go mainstream, and become more accepted.

As NLP practitioners as well as researchers, we have been aware for many years of the need for an approach to NLP that is enquiring, research-based and critical; that can acknowledge the benefits and potential of NLP without 'selling', that can identify drawbacks and blind spots without merely trashing NLP, and that can set out and discuss openly the issues in the field.

Much NLP literature, especially introductory texts, is highly repetitive, consisting of minor variations in ways of presenting a very similar body of ideas and practices. These texts describe and illustrate the contents of NLP, but seldom dig beneath the surface to question their validity, or examine issues; in the field of coaching see for example McDermott and Jago (2002), among others. The main exceptions to this, two volumes that do provide a scholarly commentary on NLP (Esser 2004; Walker 1996), are not published in the English language.[7]

That is the gap that our book aims to fill. Specifically, we aim to address questions that many people ask about the field, such as:

- What is NLP?
- Where and for what can I best use it?

- What is it based on?
- Where did it come from?
- Why is it sometimes so hard to grasp what it's about?
- Is there any research behind it?
- Does it have any theory?
- How can the claims made by practitioners be assessed?
- Is it a 'pseudoscience'?
- Why doesn't NLP seem to be interested in emotions?
- Is it manipulative?
- Is NLP a cult?
- What does it offer to HRD?

By addressing these questions we examine the contemporary issues in the field, presenting and weighing up the arguments to inform users and practitioners alike.

In doing this, we have aimed to be thorough and scholarly in our referencing, not merely to observe convention but especially to make the trail of clues through which we have interpreted the mystery of NLP available to readers. It is important to identify sources of materials and opinions in a field that is flooded with second and third-hand versions of its stories, principles and models.

Headlines

Overall we develop a view of NLP as an emergent, practical, and diverse knowledge system. What are the headline messages arising from that view?

- NLP offers a highly pragmatic and accessible approach to communication and people development that can help with a wide variety of needs for effective performance, change and learning;
- At its best NLP represents a distinctive, innovative cross-disciplinary synthesis of knowledge about human communication, especially in the subtlety of its understandings of the relationships between language, our inner worlds, and behaviour;
- NLP is often presented as if it sprang, fully-formed, from California in the 1970s, in isolation from social, cultural and historical contexts and influences. The nature of NLP as a social movement and a community of practice is under-examined;

- Contrary to what many NLP practitioners espouse, NLP *is* based on theory, but that theory is poorly articulated. Some of the ideas used within NLP exist in an intellectual time warp, so that it is prone to being both out of date and out of touch with contemporary knowledge;
- The field lacks a thorough evidence base. However, this is true also of many 'people development' practices. NLP has also lacked a research ethos, leaving it over-reliant on claims that self-evidently 'it works' and prone to operating as a self-sealing belief system;
- The prevalence of concern about the motives of practitioners is worrying. We argue that NLP *per se* is not manipulative, and there are many people using NLP in a highly ethical and sensitive way. There are also perfectly satisfactory ethical codes of conduct in the field. However we think NLP is characterised by a need to develop its ethical reasoning;
- We argue that there is also a need to revisit the designation 'practitioner', given the variations in forms and durations of training courses and the primarily commercial, self-regulated nature of the field;
- On the other hand, NLP offers a radical challenge to any form of people development through its insights into the ways in which language communicates with the unconscious, and therefore inevitably influences people. This raises a significant dimension of ethical practice that is ignored or denied by many other schools of thought;
- Altogether, we argue that NLP is at a crossroads in its development. It is a widespread field, with practitioners across the globe, that offers many benefits; yet it remains poorly linked to the world of research, and is regarded with suspicion by many people.

There are a number of things this book does not attempt:

- It is not an introductory text. There are many books available that provide this, for example, 'Magic of NLP Demystified' (Lewis & Pucelik 1990).
- It is not a 'how to' book. Reading this book is no substitute for learning NLP experientially. It is practical in the sense that it is a book about how to think systematically about NLP, and we see effective thinking as very much a part of what NLP is about.

- It is neither a polemic against NLP, nor a defence. We seek to be objective about its innovations and potential, and we also challenge the field where we feel challenge is merited.
- It is a perspective on NLP, not 'chapter and verse'. We don't claim to know NLP better than its leading practitioners, authors and developers. Ultimately, this appraisal represents our personal view of the field, one that co-exists with others and that we hope will encourage debate.

Who is it for?

Our own field of research is people development in business and adult education. Primarily therefore we are writing for:

- Human resource development (HRD) professionals, including consultants, coaches, trainers, facilitators and educators, who are seeking an informed understanding of NLP. Wilson (2005:3) describes HRD as representing 'the latest evolutionary stage in the long tradition of training, educating and developing people for the purpose of contributing towards the achievement of individual, organizational and societal objectives', and NLP is part of this stage.
- NLP practitioners in business and adult education in particular, and practitioners in general, (though we are not attempting to address specific issues that arise in psychotherapy, healthcare or school education).
- Any potential user or client of NLP and its services in these fields, including decision-makers in people development (managers, entrepreneurs, HR directors) who are considering investing time or money in NLP-based services.
- Researchers, of whom there are a growing number at doctoral level across the globe, students (most likely postgraduate), and trainees on relevant academic and professional courses.

What is our stance, and what qualifies us to write this book?

Who are we to offer these views?

We are academics who have extensive training in and experience of NLP,[8] professional educators working in the field of management learning and human resource development (HRD), as teachers and as researchers. As practitioners we use NLP in coaching and training, as well as in daily life. We have both contributed to introducing NLP into Higher Education,[9] and have published on NLP in academic journals (Tosey & Mathison 2003; Mathison & Tosey 2008), with a particular interest in how NLP can be used as a research tool. We have encouraged research in NLP and in 2008 we hosted the First International NLP Research Conference at the University of Surrey.

This gives us a privileged as well as precarious position as we are familiar both intellectually and experientially with NLP, and are not dispassionate about the subject. We are informed by our own engagement with NLP in practice through its courses, conferences, networks and communities over some twenty years. For this book we have read the NLP literature extensively, as well as related literatures, and had many conversations with key informants, including experts in the field as well as people not trained in NLP who have told of their encounters with it. Our ambition is to pursue the questions we have posed, to inform readers and to contribute to the creation of a research agenda for the field.

Chapter outlines

Part I

Part I sets the scene for the book with an introduction to the nature of NLP as a movement and as a practice.

Chapter 1: Introduction

This chapter has set out the aims of the book and our approach.

Chapter 2: What is NLP?

In this chapter we present our map of the 'six faces' of NLP. Rather than attempting a single definition, we view NLP as having multiple identities. In conclusion we offer a condensed working description of the practice.

Chapter 3: Organisational Applications of NLP

This chapter explores the incidence of NLP in business, and highlights its relevance to and potential for managers and developers, illustrated through brief examples.

Part II

Part II offers an extended treatment of the conventional story of NLP and its development through time, identifying key influences on its ideas and practices.

Chapter 4: The Road to Santa Cruz

This chapter outlines the social context in which NLP developed. It highlights the role of Robert S. Spitzer, M.D. in Richard Bandler's enquiries into the practices of Fritz Perls and Virginia Satir, and describes the early career of John Grinder.

Chapter 5: Discovering the Language of Change

In this chapter we describe what happened after Bandler and Grinder met at Kresge College, University of Santa Cruz, and how the collaboration between them and various colleagues led to the initial NLP publications. We review, and discuss the need for reappraisal of, the chief product of this phase, the NLP 'meta-model'.

Chapter 6: Exploring Inner Landscapes

A distinctive feature of NLP is its way of exploring internal worlds and their role in human functioning. Through this, the initial focus of NLP on language extended into non-verbal behaviour and the sensory structures of people's inner landscapes.

Chapter 7: The Influences of Erickson and the Palo Alto Institute

We consider NLP as one of a number of practices influenced by constructivism, a notable stream of twentieth century thought, especially through the respective influences of Milton H. Erickson, M.D., and the Palo Alto Mental Research Institute.

Chapter 8: Gregory Bateson and Cybernetics

Here we elaborate on the influence of a seminal figure, Gregory Bateson, especially through his involvement in the emergence of cybernetics through the Macy Conferences in the USA in the 1940s and 1950s. We contend that NLP as a knowledge system is founded intellectually on cybernetics, both in principle and through its lineage.

Chapter 9: The Presuppositions of NLP

In this chapter we discuss the principles often said to underpin NLP, known as 'presuppositions', and re-examine their sources. We identify a potentially significant feature that appears to be missing from most formulations of the presuppositions.

Part III

In Part III we pose a series of critical questions about NLP. These represent and address the main issues that have obscured or complicated NLP.

Chapter 10: Useful Versus True – Theory, Knowledge, and the Question of Pseudoscience

NLP typically emphasises what is useful over what is true; indeed there is a view among some practitioners that 'theory' is irrelevant to NLP. It is also charged by some authors with being a 'pseudoscience'. We discuss beliefs about the relevance of theory in NLP, and explore the relationship between the NLP and academic world as divergent communities of practice.

Chapter 11: What Does Research Say About NLP?

This chapter asks what research has to say about NLP. How much research is there into NLP, of what kinds, and what conclusions can be drawn from this? NLP appears to be over-reliant on the repetition of anecdotes or the volubility of practitioners' assertions that 'it works', yet potential support for its outlook can be found in fields such as cognitive linguistics and neuroscience.

Chapter 12: NLP and Ethics – Outcome, Ecology and Integrity

This chapter surveys key issues relevant to the ethics of NLP, given a common impression that it is 'manipulative'. We indicate that codes of ethics exist in the field, and argue that NLP *per se* is not unethical. A gap in the field is the need for more explicit ethical reasoning. On the other hand, NLP's notion that 'all communication is hypnosis' raises an ethical challenge for the use of language by practitioners in all forms of people development.

Chapter 13: NLP as Situated – Cultural Practices and Discourses

Finally in Part III, we identify various values that infuse NLP and its discourse, including ideas such as 'freedom' and the pursuit of 'excellence'. These elements of NLP as a whole appear to derive from its cultural milieu rather than from the central theories of cybernetics and constructivism.

Part IV

In Part IV we synthesise and review our arguments and revisit our questions about NLP and its future.

Chapter 14: Synthesis

Here we summarise our answers to the questions listed at the start of chapter 1. What are we saying to our audience, and what are the implications for managers and developers?

Chapter 15: Quo Vadis?

If NLP is at a crossroads, where does it go from here? We indicate three possible directions branching out from the present, one of which is a way forward based on a research agenda.

Appendices

Timeline of NLP

An historical sequence of dates and events relevant to NLP.

The NLP industry

Summarises the structure of NLP training.

Web links

Links to sources of research interest.

References

A full listing of the published sources consulted for this book.

2
What is NLP? The 'Six Faces' of the Field

NLP has proved difficult to define neatly. Various definitions exist, some enigmatic, some pithy, and some apparently competing. For example, it has been described as an attitude of curiosity, as 'the art and science of excellence' (O'Connor & Seymour 1990:17), as 'the study of the structure of subjective experience' (Dilts *et al* 1980), and more. Virtually all the definitions found in the literature have been generated by people working within NLP and, as Young (2004:60) points out, these perform a variety of functions. In contrast, Isabel Losada, who has written about her experiences of a variety of personal development and self-help methods, encapsulates NLP as 'variations on "learn how to feel great"' (Losada 2001:194).

We resist the idea that NLP should be reduced to a single definition. How, then, can a reader new to the field gain enough sense of what NLP is all about to engage with the practice? To fulfil this need we describe our map of the field, which suggests that NLP has not one, but six main 'faces'.[1]

About the title...

Before we introduce that map, what does NLP's title denote? The phrase 'Neuro-Linguistic Programming' does not appear in a published work until 1979 (Bandler and Grinder's 'Frogs Into Princes').[2] One story goes that Bandler and Grinder created it with their tongues firmly in their cheeks, and that its quasi-academic obscurity is intentionally mischievous. NLP is certainly not formally part of any established academic discipline; however, its constituent terms are neither random nor lacking entirely in connection to formal study. They use, for example, terms that resemble the interests of renowned psychologist George A. Miller (cognitive neuroscience and psycholinguistics). One of the founders, John Grinder, spent a year at Rockefeller University, where Miller was a Professor from 1968 until 1979 (Hirst 1988:269). The term 'neuro-linguistic' was, we believe, first used by Alfred Korzybski (1941:xxxix) in the 1930s, a thinker whose work appears to have been introduced to NLP's founders by Gregory Bateson (see Chapter 7).

Dilts *et al* (1980:2) offer an explanation of the title:

> For us, behaviour is programmed by combining and sequencing neural system representations – sights, sounds, feelings, smells and tastes – whether that behaviour involves making a decision, throwing a football, smiling at a member of the opposite sex, visualizing the spelling of a word or teaching physics. A given input stimulus is processed through a sequence of internal representations, and a specific behavioural outcome is generated.
>
> "Neuro" (derived from the Greek neuron for nerve) stands for the fundamental tenet that all behaviour is the result of neurological processes. "Linguistic" (derived from the Latin lingua for language) indicates that neural processes are represented, ordered and sequenced into models and strategies through language and communication systems. "Programming" refers to the process of organizing the components of a system (sensory representations in this case) to achieve specific outcomes.

The six faces of NLP

Our map of six faces is based on three main aspects that we believe characterise the field. These 'three P's' are:

- Practice: NLP as a behaviour, or practical communication – what people do;
- Philosophy: NLP as a body of ideas and principles;
- Product: NLP as a commodity that can be consumed.

These three aspects and their combinations give rise to the six faces shown on the diagram (Figure 2.1), numbered to reflect broadly the

Figure 2.1   The Six Faces of NLP

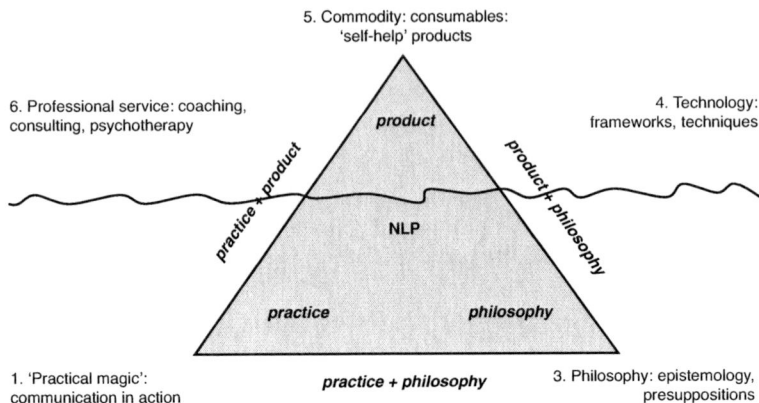

5. Commodity: consumables: 'self-help' products

6. Professional service: coaching, consulting, psychotherapy

4. Technology: frameworks, techniques

product

NLP

practice

philosophy

1. 'Practical magic': communication in action

practice + philosophy

3. Philosophy: epistemology, presuppositions

Source: © Paul Tosey & Jane Mathison 2009

way NLP has developed through time (though this is not intended as a precise chronology).

An important feature of the map is that, metaphorically, it represents NLP as an iceberg. The three faces above the waterline are more overt, and more immediately apparent to people encountering NLP afresh. The identities below the surface are less obvious, yet they comprise the main substance of the field.

Describing those six faces now will serve as an introduction to, and an overview of, the field. It will also raise numerous issues that are taken up in later chapters of this book.

'Practical Magic'[3]

NLP is essentially a 'model of human communication and behavior' (Bandler & Grinder 1979:3). Dilts *et al* (1980:preface ii) call it 'the unexpected byproduct of the collaboration of John Grinder and Richard Bandler to formalize impactful patterns of communication'. This collaboration began in the 1970s through their curiosity about how the skills of certain excellent psychotherapists, such as the influential family therapist Virginia Satir, differed from those of people who were less effective. This is a story we will describe in detail in Part II.

Those skills, which most observers regarded as 'magic', or as some unfathomable, innate ability, appeared to Bandler and Grinder to have both a structure and logic, which would enable other people to learn them; hence the titles of the first two NLP books, 'The Structure of Magic'.

NLP has gone on to identify the structure of many other naturally occurring patterns, especially strategies used by successful people. Consequently, in promotional literature NLP is often described in terms such as 'the art and science of human excellence in the areas of communicating, influencing, goal setting, managing change and understanding the use of effective language'.[4] NLP does not invent these patterns; it identifies them, strips them down to their essentials, sometimes refining and repackaging them, and makes them available for others to learn. Thus 'Neuro linguistic programming ... is the study of what works in thinking, language and behavior (*sic*). It is a way of coding and reproducing excellence that enables you to consistently achieve the results that you want both for yourself, for your business, and for your life' (Knight 2002:1).

In one sense, therefore, NLP is a collection of naturally occurring patterns of effective behaviour and communication that have been made explicit. This has given rise to the suggestion that 'if it works it's NLP' (e.g. reported by McNab 2005:17), a claim that understandably annoys people who perceive that methods developed in other fields have become appropriated by NLP on this basis. What it does indicate is that NLP offers a perspective that can be applied to all human communication, such as experiencing, learning, and so on; and that the focus of interest of NLP is, typically, 'what works'.

This also means that NLP is highly eclectic in that it draws from many diverse fields of practice; we have likened it previously to a gryphon (Tosey & Mathison 2007), a fabulous beast that is (usually) part-lion, part-eagle and part-horse. As one example, NLP is sometimes regarded as a form of accelerated learning. It has similarities to practices such as Suggestopedia, there is literature that investigates these connections (e.g. Sandhu 1994), and for a time there was much interest in photo-reading or speed reading in NLP. However, accelerated learning is a separate field of enquiry.

Dilts *et al* (1980:preface i) say that 'it could be described as an extension of linguistics, neurology, or psychology'. Our colleague Richard Churches told us of his experience working with psychologists who were initially very sceptical of NLP, yet came to realise that it offered ways of utilising knowledge of (say) behavioural conditioning that they knew as theory but had not imagined could be applied in their everyday lives. This example illustrates some of the difficulty of defining NLP's boundaries because much of the *content* of this knowledge already existed in formal psychology. What NLP supplied was an assumption that this knowledge could be applicable in practice, and offered a way of understanding how to do this.

Methodology

How did the founders of NLP identify those naturally occurring skills, and test them to ensure they had captured them effectively? They developed a method of study, which became known as 'modelling'. This gives us the second face of NLP, which is often portrayed as its essence. In fact the founders originally described NLP as a methodology (Bandler & Grinder 1975b:6), and continue to emphasise modelling as the core of the practice (Bostic St. Clair & Grinder 2001:271; Bandler 2008b:xv).

If NLP is a kind of reverse engineering, applied to human capabilities, then modelling is the procedure by which it works. It is 'the mapping of tacit knowledge into explicit knowledge' (Bostic St. Clair & Grinder 2001:271), a process that investigates the language patterns, behaviours, sequences of thought, and internal imagery that exponents use. This is why NLP is sometimes described as a form of 'study', as in 'the study of the structure of subjective experience'[5] (Dilts, Grinder, Bandler & DeLozier 1980), although its purpose is firmly pragmatic:

> The objective of the NLP modeling process is not to end up with the one 'right' or 'true' description of a particular person's thinking process, but rather to make an instrumental map that allows us to apply the strategies that we have modelled in some useful way (Dilts 1998:30).

An example of a naturally occurring skill that has been modelled in NLP is spelling. The strategy used by people who are good at spelling (e.g. Bandler & Grinder 1979:33) in essence involves three main steps:

1. visualise the word in your mind's eye
2. spell it out to yourself (i.e. not out loud)

3. check whether it is correct through feeling (e.g. a gut sense of whether it is right or not).

This sequence can be learnt by adults and children alike. Even though it is 'quite widely accepted that good spellers use internal word pictures as part of their spelling strategy' (Churches & Terry 2007:159), a phonic approach to spelling, which from an NLP perspective is likely to be a highly ineffective strategy, persists in various forms. As O'Connor and Seymour say, 'Wun wunders why foenick spelling methods arr still tort in skools' (1990:184).

The first book that describes how to model in detail is Dilts *et al*'s 'NLP Volume 1' (1980). Leslie Cameron-Bandler and her colleagues produced and wrote about a variant called 'Mental Aptitude Patterning' (Cameron-Bandler, Gordon & Lebeau 1985) . A helpful, contemporary practical guide to modelling is that by Gordon and Dawes (2005:3),[6] who for example apply these principles to identify how someone creates the experience of 'being passionate about something'.

The nature of modelling is contested within NLP today. Robert Dilts (1998) emphasises a more conscious approach that employs conceptual frameworks to analyse the activity that is being modelled, whilst Bostic St. Clair and Grinder (2001) argue that modelling is essentially an unconscious assimilation of an exemplar's capability. Dilts has used his version of the method to model a number of 'strategies of genius', based largely on an analysis of the language patterns used by historical figures such as Albert Einstein (Dilts 1994a; Dilts 1994b). One such strategy reflects the creative process used by Walt Disney, based on Disney's description of how he created stories, comprising three functions that Dilts termed 'dreamer', 'realist' and 'critic'.

In practice these two modes are often used in combination, and the validity of the distinction between them made in 'Whispering in the Wind' has been challenged by Steve Andreas (Andreas 2006a).[7] Argument about which constitutes 'true' modelling may be largely a red herring, reflecting the internal politics of NLP. Among the more significant questions that could help to develop the potential of this methodology are the extent to which modelling works – since the evidence for it is largely anecdotal – and the validity of its assumptions about human functioning, especially the idea that anyone can learn to reproduce another person's excellent performance.

Philosophy

Whilst the relevance of theory to NLP is often questioned within the field (see Chapter 10), it is clearly based on underlying ideas and views of the world. For example the belief that one *can* 'model' patterns of excellent behaviour is itself a kind of theory. These ideas often appear in NLP literature as a set of 'presuppositions', or working principles; for example, 'the meaning of your communication is the response that you get'. We explore the presuppositions in detail in Chapter 9; suffice to say here that virtually all the presuppositions pre-date NLP. So, while NLP's world view offers a particular synthesis of these sources, one can also locate NLP within the context of certain streams of twentieth century thought and practice. This counters the impression that NLP was somehow created out of thin air in the 1970s, or that it was wholly original, and makes it easier to engage with its ideas.

NLP's philosophy draws from two main areas of thought. The first is cybernetics, a cross-disciplinary view of how systems are organised based on feedback that was developed in the 1940s and 1950s, and in which Gregory Bateson was a core figure (see Chapter 8). The second is constructivism (see Chapter 7). Essentially this says that people cannot know 'reality' *per se*, so inevitably they act according to the constructions that they create. Constructivism arrives in NLP largely via the work of the Palo Alto Mental Research Institute in the 1960s, in which Bateson was also centrally involved.

We will argue in Chapter 9 that nearly all NLP's presuppositions can be traced back to these two areas, via the espoused philosophy of the figures whose practice NLP originally studied (i.e. Virginia Satir, Fritz Perls and Milton H. Erickson) and through the link with Gregory Bateson. Together, cybernetics and constructivism provide a particular approach to what we can know, and to how the world of communication functions. This is what Bateson refers to as an 'epistemology', a term found frequently in NLP literature.

To illustrate what epistemology is about, the question 'what colour is your front door?' elicits interest in the *content* of the response, a piece of information (e.g. 'red'); the question '*how do you know* that your front door is red?' is interested in the *process* of knowing, or of *how* you arrive at the response 'red' (you might, for example, have referred to a visual image of closing your front door as you went out this morning, said to yourself 'it's red', and confirmed this with a feeling of being right). NLP is interested primarily in this approach to knowing – not what we know, or what the world is 'really' like, but instead *how* we know. Based on this, NLP then explores how we may be able to change the world of our experience.

Finally, it is important to note that NLP has gone on to make use of knowledge from outside Western scientific traditions too, especially in DeLozier and Grinder's (1987) reformulation of NLP as 'New Code' in the 1980s. That book was strongly influenced, for example, by Carlos Castaneda's series about (ostensibly) the system of knowledge of Yaqui Indian sorcerers (e.g. Castaneda 1970),[8] as well as by experiences of Congolese drumming. Bateson figures again, for example through reference to his anthropological work in Bali, where he developed ideas about art as a form of knowledge (e.g. Bateson 2000a:128–152).[9]

Technology

Modelling excellent practitioners yielded certain insights into the skills and patterns of human communication. These insights became coded as various frameworks, strategies, procedures and techniques that can be learnt and used by other people. NLP's fourth 'face' is therefore as a form of practical knowledge, a *technology* comprising a wide range of models and tools that are presented in the copious popular literature and are taught in NLP training programmes. Some of the major NLP models are concerned with language patterns.

The technology of NLP can be used in many different ways. The following types of applications are common in business; (we summarise literature about known business applications in the following chapter):

- Modelling 'excellence'; this is a way of 'reverse engineering' human capabilities, that can identify the keys to excellent practice and enable others to learn how to do it themselves;
- Designing and refining outcomes, ranging from broad visions to very specific goals, and understanding the resources needed to achieve them;
- Exploring and improving communication skills (verbal and non-verbal; spoken and written);
- Increasing self-awareness (e.g. of one's behaviour patterns, of one's internal world of imagery and self-talk, and so on);

- Coaching for performance, for example to improve specific behaviours and skills, and to increase confidence and flexibility;
- Overcoming limiting beliefs, perceptions and/or patterns of behaviour.

The techniques of NLP have become voluminous. Reliable practical introductions for managers can be found in books such as those by Knight (2002), Molden (2001) and many more. Another by Churches and Terry (2007), while written for teachers, also provides an informed and lively introduction that is likely to be helpful to any professional wishing to understand more about NLP.

The tools found in NLP are to be used 'as-if' they were true, and which can be modified or rejected if they are found to be ineffective in practice. Its technology consists, in that sense, of *heuristics* – practical, working theorems. This practical, applied emphasis is often attractive to managers.

NLP's heuristics are also provisional in the sense that while there is again much anecdotal evidence about the usefulness of NLP, there is little in the way of formal evidence that demonstrates the efficacy of its claims to the public. Here we are thinking not so much of the hard-boiled sceptic who demands scientific proof for everything, more of reasonable people who are interested in the types of solutions that NLP may offer, yet who would not accept sales claims at face value. We will examine the research evidence relating to NLP in Chapter 10.

Commodity

In the late 1970s, as the range of frameworks and techniques generated by NLP grew, there was a shift from addressing the primarily psychotherapeutic audience of 'The Structure of Magic' towards making NLP available to the public at large. There is reference to NLP workshops and seminars being given in the US in 1977 by Byron Lewis (Lewis & Pucelik 1990:161) and by Robert Dilts and Terence McLendon (McLendon 1989:100). According to Merlevede (2000:63), the first practitioner and master practitioner programmes were created not by Bandler and Grinder, but by Leslie Cameron, David Gordon and Robert Dilts at 'the first NLP Institute, DOTAR (Division of Training and Research)'. McLendon (1989:113) refers to 'Not Ltd.', run by Richard Bandler, Leslie Cameron-Bandler and associates, offering training and developments workshops in 1978.

A central feature of NLP, therefore, is that its identity has evolved from asking questions (how does this work?) to offering solutions (this is how to help people change!). We regard the point at which its knowledge became packaged and sold as a system of trainings, and related artefacts such as books and audio tapes,[10] as pivotal in NLP's development. On the one hand, NLP's developers deserve credit for being excellent entrepreneurs, and for making NLP widely available rather than restricting it to the exclusive domain of established professionals. On the other hand the commercialisation of NLP seems to have had the effect of taking it further away from academic research, and of leaving purchasers free to use these powerful tools in any way they wished.

NLP training rapidly became a global phenomenon. In Europe, for example, the Austrian Training Center for NLP was founded in 1984 (Schütz 1994:49); NLP is also very popular in France, where it is known as PNL (La Programmation Neuro Linguistique). In 1990 O'Connor and Seymour (1990:201–211) listed NLP trainings in seventeen countries across four continents, North America, South America, Europe and Australia; in 2007 a practitioner training took place in India.[11] In the UK, the longest established training organisations were founded in the mid to late 1980s.[12] In 2008, more than 50 training schools were operating in the UK alone.[13] To indicate the number of certificated trainers worldwide, the website of the International NLP Trainers' Association refers to having held 40 Trainer Trainings since 2000 (and several before).

NLP now involves a large number of practitioners across the world, as well as commercial training providers, membership bodies and other organisations, conferences, discussion groups, websites, practice groups, and a wide range of publications and artefacts. It is difficult to place a figure on the number of NLP practitioners. We estimate, bearing in mind that such courses have been offered since the 1980s, and that there are many providers, that a figure of some 30,000 UK-trained NLP practitioners in the 20 years from 1985 to 2005 is not unrealistic.[14] It may be a conservative estimate; for example, O'Connor and Seymour claimed in 1990 that 100,000 people in the USA had 'done some form of NLP training' (O'Connor & Seymour 1990:23), and a profile of John Grinder on an Irish NLP training organisation's website states that globally some 20,000 people each year attend NLP seminars.[15]

NLP training is a highly competitive commercial market. It includes organisations that act both as training providers and as essentially self-appointed authorities that regulate their own particular brand of NLP certification, both directly and through other affiliated training organizations.[16, 17] For example, the website of the International NLP Trainers' Association stipulates that 'only NLP Trainers who attended an INLPTA Trainers Training are able to become members of INLPTA'.[18] A 'Consumer's Guide' to NLP training written by Connirae and Steve Andreas refers bluntly to 'commercial enterprises masquerading as professional organizations', and emphasises that 'NLP is a completely non-regulated area'.[19]

One different kind of NLP association, which attempts to put forward an independent view in the sense that it neither offers training programmes nor authorises certificates, nor is affiliated to any organisation that does so, is the UK-based Association for NLP (ANLP). Now established formally as a community interest company, it is 'dedicated to making NLP more accessible to the general public'.[20] Membership is voluntary, by subscription; practitioners who are members agree to be governed by the ANLP Code of Ethics and are encouraged to participate in their continuing professional development.[21]

The Professional Guild of NLP, an association of training organisations, was initiated in 2003 by 'a group of established NLP Training Providers' who shared an in-principle commitment to quality based on the minimum standard of 120 hours direct training, in no fewer than 18 days, for an NLP practitioner level.

Given that NLP can be seen as a commodity, some events concerning intellectual property rights in the field are relevant. In 1997, Richard Bandler initiated court action in California to assert certain rights in relation to NLP. His claims were not supported; the outcome of that action is detailed in an article by Christina Hall (Hall 2001). A release agreement issued as part of that action is reproduced in 'Whispering in the Wind' (Bostic St. Clair & Grinder 2001:376–381). In parallel, Tony Clarkson, a UK practitioner, applied to the English courts to revoke Bandler's registered trademark 'NLP'. Clarkson, who took the action as an individual but with support from NLP practitioners internationally, succeeded in 1998. This means effectively that in England and Wales 'NLP' has been declared a generic term, and it cannot therefore be trademarked.[22]

Professional service

In evolutionary terms the final face of NLP to have emerged is that of a professional service. This is ironic because, in its early days, NLP's founders emphasised its identity as a methodology that existed at one remove from the modes of psychotherapy (e.g. Gestalt) that it investigated. For example, the founders were reluctant to create the kind of belief system or 'theology' (Bandler & Grinder 1979:5) that, in their view, characterised and hampered psychology.

Today, people who have trained in NLP offer their services as executive coaches, sports coaches, consultants, trainers, psychotherapists and more. NLP can be the overt method of practice used by coaches and psychotherapists who are accredited by bodies in their respective fields.[23]

Beyond this, it may be difficult to identify exactly when, where and how NLP is being used in a professional service. Ponting (2006) identified that it is common for practitioners in business to use NLP without naming it as such. Several reasons were apparent. Sometimes practitioners were anxious that NLP could have negative connotations for clients. The word 'programming' in particular is one that many people, not just those in business, find off-putting; for example, 'I have always been wary of "programming" approaches to human development' (Mike Pedler, foreword to Molden 2003:xi). A second reason was a desire to avoid jargon. As remarked above, NLP is difficult to define. Also, for managers whose learning style preferences (Honey & Mumford 1992) are for pragmatism and action, the title appears quite theoretical – perhaps ironic in view of NLP practitioners' emphasis on what is useful and their apparent disdain for theory. Business clients typically are more interested in what a practitioner can do, and the results they can achieve, than in the theory behind a practice. For example, 'I tend to use an NLP approach and work with NLP techniques without direct reference to NLP at all – I rarely label the techniques I use in coaching' (Hayes 2006:3). Furthermore NLP can be used effectively in a conversational way, without need for its terminology to be introduced or explained. A third reason is that NLP is used by many practitioners as just one ingredient in an eclectic form of practice. They have no objection to making their use of NLP explicit, but it would be inaccurate to suggest that their approach was exclusively NLP. Finally, we are aware personally of cases where NLP has been applied extensively, yet the client organisation has insisted that their use of NLP must not be made public.

Conclusion: A working description of NLP

These six faces are, of course, not distinct in practice. Potential clients with their desires, casual viewers with their curiosities, and sceptics with their questions, all of whom experience NLP from (as it were) the outside, may encounter any of these faces, and any combination of them; similarly, those people who constitute the community of NLP may be engaged with any or all of them.[24]

Having begun this chapter with the question 'What is NLP?', and suggested that it has six diverse faces, we end with a potential working description of the practice:

> NLP is interested in **how** people communicate, perform skills and create experiences through patterns of thought and behaviour, mediated by language. NLP helps people create more preferable and useful (to them) experiences of the world, typically by attending to and modifying those patterns of thought and behaviour.

Here, as we shall discover in subsequent chapters, both 'thought' and 'behaviour' involve language in significant ways, as well as internal imagery, emotion and physiology.[25] One of NLP's distinctive features is its insights into language and its role in sense-making. It encourages the exploration of people's inner worlds, and assumes that communication, experience and performance all involve mechanisms of perception that operate outside people's conscious awareness.

According to this description, people who use NLP as practitioners have been introduced to both (a) a systematic approach to communication, and (b) methods through which it is possible to understand and influence the way people create their experience. Accordingly NLP practitioners, in whatever field they may operate, can be thought of as offering two generic services. The first is to identify how an existing outcome or effect is achieved through particular combinations of people's language, thought and behaviour. The second is to facilitate people who wish to enhance their existing behaviour and skills, or to change something they dislike about their experience, to learn relevant new combinations of thought and behaviour that will be both effective and respectful for the client and their environment. Practitioners achieve this by using language and communications skilfully and flexibly.

In the next chapter we review some of the ways in which NLP has been applied in organisational settings.

3
Organisational Applications of NLP

This chapter is an exploration of some of the ways in which NLP has been applied in organisational settings to enhance performance, drawing on our own personal experiences and published accounts. We give a brief overview of some of the ways in which NLP has been applied in organisational settings, ending with a discussion of coaching.

NLP in business: Visibility and invisibility

While NLP initially studied psychotherapists, other applications soon emerged. Because NLP is about human communication in general, its potential applications in organisations are endless. Sue Knight (Knight 1995) presciently anticipated the 'personal development explosion' in business, and wrote of NLP's potential for helping to develop learning organisations.

How much NLP is *actually* used in the business environment, and what is the evidence? While both of us have heard stories of how leading NLP trainers and innovators have used NLP in well known multi-national organisations, documented applications of NLP in organisational settings are sparse in comparison with the volume of anecdotes.

Practitioners use NLP in training (Yemm 2006), leadership development (Deering, Dilts & Russell 2002), and extensively in coaching (Grimley 2007; Linder-Pelz & Hall 2007; McDermott & Jago 2002; McLeod 2003; O'Connor & Lages 2004). Other examples of practitioners' accounts can be found in NLP magazines such as 'Rapport' and

'The Model'; the ANLP website[1] has cited applications in organisations that include Astra Zeneca, British Telecom, and Towergate Insurance. In the media, The Times has reported benefits of NLP training as experienced by PA's;[2] Fran Abrams, writing in the Times Educational Supplement in 2004, mentioned NLP courses being run for BBC staff.[3] The UK Chartered Institute of Personnel and Development includes NLP course in its training programme.[4]

The literature on NLP in academic HRD journals is minimal. Of these, an article by Dowlen (1996) attempts a critical review of NLP and its relevance to management learning. Von Bergen *et al* (1997) review NLP and other alternative training techniques from a scientific perspective. Thompson *et al* (2002) report an attempt to evaluate the impact over time of NLP training on sales and customer care in hospitality in Northern Ireland. Their findings are interesting in that, according to the measures chosen, benefits evident at six weeks after training appear largely to tail off after six months.

It is possible to indicate how NLP is used in organisations, therefore, though it is difficult to offer much in the way of evidence for its effectiveness. The sources above probably underestimate the usage of NLP. As reviewed in the previous chapter, for various reasons it is common for practitioners in business to use NLP without naming it as such. Similarly, theories and approaches derived from NLP have seeped into business and management literature, where techniques and the ideas behind them may be presented with little or no reference to their origins in NLP, leaving it less visible and acknowledged than it might be.

Yardley's 'Business Confidence' (1995) is one such case. Yardley, an NLP trainer,[5] includes references to the writings of Bandler and Grinder, Dilts, and Gregory Bateson in his bibliography, though the book itself consists mainly of formulaic advice on how to achieve more success with others in the business environment.

The first example of this phenomenon, ironically, was probably John Grinder's own adaptation of the core NLP language model for the business market, for which it was renamed 'The Precision Model' (McMaster & Grinder 1980). The book refers to its contents as the 'technology of management', and it carries a foreword from Dr. Paul Hersey of the Centre for Leadership Studies, who with Kenneth Blanchard (of 'One Minute Manager' fame) developed the well-known model of Situational Leadership. Interestingly, in relation to issues of the relationship between NLP and academic world, Hersey refers to the Precision Model as a 'useful theory' (McMaster & Grinder 1980:v). This volume offers a primer in some basics of NLP, but nowhere do the authors use the title 'Neuro-Linguistic Programming' or refer to Bandler and Grinder's previous publications. Its closest brush with this title is on the book jacket, which suggests that there is a need for management development theories to keep pace with 'breakthroughs' in fields including 'neuro-psychology'.

NLP can be applied to selling, to improving communication skills of all kinds, and to increasing confidence in one's own abilities. It can, and has been, to our knowledge, applied to goal setting, self-management, presentation skills, negotiation, leadership, team building, and interviewing. The following sections illustrate some of the typical applications.

Goal-setting

When Unipart managed a turnaround of its business against all market predictions, it did a number of things. One was to change the way that it ran meetings. Managers recognized that the emphasis in their meetings previously had been on problems, even though they were nominally called progress meetings. They acknowledged that they did not consider or imagine what they really wanted from their meetings or their projects prior to considering how to get there. So they began every meeting with a discussion of what they did really want – an outcome. (Knight 2002:280)

This example illustrates the NLP principle that when we change the language we use, we can change how we make sense of a situation, and also how we then act. Here, what Knight describes is a re-categorisation, or 'reframing' (Bandler & Grinder 1982) of the events under discussion from *problem* to *outcome*.

Secondly, the focus also switches from the present situation to the future, and enables people to construct a representation of what is wanted in recognisable and concrete terms. The kinds of questions that help people to identify the specific actions and resources needed to make their goals achievable are part of NLP's collection of language patterns.

This emphasis on the importance of paying attention to future outcomes, and how they are to be achieved, is characteristic of NLP. It is very 'outcome oriented'; it encourages managers to construct a clear image of their goals as and when they have been achieved, using whatever senses (seeing, hearing, feeling, tasting, smelling) may be the most appropriate to use to build their internal imagery.

NLP also goes beyond goal-setting by helping to access and strengthen the inner resources the person needs to achieve their goal. For example, an NLP technique known as the 'circle of excellence' (Laborde 1988:172) is designed for this purpose:

> The client accesses a number of highly positive experiences from their past, each time stepping into a vivid, imaginary circle in front of them. The combination of the positive experiences becomes linked or 'anchored' to the imagined circle. Then, whenever the person wants to access feelings of confidence and resourcefulness in future, they can imagine themselves stepping into that circle.

The potential for mental rehearsal of various kinds to influence performance is used in sports psychology. We cite support for mental rehearsal in academic literature in Chapter 11.

Selling

One of the main areas to have been influenced by NLP is that of selling. Illustrating the general approach, Robertson's *Sales: the Mind's Side* (1989) applies NLP to persuasion. Apart from lauding the pursuit of states of excellence and peak performance, and how to access them, it gives simple information about how people use their senses internally to make decisions, how some people are more 'visual' than others, and how important it is to match the other person's body language to create rapport. NLP as such is not mentioned in the main text, but the bibliography makes extensive reference to Bandler, Grinder and other developers in the field.

Washburn and Wallace's volume (1999) is enticingly entitled *Why People don't Buy Things*, and the publicity on the front cover claims that it offers the reader the opportunity of dramatically increasing their sales. It draws on a number of different sources, the first one cited in their bibliography being Bandler and Grinder's *Frogs into Princes,* even though the initials NLP are noticeable by their absence. A significant part of the content is devoted to explanations about how to identify different types of people, including those who make choices visually. Lakhani's *Subliminal Persuasion* (Lakhani 2008) is a primer of how to use NLP language patterns and hypnosis to influence people to act in particular ways, and to be motivated to then buy things.

NLP has also been promoted as a way of successfully selling over the telephone, (Zarro & Blum 1989) with advice for people on how to overcome 'phone phobia', identify visual, auditory and kinaesthetic types of 'phone responders', and how to influence people on the phone through using Ericksonian hypnotic language patterns. Knight (2002:158) describes how people who are good at telephone communication will make an internal visual image of a successful outcome to their call before they pick up the phone.

Psychological profiling through meta-programmes

NLP proposes a model of psychological and behavioural preferences, based on the way people respond to and process information. These preferences are called 'meta-programmes' (Charvet 1997) and are, metaphorically speaking, 'programmes' and motivational strategies that people run, as it were, in particular situations.

A simple example of a meta-programme is the one often referred to as 'sameness-difference'. A person whose preference is 'same-ness' may be the one that goes along with the views of the crowd, rarely disagrees, takes a broad overview of situations, and tends to repeat certain actions when faced with a problem. Someone sorting for difference, on the other hand, may be constantly scanning incoming information for what does not fit, or what he or she can disagree with. Such a preference may lead that person to seek novel solutions to problems.

Another standard meta-programme is referred to as 'towards – away from'. This describes whether a person is motivated more by wanting to avoid a particular consequence (away from), or is attracted *towards* an outcome. An 'away from' person might answer the question 'do I want a fast car?' with 'oh no! I might have an accident!' A 'towards' person might respond 'yes, rather' as she imagined the excitement of roaring along a French motorway. Applications of this model include recruitment, market research, career planning and performance management (Thompson, Courtney & Dickson 2002). The original instrument based on meta-programmes, called the Language and Behaviour (LAB) profile, was developed by Rodger Bailey. Another called 'Thinking Styles' is designed to be used in coaching (Beddoes-Jones & Miller 2007). Notably, another recent instrument called the cdaq®,[6] developed by Paul Brewerton (2004), was granted registration as a psychological test by the British Psychological Society (British Psychological Society 2007). Any approved instrument must prove its credentials rigorously, so effectively this means that the psychology establishment in the UK recognises the validity of this model. This seems significant given the criticisms sometimes aimed at NLP from academic psychology.

Leadership development

NLP has been applied to leadership in education in the UK within the Fast Track teaching programme provided by the CfBT Education Trust,[7] which provides graduate leadership development programmes that mirror fast track programmes in industry and the wider public sector. Fast Track teaching was originally developed and funded by the Department for Education and Skills in 2001 and became a National College for School Leadership programme in 2005. The programme design and content is designed and delivered by CfBT Education Trust. Training opportunities including NLP[8] are structured to support specific competency development. Since 2004, over 2,000 Fast Track teachers have had some training in NLP and by the end of 2009 nearly 800 will have done the INLPTA Diploma (Churches & West-Burnham 2008).[9] Subsequent in-house evaluation research has shown that this has had a positive impact on teacher and school leader development (Jones & Atfield 2007). NLP has also been used effectively to support headteacher development in challenging school contexts (Hutchinson, Churches & Vitae 2007) as part of the London Leadership Strategy's Consultant Leader programme. This programme identifies outstanding headteachers and gives them training and development as well as deploying them in consulting roles to support other London schools.

Modelling excellence

In Chapter 2, we described modelling as one of the six faces of NLP. The essence of modelling is to gain insights into the internal strategies used by exemplars. These insights are then used to produce a model, which identifies and maps the necessary variables needed to perform the skill. A good model is believed to enable others then to replicate this skill.

Modelling has been used to identify and map the cognitive strategies that lie behind skills that are useful in organisations such as motivating oneself, successful negotiation, effective chairing of meetings, making persuasive speeches, and many others. According to a factsheet on the CIPD website,[10] for example, 'it is possible to model any of the following:

- the ability to connect immediately with customers;
- the charisma of an inspiring business leader;
- the ability to create a compelling vision;
- the capacity to maintain motivation towards a goal;
- a state of congruence and truth;
- an ability to resolve situations of conflict;
- the skill of coaching people to achieve their best performance'.

In the 1970s, Bandler and Grinder (1979:36) referred to working for an advertising agency in order to 'clone' their most creative people by modelling the ones considered to be the most successful:

> We determined the strategy that one creative person used to create a commercial, we taught other people in that agency to use the same structure at an unconscious level. The commercials they came up with were then creative in the same way, but the content was totally unique.

Modelling has been applied in other business contexts. An interview with Charles Faulkner, an NLP trainer and author, in Robert Koppel's 'The Intuitive Trader' (Koppel 1996:71), tells how Faulkner modelled the intuitive judgements of leading traders, using the results of his modelling to become a successful trader himself. Jay Spechler claims (1995) to have modelled excellence in business, specifically in quality management; his 'When America Does It

Right' (1991) includes case studies of numerous North American corporations, including Boeing, American Express and Hewlett Packard. Unfortunately this book does not describe how Spechler used the modelling method.[11]

The NLP modeller needs to be able to ask the right questions so as to identify the particular behaviour or strategy that is the main difference between success and failure. One of us (Jane) was intrigued by the way in which a Head of a Government Department in New Zealand ran successful and productive meetings. One of the questions asked when eliciting the strategy behind his behaviour as Chair was about how he dealt with people who talked too much, went off the point or interrupted him. Here is his account of his strategy:

> If I am speaking and someone cuts in over the top of me, I stop and when they have finished, I repeat the first part of my sentence. Often the same person will cut in again at exactly the same point. I then repeat the first part of the sentence a third time. I have found that I rarely need to do that more than three times.
>
> If there is a person in the room who continually cuts in over the top of everyone I use a slightly different tactic. I simply keep talking at the same level and pace. Most people simply give up when that happens and allow the rude person to have the floor. I think it's a confidence thing. I find that if I keep talking, no one can hear either me or the other person, and it's a matter of who gives up first. I don't. Sometimes by then I am talking drivel but no one can understand it anyway with two people talking. My experience is that the person cutting in will generally stop first as they realise that they have not been given the floor. They don't do it to me a second time.

This gives a simple strategy that others could learn. Identifying the factors that make the strategy work, of course, involves investigating other dimensions as well as the exemplar's behaviour; it will be subtended by certain beliefs in his own capabilities and rights to maintain his authority, and an internal construct of what he wants to achieve from the meeting. Some of the individual skills, such as the ability to continue talking, come what may, and maintain an authoritative tone of voice, can be taught through coaching.

Coaching

The world of coaching is a rapidly expanding part of practical organisational psychology. It is estimated that the number of new coaches joining the market place is doubling every year (Rogers, preface to Hayes 2006). Coaching is part of the toolkit of many coaches in the UK, and a growth area in the applications of NLP in organisations – in 2009, 310 trained NLP practitioners were listed by the ANLP as offering a specialism in business coaching.[12]

How is NLP applied in coaching? Grimley (2007) provides a case study of an executive client who had recently been laid off. Grimley describes how he used NLP to identify the specific problems the client wanted to work on, explore new perspectives on the issues that helped him to manage his anger at being laid off, and access his own inner resources, such that the client 'felt he was truly out of his rut and moving forward in his life' (Grimley 2007:208). Grimley also stresses the need for NLP's claims to be tested in a more robust way, both quantitatively and qualitatively.

Hayes emphasises the practical aspect of coaching, observing that coaches need to work 'in the reality of the moment' (Hayes 2006:121). He expresses scepticism about many of the claims of NLP and of its community, and nevertheless states that in his work as a coach he finds in NLP an invaluable set of tools to help others to attain their goals. His book gives examples of many of the NLP techniques that can be used in coaching. For example, he describes working with Brian, a chief executive, who 'was deeply troubled when it came to presenting an argument or a report to groups of senior managers and non-executive directors'. After using, among other things, a process called the meta-mirror, which encourages a client to witness themselves as seen through other people's eyes, Brian 'recognized that the group was not, as he had assumed, conspiring to create his discomfort but was a group of individuals who wanted him to succeed and were terrified of their own embarrassment if he were to struggle to perform well in front of them' (Hayes 2006:63–64). This led to further insights that enabled Brian to learn what he needed in order to handle the situation better.

Linder-Pelz and Hall describe the work of NLP coaches as being about 'facilitating a client's performance, experience, learning and growth and about actualising goals' (Linder-Pelz & Hall 2008:43). They encourage clients to be more aware of the many dimensions to their thinking and acting, as part of acquiring insights through self-reflexivity. Using the idea of 'meta-states' (Hall 2000), they claim that it may be meaningful for the client to explore not only, for instance, how he or she views a particular situation, but also how he or she has categorised these perceptions. Does he or she feel challenged by a problematic situation, or helpless?

These authors stress the need for coaching people in organisations to become more self-reflexive so as to enable them to understand themselves and others better. A coach using this approach 'enables a client to reflect on potentials they previously may not have believed they had and on beliefs and feelings that may be holding them back' (Linder-Pelz & Hall 2008:44). Where NLP is thought to be a useful approach is that it enables the practitioner to use 'precision questioning… as well as language that induces and utilises states as well as framing, reframing and deframing meaning' (Linder-Pelz & Hall 2008:46). This highlights that a practical understanding of the powers of language to affect meaning-making is likely to receive special and detailed emphasis in the training of NLP coaches.

Some publications in this field appear to be re-hashes of NLP Practitioner and Master Practitioner training manuals, listing techniques that are said to be useful to the NLP coach but making little reference to theories of learning and human development. According to Linder-Pelz and Hall (2007), NLP coaching integrates a 'disparate but significant body of established knowledge and theory' (Linder-Pelz & Hall 2007:15) which draws on various disciplines, including Bandura's cognitive learning theory (Bandura 1986).

Conclusion

In this chapter we have described some of the ways in which NLP has been applied in organisational settings. It is used to model successful exemplars, to enable people to set compelling goals and to learn new skills, and to develop leaders. Its use in coaching is prominent. The question of the effectiveness of NLP in practice is one that we resume in Chapter 11 – this is potentially a researcher's paradise, as there is a lack of well-documented cases, and NLP's claims need to be evaluated more thoroughly.

Part II

4
The Road to Santa Cruz

The story of NLP in context

What constitutes a 'history'? The Encyclopedia of NLP, a major work, running to 1,625 large-format pages spread across two volumes, includes a section headed 'Historical Overview of NLP'. Yet within this entry, the part that recounts the 'history' is a single paragraph giving a very brief narrative account of how 'NLP was originated by John Grinder... and Richard Bandler' (Dilts & DeLozier 2000:850). Other accounts in the field, such as that by Peter Young (2004:61), are similarly sparse.

There has been relatively little published information about the specific events that led to the emergence of NLP in the early 1970s. McLendon's 'The Wild Days' is a very entertaining and informative account from someone who was directly involved. It is not necessarily accurate in detail yet, according to Bandler, it captures 'the spirit of adventure that gave birth to NLP' (McLendon 1989:ii). Then in 2001, with the publication of 'Whispering in the Wind' (Bostic St. Clair & Grinder 2001), John Grinder expanded in print on some of the events and theories that informed the development of NLP. This account is invaluable in many respects, if hard going in places and difficult to obtain.[1] As noted in Chapter 1, the two most scholarly accounts of the circumstances surrounding NLP's conception, those by Wolfgang Walker (1996) and Monique Esser (2004), are from continental Europe, and have not yet been translated into English.

Compounding this, 'serious' study of NLP has sometimes been discouraged. Whether because that is to miss the point of NLP, or because many of the details of events in the 1970s are now hazy, or because it preserves a sense of mystique and elusiveness, is a matter for debate. Grinder says, in the foreword to O'Connor and Seymour's 'Introducing NLP':

> These two men... have set out to make a coherent story out of an outrageous adventure... What you are about to read never happened, but it seems reasonable, even to me.
>
> (O'Connor & Seymour 1990:15)

Relying on NLP literature can therefore convey a very NLP-centric view of its own origins, one that is not only obscure in its detail but also stripped from its location in twentieth century culture and the ideas and practices that informed it, giving the impression that the field sprang fully formed, sometime in the early 1970s in Santa Cruz, California, from the labours of its progenitors, Bandler and Grinder. Dowlen (1996:29) says, for example, that; 'It is interesting to note the degree to which NLP is personalized in connection with these two individuals (i.e. Bandler and Grinder), with far less emphasis being accorded to either the origins of NLP or its subsequent development by others.' The NLP Story appears to some, to have become a sort of Adam and Eve 'Creation Myth'.[2]

While a focus on Bandler and Grinder is inevitable, because they are so prominent in both the literature and the practice of the field, we also aim to take a wider perspective on this reconstruction of its origins, both historically and conceptually. Can one appreciate the biography and identity of NLP without acknowledging, for example, its emergence from streams of twentieth century intellectual thought? It is difficult to see how NLP could have evolved without the theories about the ways in which people process information and understand their worlds that were developed through constructivism and cybernetics.

Also significant is the human potential movement and the cultural revolution of the 1960s. California became the epicentre of the growth movement, epitomised by the Esalen Institute that was founded at Big Sur in 1962, in which both Satir and Perls were involved.[3] The state was a hub of countercultural activity – alternative therapies, new lifestyles, experimental rock music, altered states of consciousness and a drug culture whose values were initially formed by the rejection of materialism, coupled with political dissent that was fuelled by revulsion towards the Vietnam War. McLendon says of Santa Cruz at that time, 'for those in the know about crystals, pyramids and tarot, Santa Cruz's stature is equal to that of the Bermuda Triangle, Boulder, Colorado and other high energy windows to the universe' (McLendon 1989:1). As we shall discover, NLP grew from a distinctive educational experiment happening within this context, that of Kresge College at the University of Santa Cruz.

One could take a longer-term perspective and consider NLP as an example of the type of twentieth century social movement that emerged in the USA. For example, NLP's sometimes exaggerated emphasis on the potential for the person to change themselves, and its promises of empowerment and personal success, reflect an ethos of self-improvement that can be traced back to Dale Carnegie's 'How to Win Friends and Influence People' (first published in 1936), and Norman Vincent Peale's 'Power of Positive Thinking' (from 1952). The self-help movement may have shaped the identity of NLP more than is usually acknowledged, not only in its guise as a commercial product but also in its contents. Some of these ideas sound remarkably similar to NLP, such as Carnegie's emphasis on appreciating the other person's point of view, and on adjusting one's own response in order to influence other people, and Peale's interest in boosting self-confidence.

Acknowledging this wider context, a timeline of NLP could take us at least as far back as the 1940s, as shown in Figure 4.1 (we will explain the connections to the Macy Conferences and to the Palo Alto group in the forthcoming chapters). A more detailed timeline of events is included as an Appendix.

In this and the following chapters we flesh out the bare bones of the usual stories of NLP's origins by describing how four main aspects of NLP evolved, making links backwards in time to their antecedents.[4]

The first aspect involved Bandler, then Grinder, together with various collaborators, discovering ways in which language directly influences people's thinking and their subsequent actions. This collaboration began in 1972 and led to the development of the NLP 'meta-model' (Chapters 4 and 5).

The second aspect focused on non-verbal communication. It comprised the discovery of the significance of people's 'inner

40

Figure 4.1 NLP, a Timeline

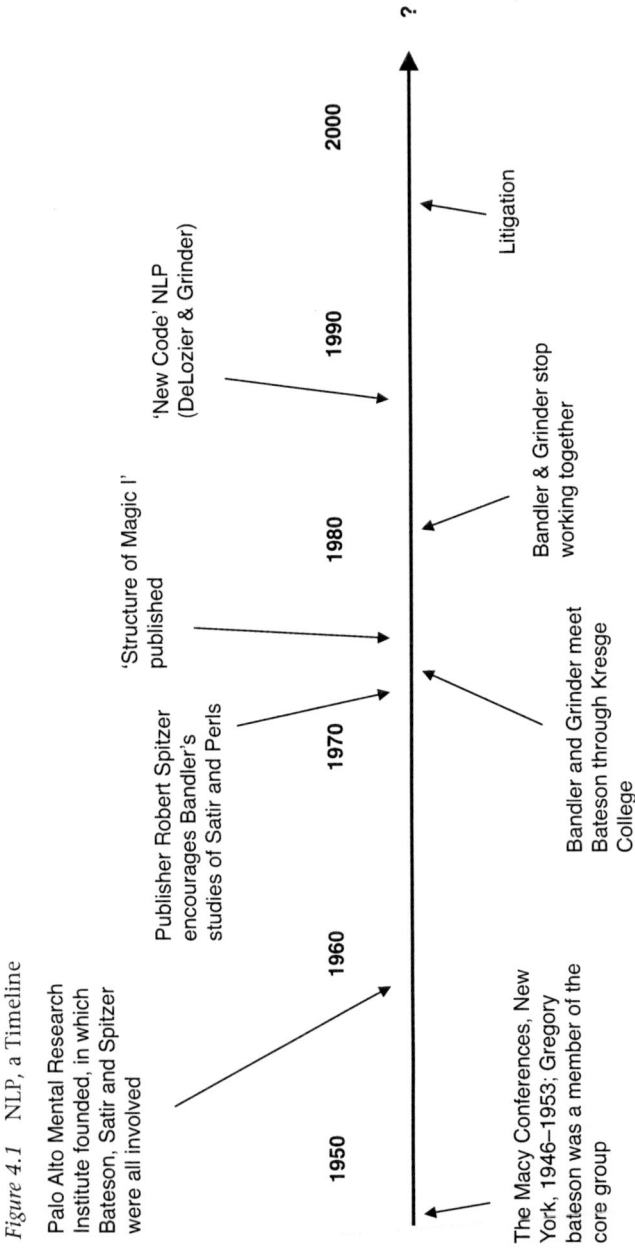

Palo Alto Mental Research Institute founded, in which Bateson, Satir and Spitzer were all involved

Publisher Robert Spitzer encourages Bandler's studies of Satir and Perls

'Structure of Magic I' published

'New Code' NLP (DeLozier & Grinder)

Litigation

1950   1960   1970   1980   1990   2000

?

The Macy Conferences, New York, 1946–1953; Gregory bateson was a member of the core group

Bandler and Grinder meet Bateson through Kresge College

Bandler & Grinder stop working together

Source: © Paul Tosey & Jane Mathison 2009

landscapes', the ways in which people re-create experience internally through inner sensory modes of vision, hearing, feeling, and more (Chapter 6).

The third aspect arose through encounters with Milton H. Erickson, the renowned hypnotherapist, who provided further insights into the unconscious effects of verbal and non-verbal communication, yielding not only an appreciation of hypnotic language structures *per se*, but also a deeper and richer understanding of language patterns and communication generally (see Chapter 7).

The fourth aspect is more dispersed in time, yet one that is central to a critical appreciation of NLP. This centres on the influence of Gregory Bateson, 'one of the most provocative social scientists of the twentieth century' (Rieber 1989), who happened to be in Santa Cruz in the 1970s. Bateson provides the link between NLP and the science of cybernetics, which we argue is foundational to any theory of NLP (see Chapter 8). This aspect links forward to 1987, when Judith DeLozier and John Grinder developed 'new code' NLP (DeLozier & Grinder 1987), an attempt to re-invent NLP as a practice more closely aligned to Bateson's ecologically-informed thinking, thereby distancing it from the mechanistic influence of early cybernetics.

While these stages only take the story of NLP up to the 1980s, they represent the main influences and events that have shaped NLP today. We update this story, and argue that today NLP is at a crossroads, in the final chapter of the book.

Bandler, Spitzer, Perls and Satir

What can be gleaned from published sources about the lives of Bandler and Grinder before the 1970s, and about the route that brought them together?

Bandler, an only child from a Jewish background (McLendon 1989:10), was born in New Jersey and grew up in the poorer quarters of San Jose, California (Walker 1996:21). At one time his family owned a restaurant, and Bandler developed 'a natural ability for cooking' (McLendon 1989:3). In 1967 the then seventeen year old Richard Bandler was an unwilling student at Freemont High School when he came to the notice of one Robert S. Spitzer.

Spitzer is a little-mentioned but important figure in the origins of NLP. For example, the dedication to 'Changing with Families'

(Bandler, Grinder & Satir 1976) reads 'To Bob Spitzer, who has made possible so much of the actualization of our creativity'. It was largely thanks to Spitzer, in fact, that Bandler had access to the people and the material that sparked his curiosity about how successful therapists achieved their results. Spitzer trained as a Freudian psychiatrist,[5] and lived in Santa Cruz, where he was a director of the publishing house Science and Behavior Books. He first met Virginia Satir at the Mental Research Institute, Palo Alto, in 1961 and, inspired by her, joined the Institute himself. He later wrote the foreword to Virginia Satir's classic book, 'Peoplemaking', which was originally published in 1972 (Satir 1978:ix–x).

Spitzer recounts (1992:1) how his wife Becky had been impressed with the musical abilities of Richard Bandler, who was a friend of their son's, and who played musical instruments, and composed jazz and rock without any formal training. They also noticed Richard's interest in philosophical questions. Recognising his potential, Spitzer initially employed him in various capacities in his publishing house. Thus the Spitzers became Bandler's unofficial mentors.

After graduating from Freemont High School, Bandler entered Foothill College, in the Los Altos Hills (McLendon 1989:4), where apparently he drove his teachers to near despair (Spitzer 1992:1) because he would not conform to its regime. Foothill College, was (and still is)[6] a college preparing students for entry into a University degree programme through accumulating credits. After two years at Foothill Bandler 'transferred to the university at Santa Cruz where he began a major in mathematics and computer sciences, later transferring his interest to the behavioural sciences' (McLendon 1989:4).

Spitzer, impressed with Bandler's work, engaged him on a new task. Fritz Perls, one of the main developers of Gestalt therapy and another of Spitzer's authors, had died in 1970, leaving behind him some unfinished work. Spitzer asked Bandler to transcribe recordings of Perls at work and contracted him to help with the editing of his uncompleted manuscripts, planning to include examples of Perls' work in a book to be published posthumously (i.e. Perls 1973). The second part of that book was mainly the result of Bandler's transcription and analysis.

Bandler immersed himself in the task, spending many hours watching and transcribing Perls' audio and filmed recordings, and running through them repeatedly to check the accuracy of his transcriptions. Spitzer wrote later that Bandler 'came out of it talking and acting like Fritz Perls. I found myself accidentally calling him Fritz on several occasions' (Spitzer 1992:2). Illustrating how Bandler had begun to use the approach that would later be called 'modelling', Spitzer says: 'He said this was how he learned music. Richard would listen to the music of someone he admired over and over until he sounded just like the person being imitated. He was not worried about imitating or losing his identity. Apparently musicians often use a form of deep identification in their learning processes' (Spitzer 1992:2).

The Spitzers owned a weekend cabin, and they agreed to let the young Bandler build his own house nearby and be caretaker for their property (Spitzer 1992:1). Richard first met Virginia Satir at a seminar she gave at the cabin, probably in 1972 (Walker 1996:31);[7] by this time Satir had moved on from the Palo Alto Mental Research Institute to become the first director of training at Esalen (Satir 1978:ix).

Spitzer then asked Bandler to tape and transcribe a month-long workshop that Satir was due to lead in Canada, intending to turn this material into a book. 'Richard was quite taken by Virginia', wrote Spitzer (1992:2), being intrigued by her abilities to elicit information from other people, and fascinated by how she achieved her results.

Incidentally, it is important to acknowledge that the practices of Satir and Perls were themselves influenced by other psychotherapists. For discussions of these types of connection, see Bolstad (2002) and Wake (2008).

Satir was also impressed with Bandler's abilities, describing him as being a brilliant young man with a fantastic intellect and a wide ranging curiosity (Walker 1996:32). Towards the end of that workshop, according to O'Connor and Seymour (1990:173), 'Virginia had set up a counselling situation and asked how the participants would deal with it, using the material that she had been teaching them. The participants seemed stuck. Richard came storming down from his room and successfully dealt with the problem... Richard found himself in the strange situation of knowing more about Virginia's therapeutic procedures than anyone else, without consciously trying to learn them at all.'

One of Satir's therapeutic tools was what she called the 'Parts Party', based on the idea that a person has a number of psychological parts, as it were, that could be harmoniously expressed in a healthy individual. At a Parts Party the therapist, or party giver, would analyse the interactions between a person's different 'parts' and guide them to take up different perspectives on each other, so that they could work co-operatively. According to Walker (1996:34), Bandler was apparently rendered speechless at the changes she facilitated in him – though Spitzer's recollection is that neither Bandler nor Grinder 'personally experienced a family reconstruction in the context of an extended training. I think such an experience for either of them would have added an (*sic*) new dimension of appreciation of Virginia and life' (Spitzer 1992:4).

John Grinder

Born in 1940 in Detroit, Michigan, John Grinder was the first of a family of nine children. He received a Catholic education and studied to bachelor's degree level 'under the tutelage of the Jesuits' at the University of San Francisco. He married and also enlisted in the US Army in 1962, serving in Germany until 1967 (Bostic St. Clair & Grinder 2001:122, 144).

Walker (1996) and Dilts and DeLozier (2000:460) both comment on Grinder's military service during which, according to McLendon (1989:9a), he worked as an interpreter and participated in covert operations. This experience seems to have been formative in the development of Grinder's non-verbal, non-cognitive approach to 'modelling'. During this time, apparently, he found that he could rapidly imitate an indigenous speaker sufficiently well to pass himself off as a native. According to McLendon (1989:9a), one language Grinder acquired in this way was Swahili.

Grinder then comments that 'for a variety of reasons, I resigned my commission as captain', then became a graduate student in Linguistics at the University of California, San Diego in 1968. He 'spent one academic year as a guest researcher in George Miller's lab at Rockefeller University (1969/70) in New York City' (Bostic St. Clair & Grinder 2001:123). Presumably resulting from this period, two of Miller's best-known ideas appear frequently in NLP. The first is the well-known dictum that the conscious mind can process at most '7 plus or minus 2' pieces of information (Miller 1956), the second is the test-operate-test-exit (TOTE) model of human behaviour (Miller, Galanter & Pribram 1960), of which we say more in Chapter 9.

After completing his doctorate at the University of San Diego (Grinder 1971) on 'deletion phenomena', an aspect of contemporary linguistics, Grinder joined the University of California, Santa Cruz as an assistant professor 'in the fall of 1970' (Bostic St. Clair & Grinder 2001:123). It was there that he and Bandler would soon come to meet.

Spitzer's influence continued after Bandler and Grinder met, though ultimately they were 'like prodigal sons who never came back' (Spitzer 1992:4). His publishing house was part of other extensive properties he owned at 1000 Alba Road,[8] Ben Lomond,[9] which he and his wife Becky rented out. There they brought together a community of people who were interested in alternative life styles. Bandler, John Grinder and Judith DeLozier would come to be neighbours at this 'intellectual hotspot' (Spitzer 1992:2); Gregory Bateson (see Chapter 8), his wife Lois, and their daughter Nora would go to live there in the summer of 1974; and Virginia Satir considered moving in too, though decided against doing so.

We continue this story in the next chapter, at the University of Santa Cruz.

5
Discovering the Language of Change[1]

Kresge College

After Foothill, Richard Bandler enrolled at Kresge College, the sixth college established at the University of Santa Cruz. Kresge was a radical experiment in education. Its founding provost, Robert Edgar, was a microbiologist who had become deeply impressed by the person-centred educational approach of Carl Rogers. Grant and Riesman comment that; 'if Kresge College could have adopted the name of its patron saint rather than its benefactor, it would have been called Carl Rogers College' (1978:77).

Kresge, which Grant and Riesman described as the University of Santa Cruz's 'most *avant garde* experiment', opened in 1970 with a 'planning year' in which staff and nearly forty students participated in a course called 'Creating Kresge College' (1978:92). Kresge's educational ethos and practices were based on T-groups, or sensitivity training, a behavioural science approach to personal growth and organisation development founded by Kurt Lewin, encapsulated in Kresge's 'Ten Commandments of T-grouping' 'Straight talk' and willingness to participate in a weekend T-group became requirements for hiring staff. Students were allocated to 'kin groups' that had both social and academic functions, but with the ethos that students and staff were co-learners As Grant and Riesman observe, these rules 'completely shake the conventions of ordinary academic discourse' (1978:84). It was intended to be 'an integrated living/learning environment shared (in principle, at any rate) by students, faculty and staff' (Bostic St. Clair & Grinder 2001:142).

46

Grant and Riesman's account, written contemporaneously in the 1970s, conveys that experiences and opinions of Kresge were complex and diverse. The approach brought tensions within the College between those fully committed to the T-group ethos and those more lukewarm or sceptical. Some students thrived, others struggled and yet benefited, still others rebelled. It also opened Kresge to attack from those outside who were either threatened by, disapproved of, or failed to understand its radical approach. By the mid 1970s Kresge had a new provost, and its ethos shifted direction. Edgar's dream had reached too far too fast, faltered and stalled, though it did not disappear.

Kresge was therefore by no means typical, either of American college education, nor even of the University of Santa Cruz. If anything it was the exception. What is most relevant in relation to NLP is that Bandler and Grinder, and later Bateson, were involved in the relatively short period during which this experiment in communal, alternative education was at its height.

A meeting of minds

The precise date of Bandler and Grinder's first encounter is unclear. According to Grinder, he and Bandler met in one of Kresge's T-Groups that he (Grinder) sponsored as a member of the faculty (Bostic St. Clair & Grinder 2001:142).

Bandler's fascination with patterns of communication and behaviour, his apparently insatiable curiosity about 'what worked', and a desire to find out how a successful therapist's communication could produce change, drove him to experiment with Gestalt Therapy himself. At that time undergraduates at Kresge could present their own work in order to gain credits. Bandler therefore started a Gestalt group on the campus in the spring of 1972, often collaborating with Frank Pucelik, in which he tried out the interventions and ideas that had emerged from his immersion in Perls' work (McLendon 1989:9–15). Gestalt therapy was at the time considered to be highly innovative. According to McLendon, Bandler needed to be supervised by a faculty member in order to deliver his course.

Bandler had by then had so much exposure to Satir's and Perls' work that he could repeat and adapt their communication patterns in order to work successfully with clients. What remained was the challenge of formalising these patterns and teaching them to others. He had noted that John Grinder, an associate professor in Linguistics, had interesting ideas about the relationship between the processes of natural language and 'the structure of the human mind' (Bostic St. Clair & Grinder 2001:143). Grinder's expertise was reflected in the doctorate he had recently completed at the University of San Diego (Grinder 1971) and a book called a *Guide to Transformational Grammar*, co-authored with Suzette Haden Elgin (Grinder & Elgin 1973).[2] Might he help Bandler understand some of the things that were happening in the experimental Gestalt groups that he and Frank Pucelik were running?

Grinder was at first reluctant to take part in the Gestalt therapy groups. However, 'a single evening was more than adequate to capture my attention... Indeed when I later compared their work with Perls' work presented on film and audiotape, I found Pucelik and Bandler's work to be significantly more effective than the model (Perls) they were imitating' (Bostic St. Clair & Grinder 2001:143). Pucelik, Grinder and Bandler then worked together for several months as Grinder applied his understanding of linguistics to puzzle out and classify these patterns.

The collaborators

At this point it is relevant to acknowledge people besides Bandler and Grinder themselves who were associated with the development of NLP, including the meta-model. We have seen already how Robert and Becky Spitzer played a significant part. Frank Pucelik is mentioned as one of the *three* men around whom 'an excited group of people' (Bostic St. Clair & Grinder 2001:173) collected to read the manuscript of 'The Structure of Magic' and assist them with their research – although apart from this and reference to his involvement in the Gestalt groups, Pucelik's contribution to NLP is scarcely mentioned.[3]

Who else appears in the NLP family constellation? Many of the early collaborators were later to become the first cadre of NLP trainers; among those mentioned in NLP literature are Leslie Cameron, Judith DeLozier, Byron Lewis, David Gordon, Terence McClendon, and Robert Dilts. Other people associated with early NLP went on to develop their own practices, such as the forms of brief therapy and solution-focused therapy that are associated with people like Steve Gilligan, Bill O'Hanlon,[4] and Steve de Shazer. The role and voice of women, especially, seems to be under-represented in the NLP story. Women in the NLP community are aware of this issue,[5] yet with the exception of Helm (1991) there does not appear to be any published discussion of gender anywhere in the field.[6]

Just three examples of the many influential women in NLP are Leslie Cameron-Bandler, Judith DeLozier, and Christina Hall.[7] Byron Lewis (Lewis & Pucelik 1990) cites Leslie Cameron and Frank Pucelik as the people who led him into NLP. Cameron, who became known as Leslie Cameron-Bandler after marrying Bandler in 1977 (McLendon 1989:109), went on to write several books. As mentioned in Chapter 2 this included one of the first to detail the core NLP methodology for mapping and reproducing competences (Cameron-Bandler, Gordon & Lebeau 1985). Cameron is called 'one of the world's most creative family therapists' in the dedication of 'The Structure of Magic II', and she played a central role in the development of NLP training. According to Patrick Merlevede, she was director of the first NLP Institute, called DOTAR (Division of Training and Research), in which Robert Dilts and David Gordon also had active roles, with Bandler and Grinder acting mainly 'as patriarchs' (2000:63).

Judith DeLozier has played a central role in NLP, virtually since its inception, and continues to do so. With a background in religious studies and anthropology, she 'got involved in NLP about the time the book *The Structure of Magic* was just a manuscript', through her friend (later her husband) John Grinder (DeLozier 1995:6). She is co-author of many NLP books (including Grinder, DeLozier & Bandler 1977; Dilts, Grinder, Bandler & DeLozier 1980; Bretto *et al* 1991) and has championed the more holistic approach to NLP known as 'new code' (DeLozier & Grinder 1987). As co-author of the 'Encyclopedia of NLP' (Dilts & DeLozier 2000), she is also jointly responsible for the major reference work produced from within the field. Therefore it may seem surprising that her contribution is not asserted more strongly in discussions of NLP.

Christina Hall is another case in point, especially since, according to her report of the legal judgement of the Superior Court in Santa Cruz (Hall 2001), she contributed substantially to the development of NLP in the late 1970s.

Accounts of NLP, such as those passed on in training courses, sometimes give the impression that there was a single community or 'meta-model group' that was engaged in this work from the beginning. It seems more the case that there were several groupings and events at different times, with fluctuating memberships, as one might expect to find in an unplanned, emergent process. Many meetings took place at friends' houses.[8] For example, McLendon (1989:39) mentions a group at Mission Street, in Santa Cruz, 'initiated by a person named Ken', and to 'Frank Pucelik, Leslie Cameron and Judith DeLozier's house in the Santa Cruz mountains' (McLendon 1989:25).

Later, there were the people among whom Bandler and Grinder circulated the manuscript of *The Structure of Magic* (which was in existence by early 1974), who helped to test and refine its contents. Another grouping comprised those who joined Bandler and Grinder in studying with Milton Erickson (see Chapter 7). It seems likely that these groupings centred on those involved in the community at 1000 Alba Road that was fostered by the Spitzers.

What is the meta-model?

The first substantive product of this period, the 'meta-model', appeared in print in 1975, titled 'The Structure of Magic I' (Bandler & Grinder 1975b)[9] and sporting a colourful image of a wizard on the front cover.[10] It carried a foreword by Gregory Bateson who, with reference to his own previous work on human communication, said: 'Grinder and Bandler have succeeded in making explicit the syntax of how people avoid change and, therefore, how to assist them in changing.' (Bateson in Bandler & Grinder 1975b:x)

The meta-model patterns were essentially a classification based on the *cognitive* or *conceptual* processes that each one involved. The meta-model, which is claimed to be 'the first complete syntactically based language model for an express purpose ever created' (Bostic St. Clair & Grinder 2001:148), conceived of grammar and syntax as mirroring cognitive processes, thus providing a means by which to understand *people's ways of making sense.*

Adopting Chomksy's ideas about transformational linguistics, the meta-model categorises certain linguistic transformations, or ways in which the 'surface structure' of verbal communication can differ from the 'deep structure', which is effectively a fuller description of experience. These transformations, which are described in detail in Bandler and Grinder (1975b), arise through the processes of deletion, distortion and generalisation, which sound undesirable but in fact help to make our communication more concise. Chomsky assumed that deep and surface structure were simply different (shorthand and more expanded respectively) versions of the same thing; asking meta-model questions could recover this detail.

A manager applying the meta-model to preparing an important presentation would start with the question; 'what processes do I want to influence in my listeners in order to enable them to understand what I'm saying in the most useful way?' The various meta-model patterns relate to processes we use to make sense, to construct meaning, and to map the worlds of our experiences on to our belief and value systems. The meta-model also identifies ways of questioning and challenging each of these patterns, and to elicit information about the cognition and conceptualisation used in formulating a problem.

We can illustrate these principles through Harry Beck's classic London Underground diagram,[11] which McDermott and Jago (2001:33) cite as an example of a map that is valuable because it is useful. As a representation of London this map *deletes* a huge amount of detail. For example it shows no streets or parks – the only geographical feature is the schematic representation of the River Thames. In terms of ease of use, for the purpose of travelling by Tube, you only have to compare Beck's map with a street map of London. On the latter it is difficult enough to identify stations, let alone to track the lines.

Second, Beck's map *distorts* in several ways. Thus the orientations of the Tube lines are stylised; they are either vertical, horizontal, or at 45° angles. Distances between stops are not to scale, so do not correspond to geographical distances. Nor are distances consistent on the map relative to each other (for example, from Piccadilly Circus to Oxford Circus is longer on the map than from, say, Baker Street to St. John's Wood; in geographical distance the reverse is true).

The third feature is *generalisation*. An example is the way that all stations are shown as one of two symbols; either a small notch of the same size adjacent to the line, or a small circle if it is an interchange. Stations are treated as quite uniform, despite large differences in size, layout and facilities.

By virtue of its judicious use of deletion, distortion and generalisation, the Tube map is both functional and aesthetic. If it were more 'accurate', in terms of maintaining proportions and features we find in physical reality, it would be much more complex and probably be far less useful, as may be seen from versions of the map that existed prior to Beck's work. Thus for travelling on the London Underground, Beck's map is excellent, while for finding one's way around the streets of London it is virtually useless.

By analogy, the meta-model provides a way to elicit the information missing from a person's map. It is a guide to enquiring about what another person is thinking or experiencing in more detail in any specific instance, through forms of question that enable specific, and perhaps uniquely situational, meanings to be revealed. For example, one category of the meta-model is called 'comparative deletions', which occur when comparatives (e.g. closer, higher, greater) are used without specifying what the comparison is with. People in Britain may remember former Prime Minister Tony Blair's election slogan, 'Things can only get better' – better than what? In that instance, the deletion helps to make the phrase effective as a political slogan. What comparison might a coaching client be making, though, if they say they want things to be 'better'? Better then ever before? Better than yesterday? Better than in a rival company? The coach and the client probably need to access the deleted information in order to make progress.

Appraising the meta-model

The meta-model remains central to NLP and continues to be referred to as the foundation (Bandler & Grinder 1979:70) of NLP. Given that more than three decades have elapsed since its discovery and publication, it is remarkable that there has been so little appraisal of it.

While a criticism of NLP is that it is under-researched and out of touch with relevant academic fields, there is a case for saying that the development of the meta-model, indeed the groundwork behind much of NLP in the 1970s, was strongly research-based. Bandler and Grinder engaged in a form of empirical research through observation, analysis, experimentation and continuous testing. This exemplified NLP's methodology of 'modelling' through the identification and repetition of the strategies and language patterns used by people who are successful in their own field. Indeed, Esser (2004) has described them as typical researchers.

Grinder's retrospective comments also indicate that there was rather more method and rigour to those early studies than was previously known; he recounts, for example, one of the ways in which they tested these patterns, through the 'Repeat Miracle Group' (Bostic St. Clair & Grinder 2001:145). Grinder would attend one of Bandler and Pucelik's groups on a Monday evening, watching how they worked with people's problems. Then he would run his own Gestalt group on the following Thursday evening, attempting to achieve similar results by using the same patterns of communication with his own participants. Grinder reports that he became able to reproduce the same 'miracles' that he had observed happening in the Monday evening group.

As another way of testing the effects of these language patterns, Bandler and Grinder devised a novel experimental procedure, which was to use a 'pseudo-therapist'. A client would be interviewed by someone who had been primed by them on exactly what questions to ask to elicit the structure of the problem, while the 'real' therapists listened in. The pseudo-therapist would then leave the client, and confer with Grinder and Bandler on the best approach to the presenting problem. Grinder wrote that 'they (the pseudo-therapist) would then be instructed by us to return and execute some intervention we determined to be relevant' (Bostic St. Clair & Grinder 2001:148). As well as their own experiments, they worked with clients sent to them by Satir (Walker 1996:34) who by then had faith in the effects they were producing.

One of the difficulties in assessing the validity of the claims made in these early publications is that the evidence and research procedures are not available for scrutiny. Other than the material that appeared in 'Structure of Magic' there appears to be no record of either the data or the validation that could be assessed independently by others. Readers of the two 'Structure of Magic' volumes will know that they do not include the methods used, the raw data, or the process of analysis and interpretation that resulted in the meta-model. Even the illuminating further detail provided in 2001 by Grinder does not provide an audit trail. Nor have the patterns identified in the meta-model been verified through systematic formal research, to our knowledge, beyond that conducted by Mathison (2003).

It must be borne in mind that Bandler and Grinder were not writing for an academic audience, therefore it would seem unfair retrospectively to impose expectations on writing that was produced for a different purpose. Nevertheless, such details might have helped respond to the critiques from studies discussed below. Despite the gaps, it is telling that this early work remains the most substantial body of evidence generated to date from within NLP for one of its own models.

It is notable that theory, specifically that of transformational grammar, Grinder's own field of expertise, provided an under-pinning to this model from the start. This is explicit in 'The Structure of Magic' (1975b:23, 40), and confirmed in 'Whispering in the Wind' (2001:78–79).

Despite the role that transformational grammar played in develop-ing the meta-model, however, it is a misconception to suggest that NLP is extensively based on Chomsky's theories. NLP adopted both the principle that language is an example of rule-governed behav-iour (Bandler & Grinder 1975b:23), and Chomsky's notion of trans-formations between surface and deep structure, an idea that is still taught in mainstream cognitive psychology textbooks today (e.g. Quinlan & Dyson 2008:513). De Shazer (1994:17–22) offers a crit-ique of this structuralist thinking, saying for example that it is erro-neous to assume that a person's 'true' meaning can be determined simply by accessing their 'deep structure'.

Grinder was also influenced by the direction in linguistic taken by Paul Postal, whom he knew from his time at Rockefeller University. Postal became a proponent of the Generative Semantics movement, with which NLP has largely lost touch despite noting its significance in both 'The Structure of Magic' and 'Changing with Families'; thus '... we suspect that some of the research currently being conducted in Generative Semantics... will be particularly useful in expanding the Meta-model further' (Bandler & Grinder 1975b:109).

At that time, many linguists were investigating the problems posed by attempting to programme machines to 'understand' human lan-guage. These included Lauri Karttunen, who lectured at the University of California, Santa Cruz. Bandler and Grinder were especially inter-ested in Karttunen's work on presuppositions (e.g. Karttunen 1974), referring to his 'series of incisive papers' (Bandler & Grinder 1975b: 221).[12] Today Karttunen[13] is a leading figure in the fields of computational linguistics and 'Natural Language Processing', which shares the acronym 'NLP'. His work, however, appears not to figure again in the Neuro-Linguistic Programming literature.

Acknowledging that 'at the present time, presuppositions are a major focus of study for a number of linguists, especially linguists who consider themselves Generative Semanticists' (Bandler & Grinder 1975b:211), they also cite someone who has become a leading thinker in the field of language and its relationship to thought, George Lakoff (e.g. Lakoff 1987). Yet with scarce exceptions (e.g. Andreas 2006b) Lakoff, and contemporary linguistics in general, appear not to have informed NLP's literature any further.

As indicated in 'The Structure of Magic', interest in the theory behind NLP's perspective on language probably needs to shift away from Chomsky's ideas, towards the sense making processes that language patterns can activate. Contemporary work in cognitive linguistics and neuroscience appears to support the central principle that the ways in which information is communicated directly influence our sense-making processes. For example, Fauconnier, to whom Bostic St. Clair and Grinder (2001:108–109) do make reference, is at the forefront of developments in cognitive linguistics. He acknowledges the principle that is fundamental in NLP, that language shapes cognition, proposing that; '... understanding grammar in its context and use ... (will) yield insights into cognitive organisation' (Fauconnier 1997:67).

The main assumption that Bandler and Grinder drew from their practical investigations was that communication activated a variety of sense-making processes, and that these could be identified. This view is also receiving support in scientific literature. For example, Richardson *et al* (2003) have shown that when people listen to certain types of words or phrases, particular neuronal networks in identifiable areas of their brains are activated. Pecher *et al* (2004) claim that words activate events in the sensory-motor system of the brain and play a critical role in understanding; Grossman *et al* (2006) believe that words that represent certain types of categories and activate different parts of the temporal-occipital part of the brain; and Yokoyama and his colleagues (2006) have demonstrated that verbs elicit greater activation of a part of the brain called the left middle temporal gyrus than do nouns.

On a broader note, Leynes *et al* (2006) believe that inviting people to remember a past experience activates different patterns of neuronal responses than asking them to imagine a future activity. Rizzolatti and his colleagues (2001) and Tettamanti *et al* (2005) believe that we understand an action (and therefore words that represent an action) because the motor representation of that action is activated in our brain by its 'mirror neurons'.[14] Whenever we communicate, we are not simply exchanging information, but directly activating certain neurological processes in ourselves and others.[15] This has considerable ethical implications, which we explore in Chapter 12.

In short, the ways in which we use language, the grammatical forms we choose together with patterns of non-verbal communication, may directly influence how people *process* the information at the neurological level. We may be influencing how people use their brains when we present them with certain types of language structures. Thus:

> An important point for cognitive scientists is that language does not directly carry meaning. Rather it serves as a powerful means of prompting dynamic on-line constructions of meaning that go far beyond anything explicitly provided by the lexical and grammatical forms.
>
> (Fauconnier 1999:615)

Conclusion

The story of NLP began to take off at Kresge College in Santa Cruz, where Bandler, Grinder and their various collaborators met, and became public in 1975 through 'The Structure of Magic'. The meta-model remains central to the field despite its subsequent lack of testing in relation to developments in linguistics. We know of no reason to suggest that this renders the meta-model language patterns themselves invalid; on the other hand, it underlines the need for NLP to refresh and update its knowledge base in the light of developments since the 1970s.

6
Exploring Inner Landscapes

Introduction

John Grinder recounts how, in the mid 1970s, after he and Bandler completed *The Structure of Magic* and while still in the creative, playful and experimental phase of their collaboration, they were driving together to the first meeting of a new group. Bandler stopped and went into a shop to buy something. When he came out, 'he was laughing. I asked what was so funny. He said (more or less), "You know John, people say the weirdest things, the woman I was talking to at the counter. She said 'I see what you're saying'." He then relapsed into convulsive laughter' (Bostic St. Clair & Grinder 2001:165).

That evening, by the time they had driven to where their new group was meeting, they had generated the hypothesis that people processed and represented information through preferred sensory systems, and that these were revealed by words they used, called 'predicates'. Thus 'see' is a visual predicate, 'hear' is an auditory predicate, and 'feel' is a kinaesthetic predicate.

When they invited each of the members of the new group to introduce themselves, Bandler and Grinder listened carefully to see if they could identify people's preferred sensory system. They had decided beforehand to have available three sheets of different coloured paper, each colour representing a particular sensory type.

This evening... as each member of the group finished their short introduction, either Richard or I would reach down, touch one of the three colors of paper lying on the floor in front of us... and present it meaningfully to the participant, naturally without explanation.

(Bostic St. Clair & Grinder 2001:165).

Bandler and Grinder then asked all the people who had received paper of the same colour to introduce themselves to each other for the first ten minutes. After that, they were to go and talk to people with a piece of paper of a different colour to theirs. The first ten minutes were animated, noisy and full of laughter. By contrast, in the second ten minutes communication appeared desultory, fragmented and interspersed with periods of silence, with low levels of eye contact and fewer movements.

This revealed another apparently significant and influential dimension of communication. Bandler and Grinder noticed that, in addition to the meta-model patterns, language also holds information about the 'ways associated with our five senses that we, as humans, have of representing our experiences' (Grinder & Bandler 1976:7). 'Things look bleak', 'it sounds awful to me', and 'it gets me down' are descriptions a person might give of the same problem, each indicating a different sensory mode and therefore a different way of experiencing that problem. Bandler and Grinder hypothesised in *The Structure of Magic II* that the way the practitioner responds, by matching or mismatching the sensory mode in their own predicates, would lead to different experiences for the person. They expected, for example, that matching predicates would enhance rapport, as in the group described by Grinder.[1]

The role of the senses in making sense

Skills of observation and calibration have played a part in NLP from the very beginning. *The Structure of Magic* is in one respect about the ability of effective psychotherapists to *calibrate* to whether a client's predicates are primarily visual, auditory or kinaesthetic. NLP takes the view that people generally under-use the potential of their sensory apparatus, and NLP training is in part an endeavour to make fuller use of abilities we already possess.

This chapter is about the ways in which NLP explored these inner landscapes of experience; specifically, how our senses actively shape and re-present the domain of experience, forming a vital part of the dynamic of our thinking processes.

According to Walker (1996:257), Perls, Satir, and Milton Erickson had all recognised that people use their senses internally as part of how they coded and processed information; the senses were used in the internal re-creation, as it were, of experience. Spitzer refers to Satir's use of sensory modalities in a video tape that he gave to Bandler and Grinder, saying that; 'These became described as representational modes in Neuro-Linguistic terminology' (1992:3–4). These modes were written up in 'Changing with Families' (Bandler, Grinder & Satir 1976), and 'The Structure of Magic II' (Grinder & Bandler 1976).

Spitzer adds that he believes Satir's awareness of different sensory modalities stemmed from deafness she experienced for several years when young; 'She taught herself lipreading and I believe learned non-verbal communications as a second language.... When hearing did eventually come back she had the opportunity to compare what added learning or confusion came from the addition of this modality' (Spitzer 1992:4).

Milton H. Erickson, from whom Bandler and Grinder went on to learn new possibilities of sensory observation, had also developed an exceptional capacity for fine sensory discrimination through experiences of illness at the age of seventeen. Thus:

> An attack of anterior poliomyelitis in 1919, shortly after my graduation from high school , rendered me almost totally paralyzed for several months, but with my vision, hearing and thinking unimpaired. Since I was quarantined at home on the farm, there was little diversion available. Fortunately, I had always been interested in human behaviour, and there was that of my parents and eight siblings, and also that of the practical nurse who was taking care of me, available for observation. My inability to move tended to restrict me to the intercommunications of those about me. Although I already knew a little about body language and other forms of non-verbal communication, I was amazed to discover the frequent, and, to me, often startling contradictions between the verbal and the non-verbal communications within a single interchange. This aroused so much of my interest that I intensified my observations at every opportunity.
>
> (Erickson, preface to Bandler & Grinder 1975a:vii)

Erickson had written (in 1961) that he had already begun to wonder about the role of the senses in hypnotic inductions in the 1920s, and explored to what extent trance could be elicited in people through commands directed at each of the patient's visual, auditory and kinaesthetic channels (Walker 1996:257).

Varela *et al* (1993) describe a similar notion from Buddhism. Frances Yates (1992) recounts how, in classical times, scholars would develop their memories by deliberately using their imagination to build complex and detailed imagined inner landscapes, buildings or conjectured palaces. They would then place the ideas or objects to be remembered in specific places, so that items to be remembered were associated with the locus or place they had been 'stored'. The publication of Yates' work produced a surge of interest in these techniques; populist Derren Brown presents these as useful 'tricks of the mind' and encourages the activation of the senses in others when using hypnotic language: 'Appeal to all the senses in your subject by referring to things you would like them to see, hear, feel, smell or even taste …. Only when these things are multi-sensory will they seem potent and real' (Brown 2007:161). Thus whenever we imagine, plan, remember, reflect or dream, we do this through a mixture of pictures, sounds, feelings, tastes, smells, and movement. Usually in NLP these sensory constructs are referred to as 'internal representations'.

Internal imagery, of course, played a significant role in Jung's psychology and related therapeutic approaches such as Roberto Assagioli's Psychosynthesis, and is used in personal development (Glouberman 1989) and sports psychology. Bandler and Grinder rediscovered this idea experientially, brought it to the foreground, made it practical and accessible, and began to develop new insights and frameworks. Gregory Bateson acknowledged this innovation when he wrote, with reference to his foregoing work with the Palo Alto group, that; 'we did not see that these various ways of coding – visual, auditory, etc. – are so far apart, so mutually different even in neurophysiologic representation, that no material in one mode can ever be of the same logical type as any material in any other mode' (Bandler & Grinder 1975b:x–xi). Bateson's recognition that visual and auditory information were of different logical types is an important distinction.

The sensory modes were formalised as the (perhaps inelegant) notion of the '4tuple' (Grinder, DeLozier & Bandler 1977:11). This denotes that whether someone is thinking of a memory, a dream, a fantasy, or an outcome, it is experienced, mostly at an unconscious level, as a kind of hologram made up of four modes of information – visual, auditory, kinaesthetic, and gustatory/olfactory (Dilts, Grinder, Bandler & DeLozier 1980:17).[2] Familiarity with the techniques for investigating and changing internal representations remains one of the mainstays of NLP Practitioner trainings. Indeed, according to Grinder, 'the application of NLP patterning to change work has as its objective <u>nothing</u> <u>more</u> than the manipulation of representations' (Bostic St. Clair & Grinder 2001:198).

The relationship between language and inner landscapes

While this domain of experience is distinct from language, language still plays a vital role in activating it. This idea appears in the work of Korzybski (1958), who first published his views in 1941 that human beings operate from their internal maps, which may be linked to language. There are certain NLP trainers, such as Christina Hall who have developed insights into this relationship that have yet to be published, but have become part of the praxis of many of her students.

Grinder states that when we attempt to understand someone's communication, we involuntarily activate what he calls our 'standard language meaning making processes'. These, he believes, are unconscious; 'To understand a word or phrase is to activate – sometimes consciously and *always unconsciously* – the set of images, sounds and feelings associated with that word or phrase' (Bostic St. Clair & Grinder 2001:157).

This, in NLP, is considered to be an essential aspect of meaning making, and many NLP interventions engage people in accessing how they have configured information at the level where they internally re-create events, (what they see, hear, feel, and so on). This is true whether using the phobia cure, or teaching poor spellers to visualise the letters of words as more vivid internal representations.

Bandler and Grinder also realised the implication that when someone is asked 'how do you feel about situation x', then that directs that person to attend to the kinaesthetic part of their internal representation about situation x. This would yield information of a different order or logical type to being asked 'how do you see situation x'. The first would most likely elicit information represented kinaesthetically, whereas the second probably would elicit visually stored data. The use of specific sensory predicates in a question could thus lead people to access information in that particular modality. With this discovery came the insight that the therapist's words could direct the client to access specific aspects of their current experiences.

Eye accessing cues

Among these developments was a set of ideas about the relationship between eye movements and internal representations that is probably among the most contentious in NLP.

In 1976, according to Dilts and DeLozier (2000:383), Bandler and Grinder had begun to notice that people who use a lot of visual predicates often looked (or accessed) upwards, when they were accessing information visually. Similarly, people who attended to sound (and therefore used a predominantly auditory predicates) tended to look sideways. Those who glanced down to the right appeared to be attending to feelings, whilst looking down to the left seemed to indicate attention to internal dialogue.

From this realisation they produced the 'eye accessing cue' model. This first appeared in the second of their books about Milton Erickson (Grinder, DeLozier & Bandler 1977:35–37), of whom we say more in the next chapter. Bostic St. Clair and Grinder say that this was an original piece of research by Bandler and Grinder, and remark on 'the amusing situation where some of those original students who were successful in meeting the challenge... of finding the eye movements themselves, have apparently come to believe that they actually were the original discoverers of this pattern' (Bostic St. Clair & Grinder 2001:193). Although accounts about who discovered the significance of eye accessing cues may vary, Robert Dilts undoubtedly made a significant contribution by going on to test eye movements at the Langley Porter Institute in San Francisco in 1977, a rare attempt from within the field to add empirical support to its claims (Dilts 1983).

According to Dilts and DeLozier (2000:382), the idea that eye movements are significant can be traced back to American psychologist William James, in 1890. According to Pierre Vermersch (1994), the possible meanings of people's eye movements were raised originally by an American psychiatrist, M. E. Day, who suggested that certain types of eye movements indicated when people were attending to their internal worlds of thought, memory and imagination. Day attempted to correlate these with cognitive functions (Day 1964; Day 1967). Vermersch (1994) has incorporated this principle into his research methodology, called 'psychophenomenology', and encourages the researcher to be aware of an interviewee's eye movements when eliciting information about their experience.

What has emerged in NLP is, similar to the insights into sensory modes of representation, a specific, practical model of the relationships between eye movements and internal processing. The principle behind the model is that the direction in which people's eyes move when they turn their attention inwards and think about something, correlates with the particular sensory system to which they are attending. However, the model's claims remain hotly debated, and we discuss the issue of the research evidence relating to it in Chapter 11.

Sub-modalities

The representations in each sensory modality also have more fine-grained characteristics; an experience may be represented visually, for instance, as in bright colours, faded, or even in black and white. Sounds may be experienced as loud or soft, harsh or melodious, and so on. There are also indications that language structures may actively influence this perceptual level of sense making[3] (Mathison 2003), though this is an area that needs far more research.

These are called 'sub-modality' distinctions, based on which people such as Bandler and MacDonald (1988), Christina Hall (personal communication) and Charles Faulkner (1999) have developed a range of NLP interventions. One of the most informative books on NLP's approach to eliciting change through working with sub-modalities is *Using your Brain for a Change* (Bandler 1985).

However the earliest explicit discussion of sub-modalities in the field – and it is an extensive treatment of the subject – appears to be that within David Gordon's 'Therapeutic Metaphors' (Gordon 1978:105–152). Indeed Gordon's book includes a valuable appendix (1978:213–243) that details relevant psychological research into the sensory modalities. Although described by Gordon as not exhaustive, this survey represents one of the few attempts in NLP literature to link its ideas to research in related fields.

This contemporary discovery of sub-modalities also has ancient echoes. Yates (1992) says that Cicero, active in the first century BC, had encouraged scholars to develop their memories by developing rich internal imagery. The following passage, taken from Yates' book, illustrates what Bandler and Grinder would describe as building internal representations:

> We ought then to set up images of a kind that can adhere longest in memory. And we shall do so if we establish similitudes as striking as possible; if we set up images that are not many and vague, but active; if we assign to them exceptional beauty or singular ugliness; if we ornament some of them, as with crowns or purple cloaks, (...) or if we somehow disfigure them ... as by introducing one stained with blood ... so that its form is more striking. But this will be essential – again and again to run over rapidly in the mind all the original places in order to refresh the images.
>
> Cicero, cited in Yates (1992:25–26)

Cicero describes variations that would make these internal representations more memorable. For example, he encouraged people to use movement and bright colours to make the imagined construction more interesting and therefore more memorable. These variations correspond directly to NLP sub-modalities, in this instance sub-modalities of the visual representational system. Re-presented sound and bodily sensations also have sub-modalities. For example, sounds may appear to be coming from near or far, from a particular location, have tonality, pitch, or volume, and may be also represented as music, or words. Bodily sensations can have location, size, temperature, duration, intensity, and more.

How are internal representations and sub-modalities (which are labelled *perceptual processes* in the language of cognitive linguistics), used in NLP? One standard exercise in NLP Practitioner training is to evoke two memories, one that has been classed as 'good' and the other as 'bad', and then to compare the two in detail. Often people find there are marked differences; for example, for some person a 'good' memory may be in colour and contain movement, and evoke a feeling of warmth in certain locations in the body. The 'bad' memory, on the other hand, may be darker, or paler, or not have so much movement, and be accompanied by loud angry voices, and a sensation of heaviness in the body. These qualities are not generalisable, since everyone appears to codify experience at this level differently.

The idea that there are distinctions in visual imagery, which is processed by the cortex, is supported by neurological evidence (Bolstad 2002:19). Bolstad also cites research that supports the idea that, neurologically speaking, size, motion and colour are mediated by separate neuronal networks, all of which are responsible for visual representations. Other functions include brightness, orientation, and binocular disparity. Bolstad reports further that there has been research showing that remembered and constructed images use the same neurological pathways as any current images being constructed.

Contemporary neurological research by Goldstone and Barsalou suggests that cognition is grounded in our perceptual processes: 'our perceptual systems have evolved to establish useful concepts' (1998:234). They suggest that perceptual processes may also play a role in how we categorise objects or events:

> For example, to decide that a particular couch belongs to the category *things that will fit through the front doorway*, a good strategy is to manipulate an analog representation of the couch's shape in reference to an analog representation of the doorway (Goldstone & Barsalou 1998:237).

Mental imagery may enable people to plan by manipulating these self-generated images. Psychologists, with support from findings in neurology, are finding this a rich seam to mine for further nuggets of information. For example, Barsalou and Wiemer-Hastings (2005) propose that there is increasing evidence that conceptual representations are grounded in sensory modalities. Neuro-imaging researchers (e.g. Pecher, Zeelenberg & Barsalou 2004) report increasingly that the different areas of the brain responsible for generating information in the form of sights, sounds, sensations, movement and so on, become active during conceptual processing, though people may not be aware of this. Barsalou (1999:64) also distinguishes automatic processing from what he terms strategic processing, which is the construction and manipulation of a novel simulation. These ideas are further developed through Barsalou's work on 'grounded cognition' (Barsalou 2008a).

Representationalism: An excursion into epistemology

As NLP clearly has used, and continues to use, the term 'representation' it would help to clarify where it stands in relation to criticisms of the notion of *representationalism*. In essence, these question the idea that our internal imagery is a representation in the sense of being like a photograph of an external reality.

First, we can only know the products of what our perceptions construct; we cannot know how those perceptions are created. At the Second Conference on Mental Health in Asia and the Pacific in 1969, Gregory Bateson asked his audience to give him a show of hands if they saw him. His response to this was, 'I see a number of hands – so I guess insanity loves company. Of course *you* don't "really" see *me*. What you "see" is a bunch of pieces of information about me, which you synthesise into a picture image of me. You make that image. It's that simple' (Bateson 2000a: 486). This 'truth' was based on Bateson's acquaintance with the perceptual experiments of Adelbert Ames:

> ... I discovered that when I see something, or hear a sound, or taste, it is my brain, or perhaps I should better say "mind" – it is I who create an image in the modality of the appropriate sense organ. My image is my aggregation and organization of information about the perceived object, aggregated and integrated by me according to rules of which I am totally unconscious. I can, thanks to Ames, know about these rules; but I cannot be conscious of the process of their working....
>
> It seems to be a universal feature of human perception, a feature of the underpinning of human epistemology, that the perceiver shall perceive only the product of his perceiving act. He shall not perceive the means by which that product was created. The product itself is a sort of work of art.
>
> (Brockman 1977:237–238)

Second, an important development in thinking since Bateson's writing, which is emphasised by Humberto Maturana among others, is that our perceptions do not merely receive and *represent* an 'external' world; instead they *create* our experience. For Maturana, 'we bring forth the world we live by living it' (Maturana & Poerkson 2004). There is 'feed forward' from both the mechanisms of perception and from our intentions and predispositions. Varela *et al* make a similar point: '... cognition is not the representation of a pre-given world... but is rather the enactment of a world' (Varela, Thompson & Rosch 1993:9).

The question of what is 'really' going on in perception is highly complex; as Bateson said, 'we wander off into philosophy if we ask, "Is there *really* a territory?"' (Brockman 1977:239). Suffice to say that, for Maturana, the idea of a 'territory' was invalid because all that could be said about it was that it was dependent on our personalities and our perception.

Similarly, Heinz von Foerster relates the work of Johannes Müller, a nineteenth century German physiologist, who discovered that 'the nerves of the different sense organs responded to different kinds of stimuli such as light, sound, and pressure in their own specific way. And this happens *independently* of the physical nature of the stimulus that triggers off the sensation' (Von Foerster & Poerksen 2002:17, emphasis in original).

What does this mean for NLP? The significance is that it dismantles the view that our perceptions are the result of a successive filtering of events in the world. Thus 'we can only know what our senses conjure up from these sensations...The only thing we know for sure is that there is a stimulus or perturbation... With these observations in mind, and they can be found in any textbook on the essentials of physiology, it is absolutely grotesque and downright stupid to talk about a representation of the outer world in the inner world' (Von Foerster & Poerksen 2002:17–18).

This has implications in particular for a map that appears in several NLP books (e.g. Molden 2003:32) of the process by which representations are supposedly produced. This map is usually called, somewhat oddly, 'the communication model'. Its origin is unclear, as it appears not to have been articulated by Bandler and Grinder themselves even though it is based on their writing about perceptual filters (e.g. Bandler & Grinder 1975b). It appears in diagrammatic form in James and Woodsmall's 'Timeline Therapy' (1988:4),[4] attributed to the work of Bandler and Grinder. This map portrays perception as a process whereby information from the 'territory' (the external world) is filtered and comes to form internal representations. James and Woodsmall emphasise that a model is 'only a description'; nowhere in NLP is the principle that 'the map is not the territory' more important to remember than with this model. Maturana's critique would appear to undermine it, because it simply neglects the way that our perceptions go forth into the world, and do not wait passively for sense impressions to arrive.

We do not regard NLP's idea of internal representations *per se* as discarded by this critique. In essence Bandler and Grinder were drawing attention to the existence of this 'inner landscape', and how it can be used for people's benefit. Hubbard (2007), for example, argues that the concept of mental representation is fundamental to studies of consciousness.

However, NLP literature, including 'Whispering in the Wind', continues to put forward a view that portrays representations as the end result of a sequence of filters, starting with some datum or event that originates in the external world.[5] Thus Bostic St. Clair and Grinder use the metaphor of 'data streaming' (2001:13) and say that what we perceive, a kind of hallucination, is actually the end result of many millions of neurological events from the point at which our receptors are stimulated by, say, a photon (in the case of visual receptors), through complex pathways, both neurological and biochemical, reaching that part of the brain which enables us to be conscious of a particular image. This view adopts the metaphor of giving *access* to the world. Yet according to the views of Maturana and others, perception does not give us 'access' *to* anything else at all; it *is* our experience. The principle that our experience is perceptually constructed, and logically distinct from whatever constitutes 'the world', is important and helpful; on the other hand, the persistence of the 'communication model' and metaphors such as 'access' is a feature of NLP that could be held to express a 'representationalist' position.

Conclusion

We began this chapter with the story of the ways in which Bandler and Grinder, and many of their collaborators, discovered the richness and complexity of the world created by the senses in our inner landscapes. This became an essential dimension of NLP, to the extent that we regard it as foundational for this knowledge system.

The way in which NLP makes specific, detailed, intentional use of this inner domain through its notions of sensory modes and submodalities is characteristic, and distinguishes it from many other approaches to learning and personal change. The internal world of the senses is a rich resource for planning, imagining, dreaming, remembering and reflecting, which deserves more investigation. An important hypothesis that emerges from this work is the idea that language can directly influence configurations in this internal domain.

We have also explored briefly some of the philosophical and epistemological puzzles that an awareness of the importance of inner landscapes produces, and have argued that whilst NLP's notion of internal representations does not constitute 'representationalism' as such, representationalist views continue to appear, epitomised by the NLP 'communication model'.

7

The Influences of Erickson and the Palo Alto Group

The next aspect of the story involves NLP's links with the psychiatrist and hypnotherapist, Milton H. Erickson M.D., and with the work of the Palo Alto Mental Research Institute (MRI). It introduces one of the underpinning streams of thought from which NLP has evolved, that of constructivism.

Milton Erickson

The manuscript of *The Structure of Magic* received an initial, unfavourable review from Jay Haley, a pioneer of family therapy, so Grinder and Bandler asked Gregory Bateson to provide a further review (Bostic St. Clair & Grinder 2001:190–191). Bateson, who was also a friend of Robert Spitzer's, was more impressed, which persuaded Spitzer to publish the book.[1]

Bateson then invited Bandler and Grinder to an evening at which they were 'treated to an intellectual feast – a remarkable and stimulating discussion with Bateson that lasted for hours' (Bostic St. Clair & Grinder 2001:173). Not only did Bateson offer to write the foreword to *The Structure of Magic* but also, because of their interest in the effects of language, he urged them to make contact with a friend and colleague of his, Milton Erickson.

Bateson and Erickson had known each other for many years,[2] because Bateson and Margaret Mead had consulted Erickson in connection with their work on Balinese trance (Lipset 1980:201; Haley 1973:9). Their acquaintance dates back at least to 1942 when Erickson addressed a meeting (on the subject of hypnotism)[3] that was the precursor of the Macy Conferences (see Chapter 8).

Bateson arranged for Bandler and Grinder to go to Phoenix, Arizona, where Erickson still lived and practised. Indeed this episode echoes events more than twenty years earlier in 1953, when Bateson had arranged for Jay Haley to attend a seminar in hypnosis given by Erickson, following which Haley and John Weakland 'began to make regular visits to Phoenix, where Dr. Erickson was in private practice. We spent many hours talking with him about the nature of hypnosis and watching him work with subjects' (Haley 1973:9). Bateson, it seemed, had long harboured the desire to understand more about Erickson's methods.

Grinder describes how, after waiting several days in Phoenix, he rang Erickson's house to arrange a meeting. He and Bandler had rehearsed what they had managed to glean about Erickson's use of language for hypnotic inductions, and used this when speaking to him on the phone for the first time. They succeeded in gaining an audience: 'you boys come over here immediately', was Erickson's response (Bostic St. Clair & Grinder 2001:177).

For the next ten months he and Bandler would spend days at a time observing and modelling Erickson at work. They distilled the language patterns through which Erickson induced trance and effected changes in his clients, then would test their mastery by trying out these patterns on other people (Bostic St. Clair & Grinder 2001:177).

As with the meta-model, there was a rigour in the way they researched Erickson's work. For example, when testing the effectiveness of particular syntactical patterns that Erickson had used, Bandler and Grinder would work with similar, paired clients, applying Erickson's patterns but leaving out a single element with one of the clients:

The key question was,

Did leaving out the particular behaviour that distinguishes the treatment offered to the two clients make a difference to the results?

If the answer is yes, the behavior involved will be maintained as a conditionally essential part of the model.
(Bostic St. Clair & Grinder 2001:181)

When satisfied that they had identified the patterns, they wrote them up as the two volumes of 'The Patterns of the Hypnotic techniques of

Milton H Erickson, M.D.' (Bandler & Grinder 1975a; Grinder, DeLozier & Bandler 1977), acknowledging the assistance of Erickson's student Rossi, who collaborated with Erickson and published some of his case studies at the same time, for providing them with many recordings and transcripts (1975a:xi). Much of the content of the two volumes of 'Patterns' was presented in a more accessible, workshop format in '*Trance*-formations' (Grinder & Bandler 1981), and Bandler has recently produced an updated version of this subject (Bandler 2008b).

While Grinder's account of this period in 'Whispering in the Wind' mentions only himself and Bandler, some of their contemporaries had also explored Erickson's methods, including the aforementioned Steve Lankton (Lankton 1980:2) and Bill O'Hanlon, Steve Gilligan, who is described as 'one of the world's most effective hypnotists' in the dedications to 'The Structure of Magic II', and David Gordon, who wrote a book on metaphor (Gordon 1978), a core feature of Erickson's work that receives little attention in the two volumes of 'Patterns'.

There is an extensive Ericksonian literature that complements many of these findings (for example, Haley 1973; Rosen 1982), so the two volumes of 'Patterns' represent only a fraction of the books about Erickson's work. However, Bandler and Grinder appear to have generated some fresh insights. In particular they recognised that Erickson's use of language bore a relationship to the meta-model – Erickson appeared to be using these same patterns, but in an inverse way. While the emphasis of the meta-model was on recovering deleted material in order to increase the information available about a client's construction of a problem, Erickson would introduce deletions purposefully, in a way that invited the client to discover their own meanings through what was termed a 'trans-derivational search' (Bandler & Grinder 1975a:220).

The main fruit of this work, known as The 'Milton Model', has become a standard feature of most NLP practitioner and master practitioner trainings. It is taught alongside the meta-model, as the basis for practising hypnotic language through techniques such as embedded commands. Most significantly, these patterns are believed to facilitate communication with the unconscious, which in this approach is reckoned to be the source of most of the resources a person needs in order to learn and change.

What of the validity of Erickson's approach, and of NLP's understanding of these techniques? Illusionist Derren Brown questions the extent to which Erickson's reputation rests on admiration and devotion inspired by anecdotes more than on substantiated results. He even goes on to describe NLP as the 'Frankenstein grandchild' of Ericksonian hypnosis (2007:128), and wonders about the extent to which people in NLP may have utilised Erickson's technique in order to construct plausible stories of NLP's credibility and efficacy as a substitute for an evidence base (an issue to which we return in Chapter 11).

Views on Erickson are divided. Jay Haley, for example, refers to Erickson's 'brilliant therapeutic techniques' (Haley 1973:9). The only published critique to which Brown refers is one by McCue (1988), which, from our reading of it, consists more of incredulity than evidenced challenge. Thus, apart from alleging some minor factual discrepancies between Erickson's accounts and those of certain other authors, McCue's argument relies on assertions that 'some of Erickson's explanations and assertions are hard to believe', and that 'his case reports probably give an exaggerated impression of their author's therapeutic prowess' (McCue 1988:265).[4] Rosen, on the other hand, says that, based on personal observation of Erickson at work, the accounts are generally factual (1982:32–34).

Critical appraisal of Erickson's work is nevertheless important, not least because the potential for influencing others through 'hypnotic language' clearly has ethical implications. Erickson used these techniques as a means to elicit and facilitate a client's change, and not (as is commonly assumed to be happening with hypnosis) as a way to impose the practitioner's views or will.

Has NLP accurately represented Erickson's work? According to Erickson, yes, except that it gives a partial view; in the preface to 'Patterns I', Erickson acknowledges its contribution to elucidating his patterns, but also described the book as 'far from being a complete description of my methodologies, as they so clearly state it is a much better explanation of how I work than I, myself, can give. I know what I do, but to explain how I do it is much too difficult for me' (Bandler & Grinder 1975a:viii). Immediately following this comment, Erickson cites his daughter Kristina's insight into how, as a medical student, she routinely used her own language skills to gain permission from her patients to rectal and hernial examinations, which they had a right to refuse. It would be surprising, indeed astonishing, given Erickson's renowned artistry with stories, if the placing of this anecdote was purely accidental. The point Erickson may have been making, dear reader, we leave to your imagination.

The Palo Alto Mental Research Institute (MRI)

Among those interested in Erickson's work specifically, and in the effects of language more widely, were the researchers at the Palo Alto Mental Research Institute. We have already noted the involvement of both Robert Spitzer and Virginia Satir at this Institute, which was founded in 1959 in Stanford, California. Developed through Gregory Bateson's decade-long (from 1952 to 1961) collaboration with John Weakland, Jay Haley, William Fry, and Donald D. Jackson, its purpose was to further the understanding of the cybernetic nature of human communication, and about ways of using this knowledge to produce therapeutic change. In contrast to NLP, there are extensive records of that collaboration (Ray & Govener 2007).

In the mid 1960s, the Mental Research Institute went through a crisis, after which many of the founders and originators went their own ways. Bateson had already moved on in 1963, Satir left in 1966, and Paul Watzlawick, took a leading role. In the same year Richard Fisch founded the Brief Therapy Institute as an adjunct to the MRI.

Bandler and Grinder, and their co-workers, knew of, and acknowledged, the work and discoveries of the MRI, for example through references to Haley, Watzlawick and others in 'Changing with Families' (Bandler, Grinder & Satir 1976). Judith DeLozier has said that the MRI's work was simply part of 'all the new stuff that was going on' that the originators of NLP absorbed.[5] Nor was the influence entirely one-way. Paul Watzlawick's 'Language of Change' (1978) makes several references to 'The Structure of Magic' and to 'Patterns I', and acknowledges Bandler and Grinder's detailed study of Erickson's work.

Like Bateson, the Palo Alto researchers were interested in the relevance of logical types and game theory to human interaction. As we shall discuss below, they also explored reframing as an approach to producing change (Watzlawick, Weakland & Fisch 1974:92). Significantly, they focused on understanding how patterns of behaviour functioned to form, maintain and resolve problems – hence their emphasis on the *pragmatics* of human communication (Watzlawick,

Beavin & Jackson 1967:13). This notion of pragmatics appears to encapsulate something of the essence of NLP too; indeed Robert Dilts notes that he once took a class by John Grinder at the University of Santa Cruz that was called 'Pragmatics of Human Communication' (1994b:ix).

The Palo Alto group also showed a fondness for the prefix 'meta' (1967:286), especially through the concept of metacommunication, that appears in NLP in numerous variations; the 'meta-model', the 'meta-mirror', 'meta-states', and 'Meta Publications'.[6] However, despite a strong interest in language – for example, their work was informed by Wittgenstein's philosophy (e.g. Watzlawick 1990) – there is no evidence that the Palo Alto group drew from the work of Chomsky, Lakoff or others. This linkage to contemporary linguistics, albeit one that was not sustained, must be regarded as Bandler and Grinder's innovation, as acknowledged in Bateson's foreword to 'The Structure of Magic'.

The Palo Alto approach fed into a number new therapies predicated on the idea that the therapist's task was to enable the client to change the *constructions* of the problematic situations for which they have sought help. These included Brief Therapy (McDermott & Jago 2001) and Provocative Therapy (Farrelly & Brandsma 1974). In Brief Therapy the emphasis is on finding solutions rather than causes, explanations or invoking past events. In Provocative Therapy the therapist deliberately challenges the patient to recognise the areas of their belief systems that are proving problematic and difficult to talk about (Farrelly & Brandsma 1974:61). Bill O'Hanlon and James Wilk refer to Bandler and Grinder in 'Shifting Contexts' (1987), another example of a constructivist approach.

While having many similarities to NLP, and sharing the interest in 'pragmatics', the work of the Palo Alto group developed through a more explicit emphasis on research, and through articulating its underlying theory, especially that of constructivism, in published works (e.g. Watzlawick 1990:131–151). This leads us to the question, what is constructivism?

Deconstructing constructivism[7]

In essence, constructivism introduces the idea that people construct their own versions of 'reality' (whatever reality means!) which then acts as the basis for their ways of understanding and operating in the world. Constructivists do not ask 'what is real?' but rather 'how do we construct our understanding of what we imagine to be real?'

Heinz von Foerster (who, as we shall describe in Chapter 7, attended many of the Macy conferences with Bateson) is considered to be one of the founders of the constructivist movement, although he argues that 'constructivism' is a word that should be eradicated from our language:[8]

> In my opinion, what is referred to as constructivism should remain a pure and simple sceptical attitude that casts doubt on the evidence of realism. (Von Foerster & Poerksen 2002: 45–46)

What is the relevance of constructivism to NLP? Like Paul Watzlawick, NLP is fundamentally interested in 'the way in which communication creates reality' (Watzlawick 1976:xi). Thus Watzlawick wrote that constructivism 'examines those processes of perception, behaviour, and communication which we human beings use to create our individual, social, scientific and ideological realities, instead of finding them ready-made in the outside world' (Watzlawick 1990:132). As we saw in Chapter 6, NLP's interest in internal representations opens up issues about what (if anything) is being represented. The stance of the radical constructivist is that our representations do not describe any outer reality (Von Foerster & Poerksen 2002); the only 'reality' is that which is produced by our acts of cognition.

Categorisation

Attending to questions of how our realities are constructed, and of how they are structured, highlights the significance of categorisation. As we shall discover, categorisation lies behind the various NLP techniques of reframing (Bandler & Grinder 1982).

In the early 1950s, one of the phenomena that intrigued Bateson was the way in which animals and humans used categories, or frames, as part of their sense-making. He was influenced by Bertrand Russell's exploration of classes of information as being of different logical types (Bateson 2000a:180). In 1954 he wrote that 'human verbal communication can operate and always does operate at many contrastive levels of abstraction' (Bateson 2000a:177–178), and that these levels of abstraction act as categories. This was a significant insight into epistemology, which is concerned with the processes involved in perceiving, understanding, making sense and explaining, and also with *how* people know instead of *what* they know.

In his seminal work, *Women, Fire and Dangerous Things,* George Lakoff (1987) explores the processes of categorisation and their philosophical implications, arguing for an essentially subjectivist view of knowledge. He suggested that how information is categorised influences how it is then perceived and responded to. Categorisation is so fundamental an epistemological process that people tended to attribute a real existence to the categories themselves, thus: 'There is nothing more basic than categorisation to our thought, perception, action and speech' (Lakoff 1987:5). Then categories are thought to act as a kind of blueprint, which contains within it templates informing subsequent behaviour and people's perceptions of cause-effect relations.

For example, Watzlawick recounts an informal experiment carried out at the Palo Alto Mental Research Institute in which Don Jackson, an internationally known psychotherapist, was asked to interview a paranoid patient who, he was told, thought he was a clinical psychologist. A 'real' clinical psychologist was asked if he would be willing to be filmed interviewing 'a paranoid patient who thought he was a psychiatrist'. The meeting was duly set up; 'Both promptly went to work treating each other for their delusions' (Watzlawick 1976:84–85). The category to which each person in the experiment was assigned indicated how they should be understood.

Categorisation can happen at a number of different levels. For example, consider the statement that a dolphin is a cetacean, which is a mammal, which is a vertebrate, which is an animal, which is a living organism, and so on. Here there are at least six different levels of categorisation, representing different levels of abstraction. As one metaphorically goes 'up' the hierarchy of levels, so more information is packed (again metaphorically) into each category. There are more 'things' in the category 'vertebrates' than there are in 'cetaceans'. This principle is used in NLP through its notions of 'chunking' up and down logical levels (e.g. O'Connor & Seymour 1990:150–152).

This line of thought suggests that categorisation is a process that is created, perpetuated and activated by language. Karl Weick, writing about the field of management, illustrates how the categorisation of a task may change people's approach to it.

> If a person justifies a decision to accept an unpleasant assignment with the explanation that it will be a challenge and an opportunity, that person often can create just such attractions and solidify the justification by the way he or she performs the assignment (Weick 2001:23).

Similarly, Cazden (1988:116) cites an example of the influence of a perceived category, transmitted through language, on the responses of schoolchildren to a command that asked them to assign an activity to a category (i.e. being a guard) as they were doing it: 'In two Soviet experiments, preschool children were able to stand still longer when asked to "be a guard" (contextualised instruction) than when asked simply to stand still.'

Another relevant contribution is that from Robert Goldstone, a cognitive psychologist, who proposes (Goldstone & Kersten 2003) that the act of interpreting any information is fundamentally an act of categorisation, and that an extremely wide variety of cognitive acts can be understood as being based on this process. There are, in his view and those of his co-workers, at least nine different perceptual effects that categorisation can potentially exert on the perceiver.[9] Research in neurobiology even suggests that our nervous systems may be metaphorically 'hard wired', as it were, to classify incoming information into abstract categories (Grossman *et al* 2006).

Developments in cognitive psychology over the last half century are increasingly in agreement that abstraction and categorisation are critical to how our cognition operates. Yet, with the exception of recent work by Steve Andreas (Andreas 2006b), there is little discussion in the literature of NLP of the contemporary thinking about categorisation by authors like Lakoff and Goldstone.

Metacommunication

Another constructivist notion that became central to the work of the Palo Alto school was that of *metacommunication*.

Communication is based on being able to use, and distinguish between, such logical levels. Bateson discovered that when animals interact, there are always signals that assign the activity they are about to engage in to a category. Animals squaring up to indulge in play fighting will transmit this information by non-verbal signals, for example; dogs will bare their teeth to show aggression but wag their tails to signal 'this is play'. Animals distinguish between play and true threat by giving each other information about the type of activity their behaviour represents, (Bateson 2000a:177–193).

Such signals are essentially a *message about the message*. Bateson's recognition, during a visit to a zoo, that monkeys that are play-fighting *know* that they are playing, and not fighting (Bateson 2000a: 179) , is regarded by Ivanovas (2007:847) as 'one of the milestones of Western science'.

As noted earlier, the technical term for this is *metacommunication*. According to Bateson and the Palo Alto school, *all* interaction involves both communication and metacommunication. Metacommunication, which is at a different logical level, is information that is exchanged between people about their relationship, or the context for their interaction. In business, it is through metacommunication that people convey messages about power and authority, culture, and so on, without needing to make these things explicit. This insight fundamentally challenges the view that 'clear communication', in which people say exactly what they mean, is possible if only people would use language with precision.

Two features complicate this. Bateson believed that while we can identify metacommunication as logically distinct in theory, and indicate how it works, in practice one cannot pull communication apart to separate out the metacommunication 'element'. Second, Bateson recognised that paradoxes and double binds were particular cases in which listeners could not undisputedly assign the information to a category.

These insights into the structures of communication enabled Bateson to develop a new approach to the treatment of schizophrenia (Bateson *et al* 1956). This was regarded as seminal work, and was continued through the Palo Alto group's research into communication patterns. Bateson's view was that the person with schizophrenia may have been exposed to double binds in their communication with significant others, usually in their own family. The result is a sometimes painful confusion of logical types, of which Watzlawick cites an elegant example:

> Give your son Marvin two sport shirts as a present. The first time he wears one of them, look at him sadly and say in your Basic Tone of Voice: 'The other one you didn't like?'
> (quoted in Watzlawick, Beavin & Jackson 1968:211).[10]

The person on the receiving end of this type of communication may begin to doubt their own ability to make sense. These patterns are not only confined to pathogenic families, though; they are also part of everyday discourse. Jane was recently working with some managers from a local organisation that had been taken over by a larger conglomerate in the previous month. The managers reported their pain and confusion after the new MD had addressed them. First he assured them that it was important to be completely transparent about the future of their part of the organisation. 'I can assure you that your jobs are safe', he told them, but then went on: 'Of course, I know things that I can't divulge about what could happen a year from now.' The conflicting messages behind the speech included 'I am transparent, and at the same time I'm not transparent' and 'your jobs are safe, but maybe they're not'. This was a typical 'double bind' structure.

Constructivist ideas in NLP

Bandler and Grinder based their work on the belief that people operate out of their individual 'maps of the world', not from reality itself; 'we operate within that world using a map or series of maps of that world to guide our behaviour in it' (Bandler & Grinder 1975b:3). Hence Craft (2001:131) argues that principally NLP 'draws on the fundamental assumptions of the theoretical framework of social constructivism'. Esser (2004) agrees that NLP is anchored in the conceptual matrix of constructivism; this is also consistent with the classification of neurolinguistic psychotherapy as an 'Experiential Constructivist' mode in the UK. On the other hand, the idea that NLP is based on social constructionism is contested by Rowan (2008).

The influence of constructivism on NLP is evident both in its broad approach, and in various specific respects. Here we focus on two, the principle that 'the map is not the territory', and the notion of reframing.

The influence of constructivist ideas on NLP is illustrated by Bandler and Grinder's references to the comparatively little-known ideas of two writers. One was Hans Vaihinger (Bandler & Grinder 1975b:7), a philosopher who was interested in how the human mind could both deform and transform itself, and who stressed the importance of imagination to healthy functioning (Esser 2004:155).

The other was Alfred Korzybski (Bandler & Grinder 1975b:5–12), from whom NLP takes the central idea that 'the map is not the territory'. Korzybski (1879–1950) was a Polish engineer who emigrated to the United States after the First World War. It seems likely that he came to the attention of Bandler and Grinder via Gregory Bateson, who had given the Nineteenth Annual Korzybski Memorial Lecture in New York in 1970 for the Institute of General Semantics (Bateson 2000a:454). Korzybski's General Semantics was an attempt to explain the relationships between people's language, thinking, and experience (Esser 2004:155). In 'Science and Sanity' (Korzybski 1958, originally published in 1933) he explored the implications of abstraction to mathematics and linguistics, and to how we know that we know.

Just as later with Bateson, Korzybski was influenced by Russell and Whitehead's theory of logical types, which proposes that there is a significant epistemological distinction to be made between an individual event, and the group or category to which it was assigned. Korzybski was writing at time when fascism was spreading, and warned of the dangers of confusing the abstract word with the real thing, echoing Whitehead and Russell's concerns about the fallacy of false concreteness, that is of assigning a concrete reality to a cognitive construct. Thus 'Fatherland' is an abstraction, which belongs to a separate logical type. To think of it in the same way as a concrete object and to act is if it were 'real' would be an example of that fallacy.

Korzybski, however, is not regarded widely as an influential thinker. Indeed Gardner (1957) describes him as someone who held his own work in high esteem, but whose ideas were often flawed and derivative. Holl (2007:1053) suggests that Korzybski's major work, 'Science and Sanity' has 'endless redundancies' and that its nearly thousand pages could be reduced to ten. Given the frequency with which Korzybski is cited in NLP, it is interesting to note that Bateson's writing actually makes very little reference to him. Harries-Jones (1995:67) observes that, according to Bateson's correspondence, he 'regarded Korzybski's ideas as a second-hand rendering' of the ideas of the philosopher Alfred North Whitehead. Bateson was interested in Korzybski's ideas about the structure of knowledge, primarily by the notion that is so familiar in NLP, 'the map is not the territory'; thus; 'language bears to the objects which it denotes a relationship comparable to that which a map bears to the territory' (Bateson 2000a:180). Incidentally, what Korzybski actually said was; 'A map is not the territory it represents, but, if correct, it has a similar structure to the territory, which accounts for its usefulness...' (Korzybski 1958:58–60) as acknowledged and quoted by Bandler and Grinder in 'Patterns I' (1975a:181).

In short, Bateson cited Korzybski's dictum in order to emphasise that the act of mapping is essentially metaphorical (Bateson 2000a:407), and that to confuse map and territory was one of the errors perpetuated by Western thought. Korzybski's work did become an extensive and central influence on 'neuro-semantics', the offshoot of NLP that is the 'brainchild' of Michael Hall and Bobby Bodenhamer.[11] Ultimately, however, NLP appears to take little from Korzybski apart from 'the map is not the territory', which is universally cited as a presupposition in the field (see Chapter 9).

Reframing

A feature of categorisation is that a change of category to which an event is assigned has significant and useful effects. This was recognised by Bateson, who explored the importance to our thinking of what he termed 'frames' (Bateson 2000a:184–189), and their effects as the contexts on perception and understanding. He suggested that these were analogous to a picture frame, which is intended to organise the way the viewer pays attention; which is picture and which is the wall it is hanging on? The intention of the frame is to instruct the observer to 'attend to what is within and do not attend to what is outside' (Bateson 2000a:187).

Bandler and Grinder incorporated the use of *reframing* in NLP as a way to elicit changes in how people thought about situations that they had construed as problematic (Bandler & Grinder 1982).

Reframing is a technique that can be used by any coach, mentor or manager. It offers new sets of lenses, as it were, through which a problematic situation can be viewed differently. The editors of 'Reframing', Steve and Connirae Andreas, point out in their introduction that one form of re-framing ('content' reframing) was widely used in contemporary family and systems therapies, citing Watzlawick and Haley at Palo Alto as well as Salvador Minuchin and therapists at the Philadelphia Child Guidance Clinic (see also Gordon 1978:48). Bandler and Grinder elaborated on this technique and added a second type, which they called 'context reframing'. This uses the principle that almost any behaviour is useful somewhere, therefore what people define as 'problematic' behaviour can be redefined by thinking of a viable alternative context. One of their favourite examples of a reframe, based on a pattern originally used by Virginia Satir, is the following:

> When the father says 'Oh my daughter is just too stubborn' and you say 'aren't you proud that she can say "no" to men with bad intentions?', that's a really valid way of looking at the situation.
> (Bandler & Grinder 1982:42)

However, their chief claim to innovation is to have introduced 'six-step reframing' (Bandler & Grinder 1979:137–157), described as NLP's 'breakthrough pattern' (Bostic St. Clair & Grinder 2001:198). Whereas both content and context reframing typically involve the conscious use of language to offer alternative meanings, six-step reframing shows Erickson's influence in the way that it engages the client's unconscious. It is used, typically, where a person is meeting a valid need through behaviour that has become inappropriate. The practitioner invites the client to communicate with his or her 'creative part', which generates new behavioural options, thereby accessing unconscious resources to resolve the situation.

Conclusion

NLP's thinking about people's 'maps of the world' has its source in constructivism. It can therefore be seen as one of a number of new approaches to therapy that were informed by constructivism via the work of the Palo Alto school, which was itself influenced by

Milton Erickson's work long before Bandler and Grinder's introduction to him. Erickson's influence on NLP is significant, and informs its beliefs about how to communicate with and work with the unconscious.

Many features of constructivism are evident in the way NLP is practised, including the slogan taken from Korzybski that 'the map is not the territory', and an emphasis on working with categories through reframing. NLP also shares the Palo Alto group's emphasis on the pragmatics of human communication. As we shall discover in the next chapter, constructivism is closely related to another foundational theory behind NLP, that of cybernetics. Where constructivism informs us about some of the features of our notions of reality, cybernetics complements this by providing a theory of how perceptions, constructions, and behaviour are organised as systems.

8
Gregory Bateson and Cybernetics

John Grinder refers to living on a plot of land in the 1970s with Judith DeLozier, where '*One of the amazing characters who we've crossed paths with was a tall, slope-shouldered Englishman by the name of Gregory Bateson*' (DeLozier & Grinder 1987:5). We have already referred to Gregory Bateson numerous times. Who was he, and what was his involvement with NLP? Significantly, Bateson provides a direct link between the founding of cybernetics in the 1940s and the origins of NLP.

Gregory Bateson

Bateson, who lived from 1904–1980, is held to be one of the most influential thinkers of the twentieth century (Harries-Jones 1995:14), if one who is neglected due to 'his refusal to stay within the bounds of single disciplines' (Charlton 2008:1). Described variously as having an 'exceptional capacity for imaginative conceptualization', 'an enormous capacity for playful conversation', and also 'a "prima donna" syndrome of some kind' (Lipset 1980:185, 255), he influenced developments in such diverse fields as family therapy and communications studies (Hawkins 2004). His stature is indicated by the fact that two academic journals, 'Kybernetes'[1] and 'Cybernetics and Human Knowing',[2] both produced special issues to mark Bateson's centennial.

As the third of three sons of the geneticist William Bateson, Gregory grew up in an intellectual family. He attended Charterhouse , a well-known English public school in Surrey, then went to Cambridge University where initially he read zoology (Lipset 1980:95). In 1925 he turned to anthropology (Lipset 1980:114). His early life was scarred by tragedy; by 1922 he had suffered the loss of both of his brothers, one killed in World War I, the other committing suicide (Lipset 1980:90–91).

In 1936 he married Margaret Mead, with whom he conducted anthropological fieldwork in New Guinea and Bali, and then in 1940 took up residency in the USA. There they were both prominent members of the Macy conferences, which began in 1946 and which laid the foundations for the science of cybernetics, which we describe in more detail below. They divorced in 1950; their daughter, Mary Catherine (Cathy) Bateson, who has described her parents' relationship in 'With a Daughter's Eye' (Bateson 1994), went on to become a professor of Anthropology and English at George Mason University. Imagined dialogues between father and daughter, based on conversations Gregory and Cathy used to have (Lipset 1980:199) appear as 'metalogues' in some of his books (e.g. Bateson 2000a:3–58). Gregory married again in 1951 and had a son, John (Lipset 1980:197), by his second wife.

In the 1950s, the dynamics of human communication became the main focus of Gregory's work when Jurgen Ruesch introduced him to psychiatric medicine (Ruesch & Bateson 1951). He began working with Don Jackson, Jay Haley and John Weakland, with whom he developed the 'double bind' theory of schizophrenia (Bateson, Jackson, Haley & Weakland 1956). He then became involved in the influential Palo Alto Mental Research Institute that Jackson founded (Lipset 1980:227). In 1961 he married for a third time; he and Lois Bateson had a daughter, Nora, in 1969 (Lipset 1980:246).

From 1965–1972 he was Associate Director for Research of the Oceanic Institute, Waimanalo, Hawaii. There he had the opportunity of observing the behaviour of dolphins, based on which he developed his theory of 'levels of learning' (Bateson 2000a:279–308), which inspired NLP author Robert Dilts to develop his well known, and contested, 'neurological levels' model (Dilts & Epstein 1995).[3]

Bateson then moved to Santa Cruz, where the events described in previous chapters unfolded, and in 1976 he was appointed to the Board of Regents of the University of California by Jerry Brown, then Governor of California (Lipset 1980:290). Bateson died in 1980, from cancer.

David Lipset, Bateson's biographer, states that Bateson, with his wife Lois and their daughter Nora, took up residence at the University of California in Santa Cruz in January 1973 (1980:280), affiliating himself with Kresge College at the end of the year.[4] Kresge's new provost, geneticist Robert Edgar, had become concerned about its lack of academic mission. He persuaded Bateson, whose 'Steps to an Ecology of Mind' had been published to some acclaim in 1972, even being reviewed in *Rolling Stone*, to join Kresge, hoping that Bateson's presence and interests might give the institution a more coherent intellectual focus. Although Bateson's role at Kresge was intended to be central, he found that many students spoke 'a horrible touchy-feely jargon' (Grant & Riesman 1978:121) and his influence was far less than Edgar had hoped (Lipset 1980:281).

Bateson and his family moved to a rented house near Ben Lomond 'after concluding the academic year of 1974' (Lipset 1980:281). According to Walker (1996:36), this was because Lois Bateson was interested in alternative childbirth, which featured in the Spitzers' community. The Batesons lived there for four years until moving to Esalen sometime after August 1978 (Lipset 1980:301).

It was at Ben Lomond that Bateson became the neighbour that Grinder describes. By the time he joined that community, Bandler and Grinder's work on the meta model had already been done, and a manuscript of 'The Structure of Magic' had been written; a letter from Bateson to Helen Kennedy of Kresge College, dated 10th January 1974,[5] refers to 'conversations about the book jointly authored by Grinder and Bandler', and prefigures Bateson's foreword to 'The Structure of Magic', with its reference to 'a rather dry and formal linguistic analysis of some psychopathologies and psychotherapeutic processes'. The letter's purpose was to support John Grinder in relation to a decision to be made by a committee, saying; 'I very much hope that Kresge will be able to take Grinder under its wing.' Bateson adds that 'it is really, I gather, since the writing of the book that John has blossomed into a very fertile thinker and talker'.

Bateson's influence on NLP

Dilts and DeLozier say that Bateson's influence on NLP 'goes largely unacknowledged' (2000:90), and Michael Hall (2001)[6] has suggested that Bateson still receives too little credit for the way his ideas have contributed to the field. Nevertheless, Bateson is probably the most-cited 'non-NLP' author in NLP literature. Works such as 'Whispering in the Wind' (Bostic St. Clair & Grinder 2001), Dilts and DeLozier's 'Encyclopedia' (2000:90–93), and 'Turtles all the Way Down' (DeLozier & Grinder 1987) discuss his ideas at length.

According to Dilts and DeLozier (2000:91): 'Key NLP concepts, such as "states," "metaphor," "conscious/unconscious relationships," "perceptual positions," "multiple descriptions," "perceptual filters," and "levels of learning and change"... were directly inspired by Bateson's work'. Hall (2001) also emphasises the significance of Bateson's interests in the relationships between language, thought and perception, or 'epistemology'.[7] Bateson also addressed the distinction between form and substance, which is reflected in the central NLP interest in the process (or structure) rather than the content of communication (e.g. Bateson 2000a:154).

What, though, was Gregory Bateson's perspective on NLP? About this, it is interesting that so little is said. Bateson's foreword to the two volumes of 'The Structure of Magic' acknowledges the advance they made on his work with his colleagues at Palo Alto: '*We already knew that most of the premises of individual psychology were useless, and we knew that we ought to classify modes of communication. But it never occurred to us to ask about the effects of modes upon interpersonal relations*' (Bateson in Bandler & Grinder 1975b:x). Apart from the foreword we have found no published comment by Bateson about either NLP or his encounters with Bandler and Grinder. Nowhere is there any evidence that Bandler and Grinder's work influenced Bateson' own writing,[8] nor is there evidence of dialogue between them after Bateson had introduced Bandler and Grinder to Milton Erickson, even though they were neighbours and knew each other well (Bostic St. Clair & Grinder 2001:173).

Furthermore their encounters at Santa Cruz are ignored in all the major literature on Bateson and his work. Not in Brockman (1977), Charlton (2008), Harries-Jones (1995), Lipset (1980), or the two journal special issues mentioned above, does there appear a single reference to Bandler, Grinder, or NLP. Lipset, for example, mentions various faculty and students at Kresge by name. He describes Bateson's meeting with English radical psychiatrist Ronnie Laing, and also refers to Bateson's links to humanistic psychology, family therapy, and Gestalt during these years. But he makes no reference whatsoever to Bandler or to Grinder, nor to any other figure associated with the early development of NLP. The Bateson archive throws no further light on the collaboration.

In terms of published comment by Bateson we are left, therefore, with one letter and Bateson's foreword to 'The Structure of Magic'. If Bateson was as convinced of the significance of Bandler and Grinder's insights as that foreword suggests, why did he not say more? Given Bateson's insistence that 'one cannot not communicate', this is intriguing, rather like the dog that did not bark in the Sherlock Holmes story, 'The Silver Blaze'.

As Grinder acknowledges, Bateson may have influenced NLP, but he did not endorse it (Bostic St. Clair & Grinder 2001:93). The most obvious explanation for Bateson's silence probably lies in his ambivalence about efforts to apply his ideas, even for apparently benign purposes. The foreword to 'The Structure of Magic' itself conveys Bateson's despair at those who had begun to count double binds. Mary Catherine Bateson says; 'even in psychiatric contexts, he resisted the transformation of his ideas into specific strategies of intervention' (Bateson 2000b:87). She comments further; 'I believe this was true of NLP as it was of the work at (the Mental Research Institute) by his close colleagues from the Palo Alto days in developing new forms of psychotherapy'.[9] For Bateson, that era had ended none too happily when his co-researchers produced a manuscript, eventually published as 'The Pragmatics of Human Communication' (Watzlawick, Beavin & Jackson 1968), that spelled out many of Bateson's ideas and clearly overlapped with a volume that he had proposed (Harries-Jones 1995:27). Bateson, who objected to the emphasis on pragmatics, distanced himself from the work of the MRI as it focused more on developing applied techniques; he saw himself primarily as a theorist researching into the epistemological conundrums posed by the complexities of human communication. Bateson also held a 'deeply passive attitude' towards human interference in nature, wondering 'if any deliberate social planning could be developed which preserved the complexity and spirit of the biological world' (Lipset 1980:287).[10]

It seems most likely therefore that NLP may have appeared too outcome-orientated, too instrumental, and simply too pragmatic, to retain Bateson's interest. Bateson also had a strong commitment to the value of theory – had NLP begun to reflect the type of intellectual paucity that Bateson encountered at Kresge?

Reference to Bateson from within the NLP community can verge on the worshipful. Yet his ideas, like any others, need critique and updating (see for example Harries-Jones 1995). There has been scant evidence of any systematic attempt at this within NLP, and the reverence shown for Bateson leads us to wonder about the extent to which he is, in effect, invoked in order to lend the discourse of NLP some intellectual gravitas. This again fuels the suspicion that NLP's ideas exist in a kind of intellectual time-warp, stuck in the 1970s. In fact, for a theoretical base for NLP we may need to begin by looking even further back, to the emergence of cybernetics in the 1940s, in which Bateson was centrally involved.

Cybernetics: The Macy Conferences

The history of cybernetics is itself complex and contested, perhaps even more so than that of NLP. What is generally acknowledged is that the Macy Conferences mark the beginnings of cybernetics as a strand of interdisciplinary intellectual endeavour. In the previous chapter we referred to the inaugural meeting that Milton Erickson addressed in 1942,[11] an event organised by Frank Fremont-Smith, head of the Macy Foundation's medical office, with the support of Laurence K. Frank, his friend and mentor. The Macy Foundation, named after the philanthropist Josiah Macy, Jr., was interested mainly in medical research (it has no connection to the famous Macy's department store in New York City).[12]

After the end of World War II, prompted by Bateson and Warren McCulloch, who were also participants in that 1942 meeting, Fremont-Smith initiated what became a series of ten conferences, held in New York[13] between 1946 and 1963. These involved a core group of about twenty 'intellectual enthusiasts' (Von Foerster & Poerksen 2002:160) from a variety of disciplines, plus invited guests. The core group included Bateson, McCulloch, Margaret Mead, von Foerster (from 1949), Norbert Wiener and John von Neumann.

This was a formidable gathering of intellects. Von Neumann and Wiener were ground-breaking mathematicians. Wiener has been portrayed as the prototype of an absent-minded professor. One story goes that he 'went to a conference and parked his car in the big lot. When the conference was over, he went to the lot but forgot where he parked his car. He even forgot what his car looked like. So he waited until all the other cars were driven away, then took the car that was left.'[14]

Bateson and Mead are referred to as 'two seemingly improbable additions to this "hard science" population'.[15] Montagnini, who describes Bateson's involvement in the Macy conferences in detail, notes that Wiener was very sceptical about including social science in this programme of work (2007:1012). Bateson and Mead, however, 'became so enthusiastic about the new ideas as to vigorously and effectively evangelize the new field outside its original natural science and engineering context'.[16]

The key achievement of the conferences was the emergence of a cross-disciplinary 'language', one that challenged the prevailing Newtonian understandings of the world. That language, which became known as cybernetics, branched out into different forms of systems thinking. It is noteworthy, given our discussion of definitions of NLP in Chapter 2, that the participants in these conferences:

> ... all eminent in their many respective fields, would go on to disseminate their individual impressions of and elaborations upon 'cybernetics' for decades thereafter. This made for a new field whose many facets make it easy to treat as a significant intellectual innovation but difficult to delineate as a coherent whole... In other words, the process' product (cybernetics itself) is many things to many people, and the process' narrative is either a mystery or a matter of hearsay. It is therefore no surprise that the coalescence of cybernetics has been mythologized by both its adherents and its critics.[17]

Von Foerster celebrates the 'absolute rainbow of attempts' to define the term, saying that it is a 'kind of thinking that allows a wide variety of approaches in a very relaxed spirit' (Von Foerster & Poerksen 2002:102).

A further resonance with NLP is in the difficulty of choosing an appropriate name for this new field. A possible title that was being discussed was 'Circular Causal and Feedback Mechanisms in Biological and Social Systems'. Heinz von Foerster, an Austrian, spoke limited English at the time and asked that the field should be called by the single term, 'cybernetics', as in the title of a book recently published by Norbert Wiener (Von Foerster & Poerksen 2002:136). This term 'is derived from the Greek *kybernetes* meaning ("steersman")'; Wiener himself defined cybernetics as the science of 'control and communication in the animal and the machine' (Capra 1996:51).

Circular causality and feedback

In retrospect, a significant loss in the adoption of Wiener's title was that the notion of *circular causality* ceased to be explicit. This principle is a key to understanding not only cybernetics (Von Foerster & Poerksen 2002:102), but also the essence of Bateson's thinking (e.g. Bateson 2000a:405–416) and, consequently, many of NLP's stated presuppositions.

How is causality 'circular'? Imagine a cat sitting on someone's lap, purring as he or she strokes it. Did the cat's purring cause the person to start stroking it? Did the stroking cause the purring? From a cybernetic view it is not possible to identify a simple, single cause. In the prevailing Newtonian ways of explaining events, however, every event, 'B', has a physical cause, 'A', that is located outside the event itself and prior to it in time – a red ball lands in the pocket of the billiard table because of the angle, velocity and force of the ball that hit it.

This explanation for events in the world of human communication has two fundamental flaws. The first is that the apparently

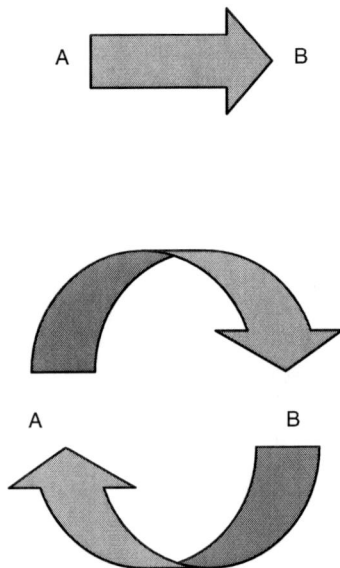

Figure 8.1   Linear and Circular Causality

linear[18] relationship between cause and effect is but a partial arc of the circuitous relations that obtain in the world of ongoing inter- action. The second flaw is the use of quasi-physical concepts, such as force and energy, as explanations (Bateson 2000a:xxix) because, in the world of human communication, events happen as the result of complex flows of information. *Circular causality* refers to the reci- procal nature of systemic processes: 'A responds to B's response to A, to which B, in turn, responds, and so on' (Flemons 1991:6).

Norbert Wiener (1965) used the image of a thermostat in a central heating system as a paradigmatic example to illustrate the basic principles of cybernetics. A thermostat responds to the temperature of the air in a room. If the temperature falls below the threshold at which the thermostat is set then the switch, governed by the thermostat, turns the heating on; if the temperature rises above the threshold, the thermostat switches it off. In a sense the thermostat 'knows' what the temperature 'should' be from its setting.

Cybernetics views all human activity as goal-directed. Thus the setting on a thermostat is determined by the occupier of the house, whose intentions (operating at a 'higher' logical level) govern the thermostat. There may be further intentions influencing the owner of the thermostat, such as the global need for energy conservation, shaped by the particular social and historical context in which the individual operates.

This gives us at least three levels of activity – thermostat, house occupier, and society. Now, which is cause, and which effect? Accord- ing to cybernetics this cannot be decided, except in the realm of how we make sense of events. The idea of explaining these as all due to one simple, linear chain of events breaks down at this point. What guides the activities of the thermostat is a complex web of information, coming, as it were, from both past present and future (i.e. the goal), and from different logical types.

In cybernetics, the concept of *feedback* is central. Bandler and Grinder clearly reflect this principle, and a cybernetic way of think- ing in general, when they say that 'the basic unit of analysis in face- to-face communication is the feedback loop' (Bandler & Grinder 1979:2). Norbert Wiener (1965) introduced the notion of feedback as information through which the system 'knows' whether or not it is on track to achieve its goal. Positive feedback confirms that it is on track; negative feedback informs it that it needs to alter course.

In the case of the thermostat, a temperature lower than the threshold at which the thermostat has been set is negative feedback; this activates the switch and turns the heating on.

These terms have, unfortunately, become loaded with implications that sabotage their original cybernetic usage. *Positive* has somehow acquired the sense of meaning 'praise', being something good and desirable, whereas *negative* is thought of as 'criticism', implying the opposite. In the cybernetic sense, both are equally necessary to the effective maintenance of a goal-directed activity. There, positive and negative have no emotional valence, but are simply two types of directives that are only meaningful in the context of the achievement of a goal. Life would be impossible without negative feedback because organisms could not regulate themselves. They would function like an electric kettle that fails to cut out – the water boils away and the system overheats, crashing and burning.

Finally, the dimension of time is also central to the cybernetic world view. A goal is generated in the system as information about a *future* event – i.e. one that has not yet happened – not as a past or present occurrence. In striving to achieve a goal, a cybernetic system necessarily compares its present activities with the goals it intends to achieve.

It is impossible to overstate the significance of these distinctions between these classical, mechanical and cybernetic modes of explanation.

Second-order cybernetics

The Macy conferences also led to a number of insights into the limitations of early cybernetic thinking. One of these was that human systems have different orders of purpose, that are not reducible to a single identifiable goal (Keeney 1983:74).[19]

A related insight was that any observer is an integral part of the system he or she is observing, and therefore all observations are information from within the system. Thus; 'You learn to understand yourself as part of the world that you wish to explain' (Von Foerster & Poerksen 2002:110). This is the central principle of what von Foerster called 'second-order cybernetics'.[20] The world previously perceived as having a separate existence 'out there' dissolves, the observer becoming at one with the observed.[21]

What matters about this distinction? It means that the ways in which we build our understanding of the worlds we inhabit have to change drastically. The notion of a pure objectivity has to be abandoned because human systems are *recursive*:

> You end up in a loop that connects the observer to the respective object that is under inspection. You not only have to explain the brain of another person, but also your own brain that is being used to work out the explanation.
>
> (Von Foerster & Poerksen 2002:110)

Bateson believed passionately that it was urgent to revise the naïve assumption that the world was separate from humanity before, in his view, we destroyed our planet. People could not operate *upon* the planet as if it were an external, disconnected object. Moreover, our maps of the world – how we *thought about* ecology – were themselves as much a part of that ecology as an oak tree growing outside the window.

These insights into the limitations of first-order cybernetics also characterise Bateson's epistemology and should – to the extent that Bateson's views are taken to be its foundation – underpin NLP. They imply, for instance, that in any interaction between a coach and their client, the coach is involved in a recursive engagement within that system, being changed by it at the same time as he or she is attempting to facilitate change in the client. The coach is not able simply to 'reprogramme' the client, because he or she is part of the 'programme' that is running in the interaction. Yet practitioners may be trained to operate as if they are external to the client system. As Keeney explains in his lucid discussion of this issue, second-order cybernetics therefore leads us into questions of ethics, a theme that we develop further in Chapter 12.

> From an ethical perspective we do not ask whether we are 'objective' or 'subjective'. Instead, we recognize the necessary connection of the observer with the observed, which leads to examination of how the observer participates in the observed.
>
> (Keeney 1983:80)

In summary, Bateson's influence on NLP is immense, to the extent that NLP seems to have grown dependent on his work for its intellectual authority. Significantly, there is a direct line from Bateson's involvement in the founding of contemporary cybernetics to the origins of NLP. Next, in Chapter 9, we examine the way that cybernetics is reflected in NLP's presuppositions.

9
The Presuppositions of NLP

Two common questions asked about NLP are, does it have any theory; and what is distinctive about it? Many NLP practitioners would probably agree with McDermott & O'Connor, that 'the root of NLP's individuality lies in its presuppositions' (1996:58).[1] What are these and where did they originate? Do they indicate that NLP has any theoretical basis?

Presuppositions are principles that are intended to be assumed or taken for granted when practising NLP; rather as the principle that 'things fall down, not up' (i.e. the law of gravity) is something we usually take for granted in our everyday lives. Expressed as maxims (e.g. 'there is no failure, only feedback') that are usually listed in NLP course manuals, they indicate the axioms or beliefs on which the practice of NLP is predicated.[2] They are the principal expression of the face of 'NLP as philosophy', and are discussed in detail by Dilts and DeLozier (2000), Wake (2008) and Young (2004), among others.

It is suggested in NLP that one makes use of these presuppositions by acting *as-if* they were true; they are not claimed to be accurate statements about how the world 'really' is. This is like saying that, although people know the earth is round, for the purposes of getting around their local area it is effective for most people to act as if the earth were flat.

In this chapter we examine the presuppositions in detail and argue that they largely reflect the principles of cybernetics. Ironically, grounding NLP in cybernetics may give it a stronger theoretical foundation than is found in many other approaches to people development, including some forms of coaching. However, we also suggest that the presuppositions reflect what became known as *first-order* cybernetics, and that NLP could usefully be positioned as a practice based on *second-order* cybernetics.

What are the presuppositions?

It is important to note that Bandler and Grinder's joint publications contain no explicit discussion of any *set* of presuppositions. They have tended to mention these principles in passing,[3] or to have embedded them in stories. In 'Frogs Into Princes' they refer not to presuppositions but to some 'organising assumptions' (Bandler & Grinder 1979:137).

Indeed, Bostic St. Clair and Grinder comment that '... *if the so-called presuppositions of NLP are to be taken seriously*, this decidedly odd collection of different logical types and levels are badly in need of revision and reorganization' (2001:202, emphasis in original). They regard them as a 'pedagogical device' that is of limited value. While we agree that the way to learn NLP in practice is not via these conceptual statements, we also believe that investigating and debating them is important for those whose goal is for NLP to become more mainstream.

The presuppositions therefore emerged as NLP developed, and were not articulated as any kind of *a priori* theory. Making the presuppositions explicit appears to have been largely Robert Dilts' project (Bostic St. Clair & Grinder 2001:202). For example, in 'Roots of NLP' (1983), Dilts articulates and explores the systemic principles underlying the emergent practice of NLP.

What are these presuppositions? There is no definitive list, and the number varies among training manuals. Here we adopt the set of fourteen identified by Wolfgang Walker (1996:111), which is reasonably representative and comparable with the sets identified by other authors. Walker suggests that all but one of these fourteen can be attributed to sources that pre-date NLP, identifying their origins as follows:

1. Every behaviour is potentially communication (Bateson, Perls, Satir, Erickson);
2. Mind and body are part of the same cybernetic system (Bateson, Perls, Satir, Erickson);

3. People have all the resources they need to make changes (Perls, Satir, Erickson);
4. People orientate themselves by their internal maps, their model of the world, and not to the world itself (Korzybski);
5. The map is not the territory (Korzybski);
6. People make the best choices that present themselves to them (Satir);
7. Choice is better than no choice (Satir);
8. Every behaviour is generated by a positive intention (Satir);
9. The meaning of a communication is the response it elicits, not the intention of the communicator (Erickson);
10. Resistance is a message about the communicator (or therapist) (Erickson);
11. If what you are doing isn't working, do something different (Erickson);
12. There is no failure, only feedback (Erickson);
13. The most flexible variable controls the system (Ashby's law of requisite variety);
14. Everything that a human being can do can be modelled (Bandler and Grinder).

(translated[4] from Walker, W. (1996:111))

First, it is salutary to note the extent to which NLP's axioms are not original creations. With one exception, according to Walker, they are all imported. Even the one presupposition that Walker says is attributable to NLP, that which proposes that 'everything a human being can do can be modelled', may be influenced by Bandura's work (e.g. Bandura 1977) and its antecedents in cognitive science. In that respect they underline the importance of appreciating the roots and influences of NLP.

Second, as instructive as Walker's analysis is, we think it can be taken a step further. Walker identifies the people from whom the presuppositions originated; one can also investigate the philosophy underlying these principles. This shows that they are not a random collection that has somehow coincidentally coalesced within NLP. In fact most of them are directly attributable to cybernetics.

The roots of NLP presuppositions in cybernetic thinking

First, we will illustrate this cybernetic dimension to NLP.[5] Later in the chapter we identify two other facets of the presuppositions, which are their use of metaphors drawn from computing, and the humanistic assumption that the unconscious is benign and wise.

Beginning with the second presupposition on Walker's list, 'Mind and body are part of the same cybernetic system'[6] affirms the relevance of a cybernetic perspective to NLP. Robert Dilts has extended this into the statement that 'life and mind are systemic processes', which echoes Bateson's thoughts.

'There is no failure only feedback' (Walker's number twelve) highlights the central cybernetic notion of feedback. Recalling the previous chapter's discussion of 'positive' and 'negative' feedback, this emphasises that feedback is information, and is value-free. It is people themselves who place such interpretations on events, and people who decide to label particular feedback as 'success' or 'failure', a judgement that is a distortion of the information itself. This presupposition conveys the sentiment of Kipling's famous lines, 'If you can meet with Triumph and Disaster, And treat those two impostors just the same'. In coaching, therefore, if a client does not respond in the way a practitioner expects, the practitioner is urged not to jump to the conclusion that they have failed. The client's response is information, and may hold the key to what the practitioner could do instead.

The first presupposition in Walker's list, 'Every behaviour is potentially communication', also reflects the cybernetician's focus on perceiving phenomena as fundamentally involving information rather than physical particles. It declares that behaviour is significant for its informational value, and represents another way to express the notion that we cannot *not* communicate (Watzlawick, Beavin & Jackson 1967:48).

The ninth presupposition, 'The meaning of a communication is the response it elicits, not the intention of the communicator' (see Bandler & Grinder 1979:61) is closely related. Returning to the classic cybernetic example of the thermostat, if the temperature in my room is not what I desired, it is nevertheless the way I set the thermostat that has led to this unwanted result (assuming of course that the thermostat is working). It is no good me going to the thermostat and complaining that it misunderstood me, or refused to do what I wanted it to, or has deliberately overheated me because it had an unhappy childhood. In relation to a thermostat this sounds obvious, yet one of NLP's insights from its very earliest days is that people can readily attribute a problem that results from ineffective communication to a fault within the system on which they are operating. Thus 'in the field of psychotherapy... you take the fact that what you do doesn't work and you blame it on the client' (Bandler & Grinder 1979:13). The coach who attributes the ineffectiveness of their interventions to the client's 'resistance', is doing the equivalent of berating a thermostat for failing to understand the intentions of the person who sets it. Presupposition number ten, 'resistance is a message about the communicator', arises from this and could be thought of as its corollary.

Bandler and Grinder say that 'one of the operating procedures of most disciplines that allows a field to grow... is a rule that if what you do doesn't work, *do something else*' (1979:13, italics in original). This is the eleventh presupposition on Walker's list, and also follows on from number nine. Again, this is more a logical derivation from cybernetic thinking than a distinctive principle. It means that practitioners need to vary their own behaviour in order to elicit a different result. If I go back to the thermostat, move the dial back and forth, but leave it back at the same setting as before – believing perhaps that I was right all along and that it will work properly next time – the output of the system (the resulting room temperature) will be no different.

Walker's eighth presupposition suggests that all behaviour, whether appropriate or not, is generated by a 'positive' intention. This is congruent with cybernetics to the extent that seeking the intention 'behind' an individual's behaviour distinguishes between two different logical types; the *behaviour* of system and its *goal*. This presupposition says that it is helpful to think of a person's behaviour as an action designed to achieve a goal (of which the agent may or may not be aware). Importantly, this cybernetic view does not *excuse* or *justify* the effects of the behaviour, nor does it mean that a person ceases to be morally responsible for their actions. It does not mean, for example, that it is morally acceptable to impose punitive controls in organisations simply because these serve a goal that is desirable for the managers. The cybernetic significance is that recognising intention as part of a system increases the information available, and provides a different perspective from which to generate options for intervention.

Note that this presupposition, as expressed in NLP, entails a non-cybernetic use of the term 'positive' (see Chapter 8). The word now denotes a judgement about what is 'good' for the system, such as its survival. It is a sign of the presuppositions edging into ethical territory. In other words it introduces the question of judgements about the rights and wrongs of people's goals, and about the means they use to achieve them.

Coupled logically with the presupposition about positive intention is number six, which proposes that, 'People make the best choices that present themselves to them'. In other words, one assumes that, however unpleasant a manager's behaviour may be for employees, it represents their 'least worst' option for achieving their goal. It implies that rather than being labelled a bad person, the manager can be perceived as being constrained by the options he or she believes to be available. Here the cybernetic logic adopted by NLP is that however irrational a person's behaviour appears to be, it will make sense in relation to the system's goals and capabilities, even though they could have inappropriate consequences in certain contexts.

'Frogs Into Princes' includes reference to both this principle (Bandler & Grinder 1979:122) and the related notion that 'you can treat every limitation that is presented to you as a unique accomplishment by a human being' (1979:67). This is an interesting idea that reframes 'problem' behaviour as a skill, just as much as a 'desirable' behaviour. NLP aims to remain curious about *how* someone manages (for example) to be late for appointments, both because understanding their strategy might give clues as to how they can change, and because the behaviour might be useful in other contexts.

According to Walker, presupposition number seven, 'Choice is better than no choice', is directly derived from the ways in which Virginia Satir approached her clients' problems. Heinz von Foerster is also known for the saying, 'Act always so as to increase the number of choices'.[7] The cybernetic principle here is that one needs to increase *variety*; in NLP parlance, this is about making choices available. Often, an NLP practitioner aims not to change the goal or 'positive intent', which is assumed to reflect a human need, but to enable the person (or system) to find new choices that will meet that intent in ways that have more beneficial effects for themselves and others in the systems in which they participate.

In essence this is the same principle as presupposition number thirteen, which is taken directly from cybernetics; Ross Ashby's 'law of requisite variety'. Hence, more choice is better because it represents an increase in variety. In fact, Ashby's law actually states that 'only variety can destroy variety' (Ashby 1965:207).

This law is interpreted within NLP as the idea that in any cybernetic system 'The element in the system with the widest range of variability will be the controlling element' (Bandler & Grinder 1979:74). This proposes that the part of a system that has the most flexibility (i.e. the most choices available) will be the most influential. However, Ashby's law could also be taken to imply almost the opposite of this interpretation; it is the very *absence* of variety in a practitioner that can most influence the outcomes for the system. As a prosaic example, if the only tool you possess is a hammer, then you treat everything as if it were a nail; the lack of variety in the hammer reduces the possible variety in the states of the system (i.e. outcomes are limited to those that can be effected by a hammer). What Bandler and Grinder argue is that a practitioner can be constrained in their own variety by (for example) professional codes of conduct or by certain beliefs; a client, who is not constrained in this way, may be more influential because they have more options available to them. In short, Ashby's law declares that there is an important *relationship* between the variety that exists within the way a system is regulated, and the variety of possible states of the system.

Based on the above discussion, we might distil down the ten cybernetic presuppositions (Walker's numbers 1, 2, 6, 7, 8, 9, 10, 11, 12 and 13) to the following:[8]

1. Every behaviour is generated by a goal or intention; behaviour and goal/intention are different logical types.
2. We can infer that people's behaviour represents the best choice available to them to satisfy that intention.
3. The meaning of a communication is the response it elicits; meaning is judged according to feedback, not according to the communicator's intent.
4. There is no failure, only feedback; 'failure' and 'success' are judgements made about the meaning of feedback.
5. 'Only variety can destroy variety' (Ashby's law of requisite variety).

The relevance of the science of cybernetics is clearly acknowledged by some NLP authors, including O'Connor and Seymour (1990:81) and Esser (2004:154). The nature of NLP as a cybernetic approach was first articulated in earnest by Robert Dilts, thus:

> The goal of Neuro-Linguistic Programming (NLP) is to *integrate the macroscopic information* about human behaviour and experience available to each of us through our *sensory experience* with the *unobservable microscopic information* of the *neurophysiology of behaviour and experience* into a useful *cybernetic model.*
>
> (Dilts 1983:3, italics in original)

However we contend that the presuppositions cited so far reflect a specific form of cybernetics, known as *first-order* cybernetics, and as such they make no *essential* distinction between thermostats and people. First-order cybernetics arose as a description of mechanical systems, such as the governor in a steam engine. Bateson, Warren McCulloch and others pointed out that it was limited to the understanding of control-based mechanical systems. As we shall go on to discuss, in the later development known as *second-order* cybernetics the practitioner is perceived as inescapably part of the changing system. He or she construes what is happening from within, and is affected recursively by their own interventions. Before we discuss the implications of that shift for the presuppositions, we address the remaining items in Walker's list.

The TOTE and computer metaphors

Another influence on NLP was the psychologist George Miller, to whose department John Grinder was seconded in the late 1960s. Miller drew from cybernetics (Miller 1970:106) and, prefiguring the combination of interests found in NLP, was also interested in psycholinguistics and problems of cognition.

Miller and his colleagues (Miller, Galanter & Pribram 1960) proposed that people continuously test or monitor what they are doing and what is happening in the environment in relation to their pursuit of a goal. Eugene Galanter recounts how their central idea of the TOTE model emerged from dissatisfaction with the 'self-imposed limits of the classical behaviourist paradigm'. An acronym standing for 'Test-Operate-Test-Exit', the TOTE represents a template of a cybernetic system, with feedback as one of its organising principles:

> ... *the three of us* (i.e. Galanter, George Miller and Karl Pribram) *were arguing about what the conceptual basis for a new theory of psychology could be. At one point, George proposed that we examine some intentional human act.*
> *'Flying a plane,' I suggested.*
> *'No – too much. How about crossing a street? An equally dangerous act in the Bay area,' Karl responded. I went to the blackboard and started a flow chart. The boxes, lines, and arrows snaked around the board as step after step was drawn.*
> *'No,' George said, 'all that stuff on the board is only a string of reentrant reflexes. Let a whole piece of action be repeated until it's finished.'*
> *'How will it know?' from Karl.*
> *'With a cybernetic test,' replied George.*
> *'But how do I draw it?' I asked.*
> *'Like this,' said George, and the TOTE replacement for the reflex was designed.*
>
> (Galanter, in Hirst 1988:40)

How does this model work? First the system *tests* or evaluates the extent of progress towards the specified goal. It then performs an *operation* designed to bring the system closer to achieving the goal. Then there is another *test*. When the goal has been achieved, then the system can *exit* the operation. The model was adopted in early NLP (Grinder, DeLozier & Bandler 1977:6) and elaborated by Dilts (Dilts, Grinder, Bandler & DeLozier 1980:26–30; Dilts 1983).

Drawing on a seminal paper by Tolman (1948), Miller, Galanter and Pribram also recognised the crucial role of internal representations (which they often referred to as *plans*) in this process, arguing that they were necessary in order for any activity to be carried out successfully. The activity of the TOTE always involves comparing the system's present state with the future outcome it is endeavouring to achieve. Without an organism's ability to (re)construct an internal representation or map, either of experience or of a *future* outcome, there could be no meaningful behaviour. Thus:

> A human being – and probably other animals as well – builds up internal representations, a model of the universe, a schema, a simulacrum, a cognitive map, an Image.
>
> (Miller, Galanter & Pribram 1960:7)

This reflects the fourth presupposition in Walker's list, 'People orientate themselves by their internal maps, their model of the world, and not to the world itself'. This, of course, is closely related to the constructivist notion taken from Korzybski that, 'the map is not the territory' (presupposition number five) that we discussed earlier.

Miller's model, added to cybernetics, emphasises the extent to which NLP has adopted an information-processing model of the person. In the 1970s, before the advent of personal computers and the spread of digital technology, information-processing and computing metaphors were both relatively fresh and meaningful, seeming to shed new light on human behaviour. Now they are somewhat stale and limiting. While cybernetics as a field remains multi-disciplinary, it is probably most associated with work on artificial intelligence and control systems. The prefix 'cyber-' has connotations of distinctly non-human systems, reflected in terms that have become familiar such as cyborgs, cybermen,[9] and cyberspace.

On the one hand, the view that human behaviour can be thought of as far more 'programmed' than people normally assume to be the case is supported in psychology, through notions such as executive control (Norman & Shallice 1986) and automaticity (e.g. Logan, Taylor & Etherton 1996). As Bandler and Grinder have noted, 'It's important for some people to have the illusion that their conscious mind controls their behaviour. It's a particularly virulent form of insanity among college professors, psychiatrists and lawyers' (1979:166). According to Halligan and Oakley (2000), 'all of the brain's information processing activities occur at an unconscious level'. Contrary to what common sense may tell us, much of our perception happens outside our conscious awareness, and people exercise conscious choice far less often than they might imagine.

A different perspective, that of discourse analysis, shows that people also behave according to socially learnt, 'customary ways of categorizing and ordering phenomena' (Willig 1999:2). These observations fit with the idea that there is more predictability, and less free will, in human behaviour than we might imagine.

On the other hand, in the 1990s the dominance of the computer metaphor in the cognitive sciences was roundly criticised by authors including Francisco Varela and colleagues (Varela, Thompson & Rosch 1993) among others.[10] They argued that while people can be thought of as functioning like computers in *some* respects, the computer is a wholly inadequate metaphor for understanding the *totality* of a person, and becomes misleading as a basis for understanding cognition. Varela instead looked to biology for a fundamental metaphor, and emphasised the notion of mind as 'embodied', with cognition as complex, emergent and active in all living beings.

The message from the work of Varela and others is that computing metaphors represent an outdated 'story' of human functioning, albeit one that still has its uses. Nevertheless, computing metaphors still infuse NLP through its terminology such as 'programming', and descriptions of people as 'hardware'; earlier we remarked on Bostic St. Clair & Grinder's usage of the metaphor 'data streaming' (2001:13). As another contemporary example, the back cover of a recent introduction to NLP (Linden & Perutz 2008) includes the following statement; 'As its name suggests, NLP is based on the idea that the human mind is a sort of computer; our verbal and body languages are the programming that allows us to change our thoughts and to influence other people'. The implication that NLP practitioners are involved in 'reprogramming' people is a source of disquiet to many, and such metaphors reinforce a first-order cybernetic view in which the practitioner can stand outside a client system and operate as an external expert.

The wisdom of the unconscious

The remaining presupposition is the third on Walker's list, the idea that 'people have all the resources they need to make changes' (see also Bandler & Grinder 1979:137). This is interesting because it seems to bear no relation to cybernetics at all. It is more a metaphysical position, a statement of faith.[11] It may originate in Virginia Satir's humanistic values and profound spiritual belief that the human unconscious contains the seeds of human psychological growth and development. In this, according to Walker (1996:227) she was in agreement with Erickson.

The assumption that 'the unconscious' will operate as a resource for the person, and is benevolent and wise, is significant and frequently articulated in NLP, though it does not feature among the presuppositions listed by Walker. While it is a notion that cannot be traced back to first-order cybernetics, Bateson regarded the unconscious as 'by far the largest, most effective, most important, and most *wise* area of mind' (Charlton 2008:36).

This assumption is especially important not to take at face value. Such a view of the unconscious, which is espoused rather uncritically within NLP literature, lacks empirical backing and clashes with other views, such as that of Carl Jung, from whose perspective it appears naïve and potentially risky to assume that the unconscious is always benign (e.g. Jung 1985:227). The concept of the unconscious as used in NLP appears to emphasise that dimension of individual processing that happens outside of conscious awareness, though could usefully be clarified. Bateson, for example, acknowledged four different usages of the term 'unconscious' (Bateson 2000a:136).

The presuppositions; a revision?

Thus far, we have argued that most of NLP's presuppositions are derived from cybernetics, or are logical derivations of cybernetic principles. We have also argued that they reflect 'first-order cybernetics' with its emphasis on control, and are related to metaphors based on information-processing or computing. The issue is, how appropriate is that perspective for working with people?

The view of the person as a mere information-processing system is limited and, according to authors like Varela, inadequate as an approach to cognition. Furthermore it has no satisfactory ethical perspective, as it is limited to relatively crude criteria concerning the necessity of survival and goal attainment.

Both these limitations could be addressed through second-order cybernetics (Von Foerster & Poerksen 2002). It seems surprising, given the frequent reference to cybernetics in NLP, that this 'second order' variety is scarcely on the NLP radar. Robert Dilts has for many years emphasised 'systemic NLP', and implicitly appears to have a profound appreciation of the chief principle of second-order cybernetics. Yet the one explicit discussion of this topic in the NLP literature, which Dilts co-authored, greatly underplays its significance, implying that it is something of a special case, 'to do with higher levels of learning and change' (Dilts & DeLozier 2000:1180). In no sense is there acknowledgement that, if Bateson's supposedly central influence is taken to heart, second-order cybernetics should probably underpin NLP.

'New Code' NLP, the direction espoused by John Grinder and Judith DeLozier in the 1980s, can also be seen as an attempt to transform the field through aspects of this second-order cybernetic thinking. In 'Turtles All The Way Down',[12] these authors refer to their efforts in 'extending and making more explicit some of the splendid work of Gregory Bateson' (DeLozier & Grinder 1987:xi–xii). They emphasise the importance of epistemology, abandon the mechanistic coding and reproduction of skills found in 'Old Code' NLP , and advocate instead the role in human development of wisdom and grace (DeLozier & Grinder 1987:6), influenced by Bateson's work in Bali.[13] The emphasis of second-order cybernetics on the notion that the observer is part of their own observations can also be discerned here, though is approached through reference to Carlos Castaneda (e.g. Castaneda 1970) rather than through the theoretical writing of people like von Foerster.

Summary

In this chapter we have discussed NLP's presuppositions, which are the most prominent manifestation of NLP's identity as a philosophy. Through analysing the presuppositions we have argued that cybernetics has a central role in the intellectual lineage of NLP, even though, as in the case of linguistics, NLP has maintained minimal contact with subsequent developments in the field. Most of its presuppositions appear to be predicated on first-order cybernetic thinking, and therefore do not adequately reflect the way Gregory Bateson's ideas developed, even though he is cited widely as influencing the philosophy of NLP. Armed only with the viewpoint of first-order cybernetics, one may be prone to treat people as equivalent to machines to be re-programmed, be they thermostats or computers. If a second-order perspective were to become more centre stage in NLP, it could unlock issues of principle, practice and ethics. If the presuppositions are taken to reflect NLP's philosophy, therefore, something may be missing. This may relate to the doubts that Bostic St. Clair and Grinder have expressed about the value of these sets of principles. Their disquiet also touches on the sometimes fractious relationship between NLP and 'theory', the theme to which we turn in the following chapter.

Part III

10

'Useful versus True' – Theory, Knowledge and Pseudoscience

People can be wary of NLP because it is seen as not academically respectable. The worlds of NLP and academe have sometimes been like ships in the night, passing each other without contact and with little awareness of the other's existence. Stereotypes appear to be common; on the one hand NLP is seen as lacking credible theory and is dismissed as 'pop' psychology or 'pseudoscience' and, on the other hand, academic theorising is seen as irrelevant to, or even antithetical to, NLP. There seem to have been more success at engagement with academic communities in countries such as France, Germany and Austria, where English is not the first language, than in the UK, the USA and Australia.

In this chapter we examine the relationship between NLP and theory, and then unpack the debate around 'pseudoscience'. In Chapter 11 we examine the related issue of the state of research into NLP. Together these chapters develop further the view of NLP as an emergent system of practical knowledge.

What is 'theory'?

We start by taking a closer look at attitudes towards the notion of theory in NLP.

A prominent question asked about NLP is whether there is any theory behind it, and if so what is it? Some NLP authors resist discussing theory altogether. One exception is Peter Young (Young 2004), whose 'unifying theory' of NLP offers interesting insights based on the work of Will McWhinney (1997). Ultimately we suggest that Young reorganises and reclassifies NLP more than articulates its underlying theory. As Young himself says, 'in this book I have rearranged the jigsaw puzzle pieces provided by NLP...' (2004:272).

Practitioners can deny that theory has any relevance to NLP at all.[1] This is ironic given NLP's reverence for Bateson, who deplored the lack of effective theory in the social sciences. Note for example the language used here: 'The NLP Presuppositions are sometimes accused of coming under the heading of NLP theory, but they can put up a strong defence against such a charge; neither theories or beliefs, they are simply invitations to imagine expanding the parameters of possibility...' (Spence 2007:14).

Dilts *et al* (1980) say that NLP 'makes no commitment to theory, but rather has the status of a model':

> A theory is taxed with the task of finding a justification of why various models seem to fit reality. We are modelers and we ask that you evaluate this work as a model, ignoring whether it is true or false, correct or incorrect, aesthetically pleasing or not, in favour of discovering whether it works or not, whether it is useful or not.
>
> (Dilts, Grinder, Bandler & DeLozier 1980: page 7 of 'Forward')

The difference between a theory and a model is not necessarily so clear cut, however. According to Chalmers, 'Theories are construed as speculative and tentative conjectures or guesses freely created by the human intellect in an attempt to overcome problems encountered by previous theories to give an adequate account of some aspects of the world or universe' (Chalmers 1999:60). This seems to describe quite well the ideas generated within early NLP about the structure behind the 'magic' of excellent communication.

The term 'theory' can have several usages. For example, it can apply to a single hypothesised explanation or conjecture (e.g. a theory about why my football team is not as successful as I would like it to be), to a set of assumptions that creates a way of perceiving events (e.g. Freud's theories of psychosexual development), or to grand schemes of ideas (e.g. Marxism).

Steve de Shazer (1994) argues that all theories are stories we construct to help us make sense of events. In the previous chapter we argued that the metaphors of computing found in NLP may represent an outdated story. As another example Evelyn Fox-Keller, exploring that twentieth century totem, the idea of the gene, points out that this notion has:

> ...carried us to the edge of a new era in biology, one that holds out the promise of even more astonishing advances. But these very advances will necessitate the introduction of other concepts, other terms, and other ways of thinking ... thereby loosening the grip that genes have had on the imagination of life scientists these many decades (Fox-Keller 2000:147).

This view of theory pervades the social sciences, where theory is considered to be a constructed point of view that offers insights and possible explanations, and not an accurate description of reality. Gareth Morgan's well-known book, 'Images of Organization' (Morgan 2006), argues that all theory is based on metaphor; that there is no such thing as pure theory because inevitably we understand one phenomenon in the world in relation to something else that we have experienced.

How, then, have some people in NLP become hostile to theory? There is an interesting range of issues behind this question that are interrelated but which, if taken together indiscriminately, may lead a practitioner to adopt the attitude that theory and NLP do not mix. By sifting through them it is easier to pinpoint some worthwhile challenges about knowledge that are posed by NLP. These issues are:

1. For the purposes of identifying effective patterns of behaviour, NLP is interested in the criterion of 'what works', not with what is 'true'.
2. NLP is concerned with studying what people actually do, not what they may believe or espouse that they do.
3. People use two modes of processing, a rational, analytic mode and a more intuitive, holistic mode. The rational mode, which is the mode that can formulate and debate theory, is ineffective for certain purposes. For example, it might not directly enable someone to act effectively.
4. In our culture, intellectual, conceptual knowledge is often privileged over practical, experiential knowledge. NLP is interested in holistic and non-conventional forms of knowledge.

Useful versus true

First, NLP literature and practices stress that it was created in order to be used. This is summed up in Bandler and Grinder's claim (1979:7) that: 'We have *no* idea about the "real" nature of things, and we're not particularly interested in what's "true". The function of modeling is to arrive at descriptions which are *useful.*'

This proposes that the core criterion for the *validity* of knowledge in NLP is that something works, not that it is an accurate description of the 'real' world. It also denotes that in NLP one is mainly concerned with *whether* something is effective; *why* it works is a separate issue.

NLP is not alone in taking such a stance. We have noted the Palo Alto group's similar emphasis on the *pragmatics* of communication (Watzlawick, Beavin & Jackson 1967:13). Dilts and DeLozier (2000:565–567) refer to William James' pragmatist philosophy, and George Kelly, the founder of Personal Construct Psychology, emphasised that the importance of constructs is not whether they are right or wrong, but whether they are useful or not (e.g. Kelly 1991:138). Bateson, commenting on everyday assumptions about the nature of the world that are, if examined, epistemologically incorrect, said, 'you and I are able to get along in the world and fly to Hawaii and read papers on psychiatry and find our places around these tables and in general function reasonably like human beings in spite of very deep error. The erroneous premises, in fact, *work'* (Bateson 2000a:486–487).

This view finds an echo in a story cited by Karl Weick, writing in the field of management and organisational theory:

A small Hungarian detachment was on military maneuvers in the Alps. Their young lieutenant sent a reconnaissance unit out into the icy wilderness just as it began to snow. It snowed for two days, and the unit did not return. The lieutenant feared that he had dispatched his people to their deaths, but the third day the unit came back. Where had they been? How had they made their way? Yes, they said, we considered ourselves lost and waited for the end, but then one of us found a map in his pocket. That calmed us down. We pitched camp, lasted out the snowstorm, and then with the map we found our bearings. And here we are. The lieutenant took a good look at this map and discovered, to his astonishment, that it was a map of the Pyrenees.

(Weick 1994:214)

Weick's story makes the point that managers do not seek, and do not require, theories that are accurate or true in a conventional sense; what they need are maps that precipitate action. A map that is wrong is better than no map at all, because the point is to do something. Through taking action, we discover ways in which the map may need to be changed in order to be more useful another time. Bandler and Grinder's pragmatic, utilitarian stance, far from being antithetical to that taken by academics, is very similar to that illustrated by Weick's story.

The difference between what do people do, and what they say they do

Secondly, NLP began with a clear interest in studying what people *do*, and paid 'very little attention to what people *say* they do' (Bandler & Grinder 1979:7). It distinguishes between observed behaviour and people's reports of their behaviour. NLP's stance is that the 'theories' people hold and through which they explain their behaviour can be mistaken, or can bear no relation to action. Bandler and Grinder (1979:8) give the example that we can all generate language; but we don't know *how* we do this.

Organisational theorist Chris Argyris (1999) makes precisely this point. He says that *all* human behaviour is guided by 'theories of action', even if those theories are tacit. Argyris distinguishes, however, between *espoused theory* and *theory-in-use*. Espoused theory is of little value in discovering how someone acts because they simply may not know; their account may include pet ideas or self-justifying claims that do not marry with their actions. Theory-in-use is the theory that can be inferred from, and accounts for, what people actually do. NLP is in tune with Argyris' thinking in attending to 'in-use' rather than 'espoused' theory as evidence for the purposes of modelling.

Dual process theories

The third strand of NLP's stance towards theory concerns the limitations on what the intellect and its conceptual thinking are useful for.

Robert Frager, who edited the third edition of Maslow's 'Motivation and Personality', tells of an incident at Esalen in the 1960s that captures the radically different styles of Maslow and Perls (Frager in Maslow 1987:xl):

> Maslow was too much of an intellectual to become a convert to the almost total emphasis on feeling and experiencing in the human potential scene. He gave his first Esalen workshop two years after Esalen began. The Institute had been gaining a national reputation as the avant-garde center for encounter groups and other intense, emotionally charged workshops. Maslow's weekend was, in complete contrast, purely intellectual. Because they were interested in his ideas, several of the Esalen staff members sat in on his talks and discussions.
>
> In the middle of Maslow's first evening talk, Fritz Perls, the founder of Gestalt therapy and enfant terrible of Esalen, got bored with the lack of emotional action. He began crawling towards an attractive woman across the room, chanting 'You are my mother; I want my mother; you are my mother.' This effectively broke up the evening session. Maslow left the room upset and offended. Characteristically, he shut himself in his cabin that night and thought through some of the differences between his own approach and the experiential emphasis prevalent at Esalen. That night he completed the outline of a classic article contrasting Apollonian control with Dionysian abandon.

While NLP has not adopted Perl's tendency to elevate the importance of feelings, it considers sensory experience to be very important. NLP recognises in particular that people use two different modes; a rational, analytical, conscious mode of thinking, and a rapid, intuitive, preconscious mode.

The analytic mode is excellent for theorising, but hopeless for producing skilled performance. Grinder says that his experiences of learning a language taught him that *'understanding is in no way a prerequisite to acting effectively in the world'* (Bostic St. Clair & Grinder 2001:144, italics in original). Similarly, 'I really believe that the face-to-face task of communicating with another human being, let alone a group of people, is far too complex to try to do consciously. You can't do it consciously. If you do, you break up the natural flow of communication' (Bandler & Grinder 1979:71). This suggests that when taking action, we just have to get into our bodies because conscious thinking will get in the way.

Of course, these ideas themselves constitute a kind of theory. Contemporary psychology has seen the development of *dual process theories* (Evans 2008), which explore the differences and interrelations between intuition (System 1) and analysis (System 2) (Stanovich & West 2000), based on the Nobel prize-winning work of Daniel Kahneman.[2] NLP publications show little evidence of being aware of this work, and of the subtleties within it. There is no established, clear agreement amongst researchers about the difference between System 1 and System 2, although Kahneman says there is a broad consensus. There is also a consensus that both modes are necessary.

Many thinkers, among them neuroscientist Antonio Damasio, have challenged the 'mind-body split', an idea reinforced by Descartes, which casts the brain (and thinking) as superior, and the body (and movement and emotion) as inferior. Damasio argues instead that a person is a whole mind-body system in which emotion is an integral part of cognition (Damasio 2006). Another contemporary expression of this principle comes through the notion of embodied knowing, as developed by Varela *et al* (1993), and by Lakoff and Johnson (1999). Bateson's view of mind, similarly, was that it resides in the relational connections through which we participate in the world, not in the organ that sits inside our skulls; he gave the example of a man chopping a tree with an axe, who is engaging in a 'circuit of mind' that includes the tree and the axe, the feel and the sound of the chopping, and so on, as a system of information in which it is impossible to delimit where the human agent begins and ends.

Alternative forms of knowledge

The fourth and final strand of this complex of issues is to do with the way the academic world, and formal education in some societies, tends to privilege intellectual, conceptual knowledge, assuming that it is superior to other forms of knowledge. Knowing *why* something happens, and being able to explain and predict events in the world, is considered a central goal of Western science.

NLP, which places greater value on 'knowing how', has refused to privilege the intellect and has discouraged the temptation to create a belief system out of conceptual knowing. Bandler and Grinder refer to the way that psychology was characterised by 'theology' of this kind (Bandler & Grinder 1979:5–6).

Instead NLP embraces and values multiple forms of knowing. One map of such forms, created by philosopher and educationalist John Heron (1992:174), shows a series of layers that start with experience, moves through symbolic or imaginative representation, becomes conceptual knowing, and moves into practical knowing.

Practical knowledge:	'Knowing how'
Propositional knowledge:	Conceptual knowing using language
Presentational knowledge:	The imaginal mode; movement, sound, colour, shape, etc. that connects perceptual imagery
Experiential knowledge:	Knowledge by acquaintance, through participation; feeling.[3]

Despite the orthodoxy that persists in formal education, propositional knowing is not superior to other forms. Heron, referring to the philosopher Gilbert Ryle, also asserts that practical knowledge cannot be reduced to propositional knowledge (Heron 1992:172). In applied fields, including management, there is increasing recognition of the importance of practical knowing, and managers themselves are typically very interested in being able to apply knowledge. We have already emphasised in this chapter that one of NLP's main areas of interest is in the sensory realm of experiential knowing. Bateson, for example, referred to dancer Isadora Duncan's response to a question about the meaning of a dance: 'If I could tell you what it meant, there would be no point in dancing it' (Bateson 2000a:137).

In relation to criteria for the quality of practical knowledge, Heron says:

Its canons of validity are canons of competence. Whatever the skill is, you need to be able to demonstrate that you can actually do it, over a significant time span, under all relevant conditions, and with an appropriate economy of means....

(Heron 1992:173)

This is so close to NLP criteria for effective modelling that it might almost have been written by an NLP author. Compare Heron's statement with the following quotation from Bandler and Grinder:

We do not test the description we arrive at for accuracy, or how it fits with neurological data, or statistics about what should be going on. All we do in order to understand whether our description is an adequate model for what we are doing is to find out whether it works or not: are you able to exhibit effectively in your behaviour the same patterns that Virginia (Satir) exhibits in hers, and get the same results?

(Bandler & Grinder 1979:10)

Another feature of NLP is an interest in indigenous forms of knowledge as an alternative to Western intellectual traditions. Judith DeLozier (1995:7) cites the influence on 'New Code' NLP of 'our African experience of drumming, dancing, singing and story-telling'. Another significant influence in this (e.g. DeLozier & Grinder 1987) was the works of Carlos Castaneda (e.g. Castaneda 1970). Castaneda, initially a graduate student at UCLA, wrote a series of books about a Yaqui sorcerer, Don Juan, that were popular in the 1970s and 1980s, and which sparked much controversy over whether they were true or fictional – or indeed whether that really mattered. Presaging the shift between 'The Structure of Magic' and 'Frogs Into Princes', while Castaneda's first book ('The Teachings of Don Juan') was written in the form of an anthropological report, he soon abandoned third-person commentary altogether and adopted first-person narratives.

David Silverman, a sociologist, used Castaneda's work with exactly the same intent as NLP, that of introducing students to issues of epistemology. Silverman comments that; 'it does not matter to me in the least whether any or all of the "events" reported by Castaneda ever "took place" ... what text is not a construction?' (1975:xi).

Anthony Grant, who is prominent in the field of coaching, offers the following comment on NLP:

A key factor in the derailment of the human potential movement in the 1960s and 1970s was a reluctance to engage with the academic community. For example, if it were not for the anti-science sentiments shown by the founders of NLP, today we could have seen the original NLP making a useful contribution to the applied psychology curriculum taught at universities – after all, the core of NLP is an often elegant application of cognitive behavioural science and linguistics. Instead we have seen some sections of the NLP community drift further and further away from solid foundations towards increasingly esoteric learnings and sometimes outright bizarre ideologies.

(Grant 2007:212)

The appearance in NLP literature of Castaneda's ideas may be one basis for Anthony Grant's reference to 'esoteric learnings' and 'bizarre ideologies'. This type of view, however, risk limiting explorations of human experience to forms of knowing that are privileged by contemporary scientific communities.

Another of the forms of knowing in Heron's model is that of presentational knowledge. This is also prevalent in NLP, reflected in the frequent use of story and metaphor by Milton Erickson. For Bateson, too, stories were no mere entertainment. They represented something important about the nature of mind, an example of the significance of the *aesthetics* of human systems, or 'responsiveness to the pattern which connects' (Bateson 1979:17):

A man wanted to know about mind, not in nature, but in his private large computer. He asked it (no doubt in his best Fortran), "Do you compute that you will ever think like a human being?" The machine then set to work to analyze its own computational habits. Finally, the machine printed its answer on a piece of paper, as such machines do. The man ran to get the answer and found, neatly typed, the words:

THAT REMINDS ME OF A STORY

(Bateson 1979:22)

NLP did not always emphasise presentational forms of knowing. As we have seen in earlier chapters, NLP evolved from within a university setting, albeit it one that was a radical experiment. It was also built upon theory from its very inception. 'The Structure of Magic' uses the terminology of transformational linguistics, complete with quasi-mathematical symbols and annotated transcripts. It is difficult to imagine how obtuse labels such as 'modal operators of necessity' and 'complex equivalence' could have come from anything other than academic theory. Bateson described it as 'a rather dry and formal linguistic analysis'.[4]

'The Structure of Magic' was not an altogether promising start on the road to becoming an 'airport psychology book', except perhaps through the appearance in the title of the provocatively unscientific term 'magic' and the gaudy covers.[5] It is often overlooked, however, that Bandler and Grinder's explicit project was to show that the abilities of charismatic practitioners, which many *perceived* to be magical, in fact had a structure and could be learnt by others (Bandler & Grinder 1975b:6). The early findings of NLP were arrived at through a process broadly recognisable as research into the 'theory-in-use' of Satir and Perls.

What happened to the conceptual approach of these early books? Once again 'Frogs into Princes' (Bandler & Grinder 1979) seems to mark a watershed at which NLP flowed into the commercial world and veered away from academic and professional communities.[6] Certainly, even before that point NLP was always concerned with practical knowledge. But its books conveyed that knowledge in the propositional terms that were familiar to its audience of, principally, professional therapists. They were more likely to overlap the interests of the academic world because they used a similar, conceptual form of discourse.

With 'Frogs Into Princes' the discourse becomes almost the inverse, or mirror image, of conventional academic writing.[7] It uses narratives of experience that enable the reader, as it were, to enter and engage with the workshop experience.

In summary, it is simply too crude to dismiss the relevance of theory to NLP altogether. Among other things, this misses certain interesting challenges to assumptions about the nature of knowledge. Denying that NLP has theory altogether, rather than embracing and exploring the *types of theorising* that are prevalent, can render NLP evasive, prone to retreat from the challenge to examine the beliefs that it promulgates. We can see that NLP engages with theory in the sense that it is usually concerned with Argyris' 'theory-in-use'; it holds a theory about modes of knowing that is broadly compatible with, but so far not informed directly by, dual process theories; and it has a theory about the value of non-conceptual forms of knowing.

Science and magic: Is NLP 'pseudoscience'?

If NLP practitioners sometimes reject academic theory, the reverse is also true. For example, NLP is sometimes dismissed as 'pseudoscience'.[8] What does this mean, and is there substance to this?[9]

The term 'pseudoscience' originated with Karl Popper, a philosopher of science who was educated in Vienna in the 1920s. According to Chalmers (1999), Popper became suspicious of the capacity of contemporary Freudians, Adlerians and Marxists to interpret any event in such a way as to support their theories; 'it seemed to Popper that these theories could never go wrong because they were sufficiently flexible to accommodate any instances of human behaviour or historical change as compatible with their theory' (Chalmers 1999:59).

Reacting to this, Popper advocated the principle that scientific theories must be falsifiable. That is, any theory should be capable of being put to the test and being shown to be false. If a theory is self-sealing, or if it rests on faith alone, then it is not scientific.

Popper's views are contested and somewhat idealistic. Chalmers goes on to explain how they could fuel a mythical view of science because theories do not evolve by falsification, they are the products of human minds continuously searching for explanatory principles. The practice of falsification may be a useful check and balance against dogma and ideology but, according to Feyerabend, history shows that; 'it is the normal case (that) theories become clear and "reasonable" only *after* incoherent parts of them have been used for a long time' (Feyerabend 1993:17). Frank Farrelly, the founder of Provocative Therapy, makes a similar point about the way many psychotherapists' theoretical systems emerged (Farrelly & Brandsma 1974:30). Chalmers notes (1999:91) that if the principle of falsification had operated strictly, Newton's gravitational theory would have been rejected by apparently contradictory observations that took some fifty years to explain. Nor do theories necessarily develop along neat, deductive lines within single disciplines. For instance, Darwin's theory of Evolution drew on population studies (Thomas Malthus), questions from Natural Theology (William Paley), and the emerging science of Geology (Charles Lyell), among other influences.

Furthermore, the positivist idea that knowledge can only be produced through the application of orthodox, scientific methods has been the subject of wide-ranging critique in the social sciences (for example, Lincoln & Guba 1985). Ironically, there is a naïve view of science among some people in the NLP community that actually reinforces belief in that view, through the hope that scientific research will 'prove' that NLP works.

The form of 'pseudoscience' allegation that originates from a positivist, falsificationist perspective by no means singles out NLP. It also challenges a wide range of training, development and organisational change practices. If applied strictly, most of these practices would probably have to be regarded as pseudoscientific too; many coaches, consultancies and training organisations would be out of business. For example, Eisner (2000) critiques not only NLP but also Gestalt therapy, Psychosynthesis and more – in short, any approach to psychotherapy that has not been supported by a dominant form of research, namely clinical trials.

Beyerstein (1990) criticised the way that 'New Age' entrepreneurs, in which he included contemporary proponents of NLP, exploited science, and specifically brain research, to lend authority to their claims. He challenged movements like NLP to produce evidence to support their claims, and to show awareness of relevant research (1990:33). We agree in sentiment, but would contest the way in which Beyerstein insists that this is done. He dismisses constructivism at a stroke and, like Eisner, insists that 'double-blind, placebo-controlled evaluations of all medical, psychological, and educational interventions are essential' (1990:34).

'It works!'

Where we think NLP could be most vulnerable to the charge of being a pseudoscience is in the lack of research and evaluation that seeks to challenge and refine its ideas. The lack of a credible, public evidence base is one of the most significant barriers to more widespread acceptance of NLP. It is wholly reasonable to seek testing of the validity of NLP's claims, without needing to subscribe to Popper's notion of falsification – even if the question of what provides for an evidence-based approach is complex and contested in many fields, including Human Resource Development (McGoldrick, Stewart & Watson 2002).

Sharpley (1987:104), noting Einspruch and Forman's (1985) statement that practitioners have 'a wealth of clinical data indicating that [NLP] is highly effective', says that if so, they 'need to provide this data for the wider professional public'. Derren Brown (2007:131) writes that much of the evidence of the efficacy of NLP 'comes from... anecdotes rather than from any actual testing or documented case histories'.[10] The experiences of practitioners do, of course, constitute a body of evidence, if one that is diffuse and difficult to assess. This is not to suggest that anecdotes are without value; see for example Isabel Losada's account (Losada 2001:200–201) of someone overcoming their fear of travelling in lifts.

A common tactic, however, is simply to assert that 'NLP works', based on the personal experience of the practitioner. Bostic St. Clair and Grinder, for example, make the breathtaking claim that the widespread dissemination of NLP 'can be accounted for by a simple observation – the patterning they (i.e. Grinder and Bandler) modeled and coded works. It works across cultures, generations, genders, age groups and fields of application' (2001:3).[11] Martin Gardner points out that L. Ron Hubbard, the founder of Dianetics, relied on exactly the same mantra (Gardner 1957:279). The claim, 'it works', should therefore be treated with scepticism, and not be accepted at face value.[12]

What are some of the difficulties with the appeal, 'I know it works'? First, we could apply several of NLP's own meta-model questions to this claim, such as, 'in what way, specifically, does it work?' Another key question is, 'how do we *know* it works?' It may seem odd that, knowing of the importance of these questions in NLP, any practitioner would encourage a client to rely on appeals to the practitioners' own experience, personal integrity or (perhaps) persuasiveness.

Secondly, within NLP there is a remarkable lack of consideration for counter-evidence. In our personal experience, NLP works some of the time but not all the time. In the field of healthcare, the standard of effectiveness is to better the rate of success of the placebo effect. To suggest that any treatment has a success rate of 100% is simply not credible. Yet where are the debates about when NLP does *not* work? There is scant evidence of acknowledgement of this, let alone enquiry into what can be learnt from such cases.

Thirdly, there is enormous potential for error in interpreting the meaning of our own experiences. For example, Beyerstein (1990:34) argues that 'the gurus of self-improvement tend to rely on their own experience and alleged insights into "what works". Much research on the fallibility of human judgement makes it clear why such affirmations are so unreliable, even if they enjoy surface plausibility'.[13] It is widely acknowledged that observation can be unreliable; we have noted that Bateson wrote about the way perception can be fooled, after experiencing the experiments of Adelbert Ames (Bateson 2000a:487).

In NLP, practitioners are taught that it is not enough to see something with one's own eyes; that, for example, 'memories' are constructed in the present, and that one's interpretation of an event depends on one's perceptual position, filters and so on. How is it that this appropriate scepticism is abandoned when advancing the claim 'it works!'?

An evidence-based, sceptical approach is typically encouraged in NLP trainings. Trainers exhort participants to test NLP's claims for themselves. Unfortunately this apparently liberal invitation is also disingenuous. Let us say that the NLP practitioner does genuinely attempt to test NLP's claims for him or herself. What are some obvious barriers to making such an evaluation systematic and reliable in research terms? A relatively straightforward issue is of how rigorous and systematic participants will be in record-keeping. For example, will they notice successes but ignore failures?

Then, as with any movement, and as with any business organisation, NLP is prone to tendencies towards social conformity, not just conformity about evidence but potentially *despite* the evidence. This phenomenon is illustrated graphically by the experiment conducted by Professor Solomon Asch (Watzlawick 1976:85–89). Asch showed that over a third of people (36.8% in his experiment) will change their view of something as simple and apparently objective as the relative length of two lines in order to avoid being out of step with a majority opinion. A recent re-run of the Asch experiment, led by Dr Gregory Berns (Berns *et al* 2005), used MRI scanners to show that peer pressure can neurologically alter our very perceptions.[14] In other words people do not just know privately that the lines are of different lengths, but choose consciously to modify their declared view in order to fit in. Instead, peer pressure seems to change perception itself.

Added pressures include that fact that participants are often paying significant amounts of money for their training; most people will assert the value of a purchase rather than appear to be a fool for having parted with their money. NLP trainings offer certificates, for which participants are assessed by trainers. It is well known in education that there is unequal power between assessors and assessed, and that participants will often be obedient to, or seek to stay on the right side of, perceived authority figures.

Finally, from a more sociological perspective, a training course in NLP can be seen less as a process of acquiring specific competencies, and more as a rite of passage towards being accepted into a particular community of practitioners, or 'NLP-ers'. To the extent that participants value this outcome, they are less likely to risk flouting the norms of that community.

None of these concerns is unique to NLP; they are based on established knowledge in the social sciences and apply to any form of organised learning, including university education. The issue is that apparently plain-speaking appeals to personal experience to validate the efficacy of NLP are unreliable. One way to enhance the credibility of NLP, therefore, could be to show how this issue is being addressed, instead of relying on the mantra 'it works!' to assert efficacy.

Conclusion

As a knowledge system NLP is characterised by a distinction between what is 'useful' and what is 'true'. NLP is not as lacking in theory as it may seem; it also emphasises practical knowledge, employs presentational knowledge, and has explored alternative unorthodox (in Western scientific terms) forms of knowing. Accusations that NLP is 'pseudoscience' need to be scrutinised as they tend to emanate from a particular view of science. However, they also highlight a lack of research activity in NLP, which surely has relied too much on the mantra 'it works!'

11
What Does Research Say About NLP?

Many people who come across NLP want to know whether it is backed up by research. 'Even its greatest enthusiasts are hard-pressed to find serious scientific research that backs up its wilder claims', wrote Fran Abrams of NLP in the Times Educational Supplement in 2004.[1] Is this a fair comment? In this chapter we examine the research that is available into, and relevant to, NLP.

Findings from relevant disciplines

There are three main types of research to be concerned with:

1. Indirect research – findings from relevant disciplines
2. Evaluation from within NLP
3. Independent research into NLP's claims.

Of these, the first is the area that may offer most support to NLP's ideas and practices. We have cited, for example, the work of Lawrence Barsalou on the role of the senses in cognition, as supporting NLP's perspective on the role and significance of internal representations (Barsalou 2008b); that of Robert Goldstone on categorisation as supporting NLP's stance on the relationship between language and thinking (Goldstone & Kersten 2003); and that of neuroscientists as giving insights into the dynamics of, for example, rapport through work on 'mirror neurons' (e.g. Rizzolatti & Craighero 2004).

There is a growing trend in recent NLP literature for authors to specify relevant research findings from mainstream psychology and other disciplines;[2] examples of publications in which this is done include Bolstad (2002),[3] Churches and Terry (2007), Linder-Pelz and Hall (2007) and Wake (2008). This marks a shift of attitude towards research, and usefully counters a tendency for NLP training courses and literature to recycle knowledge that has been in circulation since the 1970s. This trend might also help to counter the propagation of myths or misconceptions about what various pieces of research actually say.[4] Finally, it also reflects the fact that many people in the NLP community are genuinely interested in how research findings (regardless of whether they directly concern NLP) can inform and improve their practice.

Evaluation from within NLP

Moving on to the second category of research, as noted in Chapter 10 the evidence base created within the field of NLP is especially in need of development. Unlike related practices such as Solution-Focused Therapy, and with the exception of research into NLP psychotherapy promoted in Europe (by the EANLPt) and the USA (by the NLP Research and Recognition Project), NLP has done little to open itself up to independent evaluation.[5]

Why is this? One possible reason is that the people who have developed and promulgated NLP regard themselves, in Judith DeLozier's words, as 'searchers not researchers'.[6] In other words their motivation is to explore and to develop new ideas. They are simply not drawn to the different type of endeavour that research involves, though they have no objection to this being done by other people. Based on their written output, of the long-established NLP trainers it is probably Robert Dilts and John McWhirter who have shown the greatest inclination to be researchers as well as searchers.

However the same ambivalence towards and stereotyping of theory that we described in Chapter 10 also affects research. Statements like 'there's a whole body of people called "researchers" who will *not associate* with the people who are practicing!' (Bandler & Grinder 1979:6, italics and spelling as in original) appear to have influenced some NLP practitioners' attitudes towards research.[7] Platt (2001) reports his experience that 'people who practise NLP are not receptive or even prepared to countenance critical reviews of the field'. We had the experience of being told by a leading UK trainer that NLP did not need to be researched, and being chided for hosting an NLP research conference.

As mentioned in Chapter 10, NLP has relied a great deal on informal research by its thousands of practitioners who have been encouraged to test NLP in practice for themselves. There is, on the other hand, a strand of research-mindedness that runs through NLP from its very beginnings. We have described the research that informed the NLP publications of the 1970s, even though it left no effective audit trail. A case book called 'Leaves in the Wind' (Bretto, DeLozier, Grinder & Topel 1991) includes research-based reports. A journal called 'NLP World', founded and edited by G. Peter Winnington, and published between 1994 and 2001, was notable for encouraging more scholarly writing in the field.[8] The journal carried many conceptual articles and some examples of the type of scholarly critique that might have helped move the field forward. Other articles began to contribute to an evidence base for NLP.[9] It is noteworthy that more than 35% of the authors of its articles held PhD's, from a variety of disciplines.[10] Ultimately this journal failed to make an impact beyond the NLP community. Judging by its list of reviewers it probably relied too much on evaluation by NLP practitioners and authors, another example of the inward focus of the field. Nevertheless, Peter Winnington deserves great credit for this contribution to research in NLP.

Despite this work, the 'trail of techniques' left in the wake of the early developments in Santa Cruz has been over-sold and under-tested. For example, anecdotes about modelling may give the impression that through this method one can 'speed-learn' capabilities such as that of fluency in a foreign language. John Grinder's apparent claims in this respect ('While I myself have long journeys ahead of me to mastery, I have working competency in some eight languages')[11] may well be true, but they have not, to our knowledge, been evidenced or corroborated in published form. Nor have these claims been specified; thus, what is 'working competency'? While it seems plausible that one could learn to *act* as native speaker, perhaps through appropriate non-verbal behaviour and armed with phrases suitable for everyday interaction, it seems far less plausible that one could bypass the trial and error that would usually be involved in learning a language in depth.

Another issue is that genuine applications of NLP sometimes do not come to light. We know personally of someone who organised a new way of training volunteers for an international organisation, but who has never mentioned NLP in any of that organisation's publications; and of a psychiatrist who used NLP to model how people who had experienced a certain form of trauma were able to access their coping mechanisms, but omitted any reference to Bandler and Grinder in order to be taken seriously by medical colleagues. Our own explicit reference to NLP has sometimes raised eyebrows, and we have been gently advised on occasion to re-brand our interest.

In recent years, on the other hand, there have been signs of greater engagement with the academic world, providing some of what Hancox and Bass (1995a:43) have described as 'cultural pacing'. First, there has been a growing voice in NLP publications advocating the need for research in a plurality of modes (Hancox & Bass 1995b; Hollander 1999; McKergow 2000; Miller 2005). Secondly, there are welcome, contemporary examples of systematic efforts by practitioners to evaluate their work (e.g. Hutchinson, Churches & Vitae 2007). As mentioned in Chapter 3, one NLP model, that known as 'meta-programmes', has been tested to the extent that it is now the basis of a validated psychological instrument (Brewerton 2004). It has also been used as a research method by Nigel Brown (e.g. Brown 2001). Thirdly, at the time of writing there are many PhDs under way in established universities that are investigating NLP in fields that include management, education (Day 2008) and engineering.

Independent research into NLP's claims

The third and final category is independent research into NLP. Perhaps surprisingly, little formal academic research has been done. Most of the research studies of NLP that do exist were conducted in the 1980s and 1990s by researchers in experimental psychology who tested some of the assertions made in NLP publications in the 1970s. While that research generally does not support the claims that were tested, this is not the same as saying that research has rejected or disproved NLP as a whole field. For example, some commentators have questioned whether those studies have provided valid and reliable tests. Also, the findings that do exist were regarded as interim. What do these findings say?

The view that research has discredited NLP appears to stem mainly from a chapter written in the late 1980s in an edited book on hypnosis (Heap 1988). Heap wrote what is called a 'meta-evaluation', in which he summarised the results of sixty-two studies of NLP. These studies were principally psychological experiments that were concerned with testing three main notions in NLP. These were, first, 'primary representational system', according to which individuals have a preferred sensory mode of internal representation; secondly, the principle that matching sensory predicates enhances rapport (for example between a practitioner and a client); and thirdly, the 'eye movement' model, which suggest that the direction of a person's gaze corresponds to the sensory mode in which they are processing information. Details of most of these studies are accessible via a database developed by Dr Daniele Kammer at the University of Bielefeld in Germany.[12] It is interesting that the meta-model, which is typically portrayed as the core of NLP, was not the subject of any of the empirical studies reviewed by Heap.

Significantly, Heap described his conclusion as an 'interim verdict', declaring that Einspruch and Forman (1985) were 'probably correct in insisting that the effectiveness of NLP therapy undertaken in authentic clinical contexts of trained practitioners has not yet been properly investigated' (Heap 1988:276). Nevertheless Heap is quite definite in his conclusion:

> ... the assertions of NLP writers concerning representational systems have been objectively and fairly investigated and found to be lacking. These assertions are stated in unequivocal terms by the originators of NLP and it is clear from their writings that phenomena such as representational systems, predicate preferences and eye movement patterns are claimed to be potent psychological processes, easily and convincingly demonstrable on training courses by tutors and trainees following simple instructions, and, indeed in everyday life.... It may well be appropriate now to conclude that there is not, and never has been, any substance to the conjecture that people represent their world internally in a preferred mode which may be inferred from their choice of predicates and from their eye movements.
>
> (Heap 1988:275)

While there are some qualifications to add, Heap's broad conclusion is a fair summary of the findings of studies prior to 1988 which, in short, was unfavourable to NLP. Should that interim conclusion suffice to dismiss the entire field? Logically, these findings should be a stimulus for further research. However, in the 1990s direct research into NLP began to dry up and it is only now beginning to reappear.

Heap's interim conclusion can be qualified in several respects. First, the quantity of publications available to Heap was very limited by academic standards. As a quick comparison with a related contemporary research theme in HRD, an online search on a management database for academic journal articles with 'coaching' in the title between 2000 and 2006 returned one hundred and sixty-nine 'hits', representing nearly seventeen journal articles per year. This compares with fewer than three per year for NLP research in the period that Heap considered. Despite this greater volume of studies, so far as we are aware, no definitive conclusions have been reached about coaching.

Secondly, of the sixty-two studies cited by Heap, thirty-six are postgraduate dissertations (mostly at Masters level) and only twenty-six are published journal articles. According to the information provided on the aforementioned Bielefeld site, and by Heap's references, the authors of only five of these dissertations can also be identified as an author or co-author of a subsequent journal article. Thirty-one studies, for whatever reason, were apparently not developed into academic articles.

Significantly, it appears that Heap's review was based on only the abstracts of the dissertation studies included in his meta-evaluation, not on the dissertations themselves.[13] Typically the abstracts consist of a synopsis of two hundred words or less. There is no indication that Heap undertook any critical appraisal of the methodologies used by these studies, or that he assessed their validity.

While Heap's chapter appears to have taken the merits of these studies at face value, other researchers have voiced concern about their quality and validity. Beck and Beck (1984) and Einspruch and Forman (1985) have argued that many of these studies suffer from problems including inadequate interviewer training and misunderstanding of the NLP approach. Sharpley (1987), on the other hand, rejects these criticisms. For example, he points out that researchers have not reinterpreted NLP, but have investigated specific claims stated by Bandler and Grinder in publications.

Subsequent to Heap's meta-evaluation, Baddeley and Predebon (1991) reviewed seven previous studies and found that 'all studies except that of Buckner *et al* (1987) had consisted of significant misinterpretations of the NLP hypothesis.... Even the Buckner study can be faulted on design errors which call into question the validity of the findings' (1991:4–5). For example, some research reported that when some people looked up, they did not necessarily use a 'visual' word ('I see what you mean'), but perhaps an auditory or kinaesthetic predicate, ('that sounds good', or 'that's my feeling'). This could be explained by Bandler and Grinder's notion of a *lead system*, which means that a person could be looking up, accessing an internal image, but paying attention to their feelings about the image. In this case they are using their *lead system* (visual) only as a gateway to the sensory mode (kinaesethic) that generates the predicate. Baddeley and Predebon concluded that more innovative investigation was needed to develop a sufficiently complex account of the eye movement phenomenon.[14]

It is important to note also that although this research rejects the *specific* claims made by Bandler and Grinder, it does not contest the *phenomenon* of eye movements *per se*. For example, Heap does not question the fact that eye movements are considered generally to be related to internal cognitive processing. For example we mentioned in Chapter 5 the American psychiatrist, M. E. Day, who suggested that certain types of eye movements indicate when people were attending to their internal worlds of thought, memory and imagination, and attempted to correlate these with cognitive functions (Day 1964; Day 1967). Heap's criticism, like that of Baddeley and Predebon (1991), is of the particular correlations that are put forward in 'Frogs into Princes', as well as Bandler and Grinder's failure to refer to an existing literature on 'Lateral Eye Movement'.[15]

This research probably calls for a revised, testable 'eye movement hypothesis' that clarifies what NLP is claiming about the relationship between predicates in a question that is posed by one person, and the respondent's subsequent eye movements. Some NLP authors claim that this model is *only* a map that can be used 'as-if' it is true (O'Connor & McDermott 2003). Yet this conflicts with explicit reference to the eye movement model as a 'discovery' (Bostic St. Clair & Grinder 2001:171) of a phenomenon of human behaviour. Experimental studies have interpreted the claim as indicating a stimulus-response relationship, which therefore should yield correlations between questions and eye movements. Beck and Beck on the other hand, say; 'Eye movement in neurolinguistic programming is viewed not as a response to a stimulus but as an indication of the person's internal processing of information' (1984:176). This implies a somewhat different claim, purporting a correlation between eye movement and internal processing; the relationship between questions and eye movements may therefore be uncertain.

Similar arguments apply to studies reviewed by Heap about internal representations (see Chapter 6). The notion that people make such representations, and that these make use of sensory modes, is not at issue. The appearance of sensory predicates in language is undoubtedly an everyday phenomenon, illustrated by conversations, e-mails, media interviews, novels, and so on; the question is what, precisely, do they tell us about cognitive processes?

What the research queries is the notion that a person has a *primary* or *preferred* representational system. A reading of Heap's chapter suggests that he took Bandler and Grinder to be proposing a trait theory, rather than treating people's preference for representational systems as contextual and variable. Once again it would be helpful for NLP to have developed a more precise, refined statement of such claims, perhaps making clearer the distinctions between lead system, representational system, and reference system (Bandler & Grinder 1979:28).

The National Research Council studies

Besides Heap's review there is a second strand of research to address. Conducted in the USA by the National Research Council (NRC), chaired by John Swets (Druckman 2004:2234), this used an orthodox scientific approach to test methods of performance improvement for application in the US Army. Beyerstein comments that in relation to the efficacy of NLP, the NRC's original investigation 'could unearth no hard evidence in its favour, or even a succinct statement of its underlying theory' (1990:28). Druckman comments that the NRC's initial experiences with NLP led to two conclusions:

> On the one hand, we found little, if any evidence to support NLP's assumptions or to indicate that it is effective as a strategy for social

influence. It assumes that by tracking another's eye movements and language, an NLP trainer can shape the person's thoughts, feelings and opinions (Dilts 1983). There is no scientific support for these assumptions. On the other hand, we were impressed with the modeling approach used to develop the technique. The technique was developed from careful observations of the way three master psychotherapists conducted their sessions, emphasizing imitation of verbal and nonverbal behaviours (Druckman & Swets 1988, Chapter 8). This then led the committee to take up the topic of expert modelling in the second phase of its work.

(Druckman 2004:2245)

The first conclusion is consistent with Heap's meta-analysis. The second, the comment that these researchers were impressed with NLP's method of modelling, is interesting, and supports the potential of NLP as a methodology.

A proposed subsequent program on NLP was not implemented. The NRC then engaged in a further twelve years of work, which reported findings about the use of techniques of visualisation and mental rehearsal; 'A comprehensive review of experiments showed that mental practice does contribute to gains in performance. These gains are stronger for motor tasks that have cognitive components and when it is combined with physical practice (Feltz & Landers 1983)' (Druckman 2004:2240).

With regard to mental rehearsal, a study of basketball players is often cited in NLP trainings. This refers to a paper by Clark (1960),[16] who reported that mental rehearsal of a specific basketball shot proved to be almost as effective as actual rehearsal for two groups of college students who were already familiar with this type of shot. It was less effective for novice players, which may be explained by the fact that this group had yet to develop the physiological and neurological pathways involved in making the shot. According not only to Feltz and Landers, but also to Driskell *et al* (1994), Clark's findings are broadly supported by subsequent work in the field.

Of relevance to the NLP practice through which one person 'mirrors' another persons body language, Druckman reports that; 'The committee's work on socially induced affect showed that one person's expressed feelings can influence another's feelings... This process has implications for other topics studied by the committee, such as influence through mimicry, group cohesion, self-confidence, cooperative learning, and team training' (Druckman 2004:2244). This principle is taken up by Goleman and Boyatzis' (2008) notion of 'social intelligence', in which they suggest that a leader's demeanour has a direct influence on the climate of their workplace. Related findings affirm the impact on performance of confidence and self-efficacy beliefs, which have been of interest to NLP (Dilts & DeLozier 2000).

In conclusion, there is little substantive support for NLP from the independent research conducted to date. Yet that body of research is not only small but also methodologically narrow. Its findings tend to be repeated (e.g. von Bergen *et al* 1997), to the extent that the volume of repetition drowns out relevant detail, such as the concern that Heap's 1988 evaluation appears to have taken the results of student dissertations at face value. The additional research that could have developed Heap's interim conclusion into a more definitive statement has simply not yet been conducted. NLP has been in something of a Catch-22; it is dismissed because it is said that there is no evidence for it, yet there is no evidence for it at least in part because research is not being done, and research is not being done because the field is dismissed. Why? Because there is no evidence to support it.... The research questions noted above have therefore become marooned, abandoned by researchers who assume that they are not worthy of investigation, treated as matters of primarily theoretical interest in fields such as cognitive linguistics, and regarded by NLP practitioners as irrelevant or not in need of further investigation.

Review

Based on the above analysis, the comment from Fran Abrams at the start of this chapter, while offering a relevant challenge to articulate NLP's evidence base, seems to overstate the case. Even Derren Brown, who can be scathingly critical of NLP, says '... there are some sensible enough tools and techniques from that world which are worth knowing about, as long as you don't become a True Believer'. (Brown 2007:188). Brown goes on over the next twenty-five pages or so to attest to the validity and utility of much of the practitioner level contents of NLP.[17]

It is also important to say that NLP should be judged on a level playing field with other practices in HRD. Models and practices that are not supported by research evidence are, if anything, the norm. For example, what is generally known as the Tavistock approach to human relations (e.g. Miller 1993) has no 'hard science' evidence to support its theories. What it does have is accumulated case evidence that has been reviewed over many years through critical dialogue. Sharpley, one of the strongest critics of NLP, acknowledges the possibility that NLP principles 'are not amenable to research evaluation', and points out that:

> This does not necessarily reduce NLP to worthlessness for counselling practice. Rather, it puts NLP in the same category as psychoanalysis, that is, with principles not easily demonstrated in laboratory settings but, nevertheless, strongly supported by clinicians in the field. (1987:105)

As another example, it is commonly estimated that organisational change strategies fail to deliver their outcomes 70% of the time (e.g. Beer & Nohria 2000). Yet business organisations surely spend vastly more on organisational change than they do on NLP; the use of organisational change strategies probably impacts on more people, and more deeply, than current use of NLP in the field. While there are plenty of critics of organisational change and related consultancy practices, there is scarcely the vehement opposition to them that the lack of evidence behind NLP seems to attract. This does not avoid the need for a more research-informed NLP, but it does suggest that NLP should not be singled out for criticism in this respect.

An important feature of this debate is that the body of research discussed above took a positivistic approach, which in Chapter 10 we identified as being a particular, rather than a universal form of research. In particular it is based on a cause-effect model; consequently, it treats a learner or client as an object who will be affected by the technique being used regardless of their participation in the process, and regardless of their meaning-making about the situation. From the perspective of cybernetics, with its central notion of circular causality, and especially from second-order cybernetics, which regards not only the practitioner but also the researcher as part of the system under investigation, this approach is highly problematic. For example, as O'Connor and McDermott (2003) point out, while the positivist approach aims to isolate variables and test their effects, in any experiment the context, including the relationship between researcher and participant, cannot be neutral and will affect the phenomenon being studied.

This means that research into eye movements, for instance, will have a dual layer. The first is the purported relationship between eye movements and internal processing, which should be capable of being investigated through conventional methods, as in Dilts' (1983) use of EEG recordings. The second layer is the relational context involving the researcher, the respondent, the purpose at hand, and the interaction through which these all influence each other. Most experimental research regards this layer as an extraneous factor that can be controlled so that its impact is rendered neutral. Bateson's views about the significance of relationship and metacommunication not only offer a fundamental challenge to this assumption, but also regard this layer as the more interesting to study. Thus Bateson;

> knew in a very deep way that the 19th and 20th century methodological seduction of psychology by the pre-eminently successful physical sciences was a historical tragedy... an error of both logical typing and logical level... his task was to demonstrate that there are fundamental differences between the patterns of the physical, sensible world and the patterns of the world of mind without falling into mysticism.
>
> (DeLozier & Grinder 1987:xi–xii)

This means that it is problematic for the outcomes of processes like coaching, which result from processes involving circular causality, to be regarded as straightforward 'effects' for which one can identify simple, single causes. In short, from a cybernetic perspective what we call 'change' and 'learning' need to be understood as *emergent*, in that they are consequences that cannot be predicted.

This argument is linked to wider contemporary debate in other fields of people development about how to evaluate efficacy. For example, in relation to psychotherapy, Wampold (2001) rejects the dominant 'medical model' that seeks objective findings about techniques, and instead argues that the evidence shows that all psychotherapies are virtually equal in their efficacy. This, he says, needs to be explained through understanding psychotherapy from a contextual perspective, which shifts from the metaphor of a 'cure' provided by an expert, to one of a human relationship from which 'healing' can arise (Glass, in Wampold 2001:ix). Martin Seligman, one of the founders of 'positive psychology', offers a similar challenge to the assumptions behind the conventional, experimental efficacy study, because *'it omits too many crucial elements of what is done in the field'* (Seligman 1995:italics in original).

Does this mean that positivistic, conventional science is irrelevant to NLP? No, because if NLP authors and practitioners make claims for the objective existence of certain phenomena (e.g. eye movements), or for the reliable efficacy of certain procedures (e.g. the phobia cure), it is fair to expect that these claims should be available for testing. Even if one accepts that the outcomes of coaching are essentially emergent, discrepancies between published research findings about NLP and its claims should prompt further enquiry. To reject or ignore unfavourable findings by suggesting that research in general is not relevant to NLP creates a worryingly closed system that could serve to maintain its existing model of the world. Any field of practice needs to be alert to discrepant findings, which can mean that something new has been discovered, and that existing knowledge can be refined.

Other types of research into NLP will also be important. A voice that is strikingly absent from the field is that of the user, or client. The few published examples of users' accounts are rather drowned out by the publicity offered by practitioners, which may be thought surprising given the value espoused in NLP of considering multiple perceptual positions. Published accounts by users, which are few in number and often by journalists, generally attest to finding value in NLP. For example, Robert Crampton reported benefits of NLP therapy in The Times in 2002.[18] The potential gains from NLP are illustrated in a balanced way by Isabel Losada (Losada 2001).

Even if the weight of anecdotal reports of its efficacy suggest that something of value is being experienced, the desirability for NLP of providing more credible evidence should be clear. Without this type of evidence, people may continue to wonder whether enthusiasm for NLP is anything more than a contemporary case of 'The Emperor's New Clothes'. There is great scope for evaluating users' experiences and the benefits they gain from NLP.

Communities of practice

Finally in this chapter we return to the relationship between NLP and academe.

John Ziman (2000) points out that science is a culture, not a method, one that is characterised by a particular belief system and social practices. As an alternative to focusing exclusively on the merits of their substantive contents, we can consider NLP and the academic world as different communities of practice. NLP author Lucas Derks acknowledges this perspective when he says that a new idea 'stands or falls by the location of its originator in the social panoramas of the scientific community' (Derks 2005:viii).[19] Of course there is no single 'scientific community', it is more a multiplicity of intersecting interest groups. Similarly when we talk of an 'NLP community', it means this kind of loose network of practitioners – a very different kind of community from a small village whose inhabitants interact daily.

In some respects, NLP practitioners and academics share more in the way of concerns and approaches than may commonly be appreciated. For example, in their own ways they are both intensely interested in how people construct understandings through language; in questioning forms of knowing; and in creating useful, valid knowledge. NLP studies behaviour to find regularities and patterns within it, and to enable action to be taken based on these patterns. NLP and academic communities could therefore be seen as complementary, not opposed, investigating similar concerns but through diverse spectacles and practices.

One difficulty for NLP practitioners wishing to participate in academic communities is that NLP has no established disciplinary home in universities. Although its founders originally identified NLP as broadly associated with the concerns and endeavours of psychology (Bandler & Grinder 1975b:1), NLP is not the obvious remit of that or any other discipline, and in many respects it is transdisciplinary. Even constructivism and cybernetics, which we have argued provide the intellectual foundations of NLP, tend to be perspectives taken by individual academics, rather than the identities of whole university departments.

This suggests that one way to accelerate the 'mainstreaming' of NLP, therefore, could be to engage with the structures and processes of academic debate – which is one of the points made by Anthony Grant (see Chapter 10). Probably more important than 'proof' would be for NLP to become discussed routinely within research communities. There are some examples of increasing engagement, especially through the emergent doctoral research in NLP that we acknowledged above.

Conclusion

Thirty years after its inception, and twenty years after Heap's meta-analysis, research into NLP remains in its infancy. The existing body of empirical research makes for uncomfortable reading for NLP practitioners and gives no substantive support for NLP. It is, however, methodologically narrow and unfortunately has not led to further enquiry through refinements of NLP's claims and evaluations of its practice. We resist and challenge the view that the provision of 'proof' should be the primary purpose of research into NLP, or that conventional science is the only legitimate method to use. There remains a desperate need for an evidence base arrived at through quality evaluation. It is especially notable, and unfortunate, that there is an almost total silence from users.

The worlds of NLP and academe can be seen as communities of practice that to date have operated largely at a distance; we believe these worlds can gain from each other, and are beginning to do so more.

Ultimately our position is that research into NLP is not only merited, but also important, because it is so prevalent in HRD. It would seem short-sighted to neglect further research when its use is widespread; this does no useful service to its many existing, and prospective, clients and users.

12
NLP and Ethics – Outcome, Ecology and Integrity

Introduction

As we have seen, NLP makes a number of claims about the ways in which communication can influence people. The meta-model is essentially a model of the relationship between language, and how people have constructed information about events at a level of which they may not be aware. In selling, NLP is used to influence people's views about products and services. Ericksonian language patterns, which are an integral part of the armoury of NLP practitioners, are claimed to enable the user to bypass the listener's conscious, analytical mind, and exert an unconscious influence.

These are claims which have considerable ethical implications. Yet with few exceptions, such as an entry Dilts and DeLozier's encyclopedia (2000:372–373), there is little explicit discussion of ethics in NLP. In the late 1970s Bandler and Grinder acknowledged people's discomfort about using an approach that 'did specific things to get specific outcomes' (1979:7), even if those same people were seeking to become more effective professional communicators. This has turned out to be prophetic.

We cannot escape the fact that there are worrying reports about how NLP is used. There is an element of sensationalism in some accounts; for example, it has been linked to teaching people seduction techniques, and to promises of gaining power, earning a fortune, or easily changing people's lives. Some people – mostly conspiracy theorists, it would appear – even believe that NLP helped Barack Obama win his presidential election campaign in 2008.[1]

Not every criticism of NLP in this respect merits serious attention. We referred earlier to a newspaper article (in which NLP was called the 'refuge of the socially inadequate'), which seemed to be based more on the author's emotional response to NLP than on reasoned consideration. This is mild compared to Megginson and Clutterbuck (2005) who imply an analogy (which seems to us to be odious) between NLP and an instrument of genocide.[2]

The existence of extreme views like these, however, does not alter the fact that it is crucial to consider ethics in relation to NLP, not least because of existing and impending government regulation in the USA and UK. As we shall see, much has been achieved already within the field to deal with issues of standards and ethical codes that are compatible with other methods of people development. Nevertheless this is an area that needs more explicit attention within the NLP community.

'Manufacturing' trust

According to published accounts there is evidence that people find NLP skills and insights helpful, both professionally and personally. Despite this many people, when asked about their impressions of NLP, say that they have heard that it can be 'manipulative', or have had an experience where they sensed they were being manipulated. Charles Tart, whose field of expertise is the study of altered states of consciousness, wrote:

> I must confess to some ambivalence about Neurolinguistic Programming, as the movement it has become shows a manipulative and power-seeking attitude in some cases, but the technical developments are well worth following.
>
> (Tart 1990:280)

NLP is sometimes stereotyped as being about manipulating another person by mimicking their non-verbal behaviour in order to generate 'rapport' artificially. This process was in fact discussed originally in NLP as a matter of 'trust' rather than of 'rapport' (Grinder & Bandler 1976:14). The importance of trust is well established in the fields of helping. Lewis refers to research by Strupp *et al* that showed the patient's trust in the therapist to be a 'singularly important variable' (Lewis & Pucelik 1990:14), and cites Jerome Frank, who emphasises the significance of trust in rendering the client suscept-ible to the therapist's influence.

Jane's first experience of attending an NLP Practitioner course cer-tainly raised concerns for her about the way she was asked to use rapport:

> The particular trainer in question wished to familiarise us with Ericksonian Language Patterns. First he recounted how he used them to trick people into believing that he could read palms. It was, he said, particularly useful on long haul flights, where he would charm the members of the aircrew handing out drinks into believ-ing in his special powers, so that he could get more free drinks, as they listened to his authoritative insights and prognostication. We were instructed in how to take someone's hand, focus their atten-tion on their palm, induce a light trance and then explain to them that the lines on their palm made a letter of the alphabet which must signify something or someone important to them, and thus send them on a trans-derivational search. We were told to calibrate to their responses to our suggestions couched in vague and abstract terms. After this exposition the whole group was sent out to a weekly market in the town, to see how far they could go in con-vincing innocent members of the public of their special powers, even getting them to co-operate further by allowing members of our group to engage them in ear-reading, and even sole-of-the-foot reading. I refused to do this, but watched in some horror as my fellow students persuaded innocent market goers of their special powers. The following day the lead trainer took me to one side, and suggested that as I was having difficulties with learning NLP, perhaps I would like to make do with just an attendance certificate?

On the other hand, NLP highlights something that common sense too easily forgets; for example that aspects of being 'authentic' are learnt skills, or 'programmes', and may be more socially conditioned and less' natural' than people typically assume. Many rituals that may help to enhance rapport, such as asking a person one meets how they are, complementing someone on their appearance, or showing sympathy for a misfortune – are regarded as 'natural' and 'authentic' because they are socially and culturally familiar. Attend-ing to this dimension of interaction consciously in order to improve one's social ability may be seen as inauthentic. Yet this creates a bind for someone who recognises that their skills could be improved, or to whom the notion of rapport is a genuinely helpful insight into the nature of social interaction. Are they then perceived as calculating just because they seek to be more effective at relating to people?

As explained in Chapter 9, it is also a myth that people's behaviour is always the result of conscious choice. People overestimate the degree to which they operate by conscious choice in daily life. NLP holds that it is possible to learn alternative 'programmes', and to establish these in such a way that a preferred programme will run automatically in a real-life setting; an example could be a 'programme' to feel confident when walking into a meeting – noting that Derren Brown celebrates the fact that 'Confidence can be faked. It's not real' (Brown 2007:209).

All communication is hypnosis

Next we turn to a way in which NLP may in fact show a *greater* ethical sensibility than many other modes of people development. Lewis and Pucelik (1990:iii) cite Edward T. Hall's comment:

> ...we must learn to understand the 'out of awareness' aspects of communication. We must never assume that we are fully aware of what we communicate to someone else. There exists in the world today tremendous distortions in meaning as men try to communicate with one another.

There are critics who appear to assume that it is only NLP trained people who seek to influence others through language. This misconception seems (based on our personal experience) to be common amongst practitioners who naïvely assume that being 'non-directive' somehow means that all influencing can be avoided. Bolstad cites two examples of ways in which Carl Roger, the epitome of the client-centred practitioner, unwittingly influenced his client during a film in which Rogers, Fritz Perls and Albert Ellis each work with a client called Gloria (Bolstad 2002:56, 65).

Furthermore, anyone who tries to avoid influencing risks being ineffective in a work role; who would neglect to design a presentation so that it is persuasive, or put across an argument at a meeting in such a way so that they are understood, or tell a story or a joke to put their audience at ease? The use of influence in the world of management is accepted as commonplace. Lakhani (2008:48), for example, says:

> The most effective marketers and persuaders are carefully crafting, positioning, and packaging stories to make them most believable and credible to the public.

The founders of NLP became convinced that 'all communication is hypnosis' from their time studying Erickson (Grinder & Bandler 1981:1).[3] Isabel Losada understood this from her direct experience of NLP; 'It's a scary thought, but we hypnotise each other in this way all the time. This is what you do when you say to people, "You're looking tired" and they had been feeling OK until you told them they weren't' (Losada 2001:199). Richard Bandler, writing about Virginia Satir, says: 'Virginia was an exquisite hypnotist, something she strongly denied at first. I showed her videotapes of her and Erickson, and for the first ten minutes they said exactly the same thing... It was superb hypnosis, but she said it was just a centering exercise' (Bandler 2008a:40).

That we necessarily and inevitably communicate with our own unconscious, and that of others, in our everyday interactions as a general phenomenon is increasingly supported by evidence from neurological studies about how the brain processes information and makes sense of language.

Furthermore, recent discoveries in this field indicate that both words and actions are processed by recognisable patterns of activity in our neurology;[4] the words that we read or hear have physiological and neurological effects, yet we are not consciously aware of the responses they evoke. In effect this means also that mild forms of trance state are everyday phenomena. Lankton (1980:171) explains, with reference to Charles Tart's classic work on altered states of consciousness, that:

> In fact, most of us alter our states so frequently that we fail to discriminate between them. For example, a different state of consciousness is operating while you are at work than when you are swimming, fishing or picnicking... Daydreaming is easily distin-

guished from the quality of attention you would bring to flying an airplane. For most people being immersed in an internal dialogue is subjectively unlike a direct conversation with a friend.

NLP's 'Milton Model', based on verbal patterns used by Milton Erickson, enables us to identify these types of verbal exchanges, regardless of whether the speaker has any knowledge of NLP. For example, Paul and a colleague were talking together about preparing feedback on drafts written by a student whom they were supervising together. The colleague, who is not trained in NLP, said to Paul, 'I don't know when you'll get around to reading them' (i.e. the chapters). Unbeknown to her, she had used an embedded command (i.e. 'get around to reading them') and a presupposition (i.e. that Paul would indeed read them). Paul reflected back that there seemed to be an assumption or two in her statement, at which she laughed.

From this perspective, any facilitator needs to develop an awareness of, and take responsibility for, the way they communicate and influence other people at the unconscious level. It is impossible for all communication to be overt and conscious. Clearly, this contrasts dramatically with the views of people who maintain that it is inappropriate or unethical to communicate with another person's unconscious without their knowledge and consent, and who believe that some forms of coaching are free from the taint of any influence on a client.

We need to talk, therefore, not about *whether or not* people exercise influence in the first place, but about *how* someone influences other people through their communication. Nobody can choose not to influence other people because of the nature of communication itself. This means that all who interact with others, professionally and personally, do so at both conscious and unconscious levels, and for good or ill. Thus there is a complex ethical dimension to all human interaction.

Ethical codes and ethical reasoning

Since communication cannot help but influence, the issue is about the way the practitioner uses that influence. Given that NLP acknowledges this influence and makes it an explicit part of the practice, it offers the potential advantage that the practitioner can make informed choices. What perspectives could help to identify the types of choice to be made? What are the key issues of ethics in NLP, and how do we know when an action is 'ethical'? These are complex questions.

First, it is helpful to distinguish between ethical codes of conduct, and ethical reasoning. Many practitioners, if asked about ethics, would refer to their espoused code of practice, of which there are plentiful examples within the field of NLP itself.[5] The Association for NLP has had a code of ethics for many years (Brion 1995). This makes explicit reference to respecting 'the dignity and worth of every human being, and their right to self-determination'; and to striving 'to act with integrity, independence and impartiality, avoiding conflicts of interests and acting in accordance with the pre-suppositions of NLP'.[6] Associations such as the Guild of NLP, and the International NLP Trainer's Association, have also developed codes of practice. Specific codes of ethics exist in professions in which NLP is an accepted mode of practice, such as psychotherapy.[7] In Human Resource Development relevant associations to which NLP practitioners may belong include the Chartered Institute of Personnel and Development, the British Psychological Society, the European Mentoring and Coaching Council, and more.

There is a high degree of consensus in professional literatures about the types of principles that comprise ethical codes; for example in counselling (Jones *et al* 2000:9), and in nursing (Fry & Johnstone 2002:21). The codes that exist in NLP seem to be consistent with Rowson's 'framework for ethical thinking in the professions' which uses the acronym FAIR to distil the most commonly cited ethical principles:

- To treat individuals justly and fairly
- To respect people's autonomy
- To act with integrity
- To seek the best results.

(Rowson 2006:151)

There are two main problems with codes of practice. First, such codes may have little to do with ethics as such; according to Gregory (2008) they can be more about controlling the behaviour of people who are not ethically or morally mature.

There is also view that, despite the rhetoric of protection of the client or consumer, in practice these arrangements tend to serve the interests of the professional themselves. This is a complex matter which is currently taxing fields such as coaching. Postle (2007) argues that regulation reflects an agenda of state control and dominance of established professions which, among other things, could militate against the emergence of new fields.

The second problem is the question of whether, even if a code of ethics exists, there is effective accountability. Most codes of conduct in NLP itself are adhered to voluntarily; they are not universal. At present, practitioners are more likely to be held accountable by the codes of conduct of their other professions, rather than by NLP itself.

Codes of conduct, therefore, are prescriptions defining right action originating from a source external to the practitioner. Authors like Monica Lee (2003) and Richard Rowson (2006) argue that while the existence of codes of conduct is important, and may be required for legal purposes, they are not a substitute for moral development and the capacity of the individual practitioner to engage in ethical reasoning. Indeed there is a risk that compliance with such a code is taken to be all that a practitioner needs to do; ethics is then reduced to rule-following.[8] According to Rowson, 'the ethical obligation of mature people' includes 'an element of *judging* for themselves what they ought to do in particular circumstances' (2006:49).

So, what are the bases on which individuals can make such judgements?

A conceptual framework

This is not a book about ethics. We are, however, concerned with promoting mature ethical reasoning and awareness in the field and, in order to explore some of the main issues further, we venture briefly into the terrain of moral philosophy. There are two branches of moral philosophy that may help with this mapping, known as Consequential Ethics, often referred to as the utilitarian approach, summed up by the saying, 'the end justifies the means'; and Deontological Ethics, which is concerned with the intrinsic rightness of an action. We will link these philosophical positions to the influence of Satir, Perls, Bateson and Erickson, and the way their ideas were subsequently developed in NLP.

We suggest that there are three main types of ethical judgement evident from NLP literature and practice, to do with the 'ecology' of the client's outcome; the consequences of the practitioner's intervention; and the 'integrity' of the practitioner. Practitioners may be exercising all or none of these types of judgement. It is not our intention here to say what judgements *should* be made; our purpose is to offer a map of this particular territory that may be useful to practitioners and clients alike.

Outcome and ecology

In consequential ethics, an action can be justified as ethically acceptable if it is thought usefully to fulfil a purpose. How do we know that what a client wants at a particular time is a suitable purpose?

Outcomes, of course, can vary tremendously in scope and scale, from a local, practical goal desired by an individual client through to an ideal such as 'the wealth of the nation'. In effect the notion of outcome can be extended in time and space, becoming concerned with consequences and meanings for others, and not solely for the client.

Consequential ethics is therefore often concerned with notions of the greater good for the greatest number. How much greater, and who can judge what is 'good', are of course the very issues to be wrestled with. The notion of 'the greater good' has led to the establishment of the National Health Service, but also to totalitarian regimes. How wide and far do we draw the scope, and from what perspective do we view the outcome? For example, do we consider the impact on the client and their family over the next week? On humanity for the next 50 years? On the universe for eternity? And who decides what constitutes the 'greater good' for humanity?

How is this type of judgement approached in NLP? One possibility is simply to accept the client's outcome at face value. At this level the ethic of NLP is quite simple; to enable the client to achieve their outcome. Yet things are rarely that simple, and there are ways in which NLP practitioners encourage clients to assess the likely consequences of their outcome. A prominent principle in NLP that relates to the idea of 'the greater good' is that of 'ecology'. Thus 'the ecological check is our explicit recognition that... each one of us is a really complex and balanced organism. For us to make a change in pattern X and not to take into account all the repercussions in other parts of (his) experience behaviour would be foolhardy' (Bandler & Grinder 1979:147).

Influenced by Bateson's views about the ecology of human systems, this entails the idea that an intervention must not have deleterious consequences on either clients or their environment, including the people in it. It is also reflected in the idea that an outcome should result in a win-win situation for the people involved.

One way in which this is addressed in NLP is to begin with the client's stated outcome, and to rely on the client's own awareness of its suitability or otherwise for them to emerge. I might start by saying that my outcome is to gain a promotion, but through exploring it I have come to appreciate more of what I could also lose (perhaps more of my evenings and weekends will be taken up by work issues). My sense of whether the prospective rewards will make such sacrifices worthwhile then becomes the 'ecology check'.

A second way is through Erickson's belief that a person's unconscious is a more reliable guide to what is ecological *for them* than their conscious mind. Erickson's own writing is full of examples (Rosen 1982), and this principle is utilised in NLP's 'six step reframing' (Chapter 7).

Another stance is that described in 'Whispering in the Wind' (Bostic St. Clair & Grinder 2001:208), which proposes that the ethics of NLP should be to develop a client's independence so that he or she recognises that they are 'the source of the resources and have the ability to participate fully in the processes of change initially managed by the agent of change'. This links the ethical consequence to one of NLP's own presuppositions (e.g. 'People have all the resources they need to make changes'). A potential difficulty of this stance is that it involves a value judgement by the practitioner about what is good for the client, even if at a high level.

The point that Bateson makes, however, is that we cannot know with any certainty what will be 'ecological'. Our conscious minds perceive only limited parts of the subtle and complex connections involved in any system; we then assume that we can act on those limited parts in a linear, cause-effect way in order to achieve some goal, *and that our action will only affect that part*. This assumption, according to Bateson, is not only profoundly mistaken but also dangerous. He believed that our instrumental actions are likely to do harm to, or at least have unanticipated consequences for, the wider ecology.

Bateson's own position became one in which nature, not human-kind, was the focus; 'the ethical unit is the *relating between* two or more people and their *relating to* the larger environment' (Charlton 2008:202). Instead of making this type of judgement through the rational, conscious mind, Bateson favoured the idea that it would be based on aesthetics. Thus Mary Catherine Bateson explains: 'There ... is something like a template within the self that makes possible the recognition of aesthetic order in the other. We reveal something about ourselves in judging something beautiful' (Bateson 2000b:89).

In order to make an ethical judgement about consequences, there-fore, one may be involved in considering the scope of the outcome, and in choosing perspectives from which to view its consequences. In NLP literature we can see that this type of judgement is made in various ways.

Ends and means

The second category of judgement is about the likely consequences of the practitioner's intervention, and whether the end justifies the means.

Taken simplistically, the logical implication of making the client's outcome central is that the end always justifies the means. However, things are not so simple and interventions have other consequences. An illustration is Losada's account of the way she experienced fear being used as a means of control in the workshop she attended and felt troubled by the lack of compassion she experienced in this inci-dent, even though she went on to say, '... I still want to go back. I was learning a huge amount and I'd laughed more this week than I ever remember laughing before' (Losada 2001:204).

To what extent, therefore, does the end justify the means? This question has a lineage prior to NLP. Fritz Perls was prepared to be outrageous if it would serve a client's needs. Frank Farrelly, the founder of 'Provocative Therapy', developed his approach because he came to realise that his Rogerian training often did not work. Many clients had constructed elaborate, entirely reasonable justi-fications for why they couldn't change and, in Farrelly's experience,

Rogerian sensitivity and empathy only served to elicit these jus-
tifications. Farrelly believed, at root, that people *will not*, rather
than *cannot*, change (Farrelly & Brandsma 1974:37). He sought to
expose this by outwitting clients' problematic patterns of thinking
and behaving.

Erickson's approach was clearly utilitarian in many respects,
including that he would use verbal and non-verbal communication
in any way that he believed would help therapeutically. He often
used indirect or embedded hypnotic commands targeted at the
patient's unconscious, and stressed the importance of the idea of
'utilisation' (Walker 1996:2), which meant that the therapist could
'utilise' any of the client's beliefs and values to achieve the necessary therapeutic goals. He would, for example, employ double
binds (Erickson & Rossi 1975) therapeutically. The Palo Alto group
would also use an apparently irrational method called a *paradoxical
injunction* (Watzlawick, Beavin & Jackson 1967:194). For example, a
client in a therapy group claimed that she could not say 'no' to
other people. The therapist instructed her to say 'no' to everyone
in the group – an injunction she could only avoid by saying 'no' to
the therapist.

What NLP has taken from sources such as these is the principle
that unconventional methods are sometimes necessary to achieve
the client's outcome because more conventional, apparently reasonable interventions are ineffective. Outrageous and challenging behaviour is often encouraged, especially for trainers; the
reason given is so that whatever is being communicated is more
memorable.

It is, of course, possible to take the idea that the end justifies
the means to extremes, or even to adopt outrageous behaviour
as a posture that serves the practitioner more than the client. The
more excessive side of Perls' behaviour has been downplayed in
Gestalt circles since, and the confrontive tenor of 1960s Gestalt
psychotherapy revised, in order to render it a more respectable, contemporary approach within the psychotherapy community.

Ingredients in the judgements made by practitioners about
whether the end justifies the means may therefore include whether the practitioner, cognisant of the implications of metacommunication, is able to consider the wider consequences of their
interventions.

Integrity

The third category of judgement relates to the notion of *intrinsic purpose* that is found in Deontological ethics, which concerns a practitioner's own ability to apply moral reasoning, and their own mature moral sense to a situation for which they take responsibility.

Intrinsic purpose puts the onus on the practitioner to become more aware of his or her own moral and ethical assumptions, and to be open to critically reflecting on them. This ethical stance therefore assumes that the practitioner will have developed a consistent value system for themselves.

Deontological ethics focuses on the rightness or wrongness of the intentions or motives behind people's actions, instead of trying to anticipate their consequences. Here the moral stance is more about 'doing the right thing' than 'doing things right', and may be based on respect for people's rights, or on duties or principles. This is a central feature, for example, of Stephen Covey's view (Covey 1992) that effective people tend to be principle-centred.

Within NLP this stance is epitomised by Virginia Satir, who believed deeply in the importance of humanism, where the individual was perceived as a valuable part of the creation, and regretted the lack of intrinsic values in the modern scientific world view, with its inability to provide people with a more spiritual meaning for life (Walker 1996:171).

In Erickson's practice also we can find examples of 'doing the right thing'. He lived simply, in an unassuming house, and has been described as someone who put the interests and wellbeing of his patients and clients above his own economic needs, often charging only what he thought his clients could afford (J. Zeig, cited in Walker 1996:212). His students were able to attend his seminars for four dollars. If a person was in need, but did not have the means to pay him, there was no charge, provided that such clients were motivated to work with him therapeutically.

Notions of 'integrity' (Laborde 1983) and 'wisdom' are probably the most common expressions of a deontological, principle-centred ethic in NLP. McNab (2005:146) for example, implies that concerns about 'manipulation' can be answered through an appeal to 'integrity'. Judith DeLozier, writing about 'New Code' NLP, said that: 'there is no wisdom in a piece of technology. Wisdom has to be the carrier of that information' (DeLozier 1995:7). This view implies that a practitioner applies ethical judgements, and is not just making technical decisions about how best to 'reprogramme' a client to achieve an outcome.

The difficulty here, of course, is in knowing what is meant by nominalisations such as 'integrity'; how can we know that a practitioner's claim to be acting with integrity is not an empty self-justification? From an NLP perspective, too, we will be more interested in how, specifically, exemplars act with integrity than in semantic debate about the concept.

Influencing ethically

So far we have argued that NLP practitioners may be making up to three different *types* of ethical judgement, all of which are complex and call for ethical reasoning. As illustrated above, the people who most influenced the development of NLP had their own particular perspectives in relation to ethics, which remain evident in NLP today; Satir's profoundly humanistic approach, Perls' combination of humanism with outrageousness, Erickson's pragmatic utilitarianism, supported by a deep commitment to healing, apparently above his own economic needs, and Bateson's ecological mysticism, coupled with a concern for the harm that a naïve epistemology would do to the planet and its inhabitants.

Is there a way to bring these threads together? One option is to conclude that we can only rely on the individual's choices. O'Connor and McDermott say, 'we each apply our own morality and ethics to both our outcomes and the means we choose to achieve them. The basis for the ethics is our common humanity and our deepest essence as human beings' (O'Connor & McDermott 1996:133–134). Ultimately, this is all we can rely upon. According to Hayes (2006:12), 'the key is to be able to identify those who work well and ethically within NLP – thankfully, they can be found'. Based on our own experience, we agree; yet there would appear to be a pressing issue of the extent to which NLP practitioners are perceived as trustworthy.

Within NLP, for example, there is the issue that lay people are being trained to make interventions and to help prospective clients achieve outcomes. The route to becoming an NLP practitioner is somewhat short compared, for example, with the years of training involved in becoming a Jungian analyst.[9] An NLP training can be perceived by participants as constituting a license to practice, and such people are at liberty, under current law, to market themselves as (for example) coaches and consultants. While some NLP courses are designed as a dedicated training for coaches, most are generic and cater for learners with a variety of interests and backgrounds. There is little or no screening of the people wishing to take part in these courses, who may wish to learn how to influence others for any purpose they choose.

How trainees are then assessed is another matter. There is no standardised form of assessment and the extent to which an NLP certificate is a reliable mark of competence must be open to question.[10] This is of concern to Steve Andreas, who also perceives the need for sufficient training and an informed ethical stance for practitioners, and is critical of the current fashion for very streamlined forms of practitioner trainings.[11]

What ethical issues are raised by this, and how can people be guided on how to make ethical choices when they use NLP? We conclude this chapter with four recommendations.

First, one approach to ethics taken in NLP is to suggest that practitioners should be have a duty to act *as-if* the field's presuppositions were true. This is one component of the ethical guidance adopted by, for example the ANLP and the Professional Guild of NLP. It is a good recommendation so far as it goes, as it would be a concern to find a practitioner conspicuously flouting the presuppositions, for example by practising NLP in pursuit of their personal goal at the expense of their clients. The limitation is that, as we have argued in Chapter 9, the existing presuppositions do not go far enough because they reflect the perspective of first-order cybernetics, and practitioners may be trained to operate as if they were external to the client system. To become a more comprehensive set of ethical principles, they could emphasise (say) circular causality, such that person A's action towards person B has consequences for person A.

Secondly, we suggest the time is ripe for a re-appraisal of the designation of people as 'practitioner' on the basis of completing a basic training alone.

Third, a principle on which we are keen is that of complementarity. This entails the idea that NLP may be used most ethically by people who have training in, or experience of, a complementary mode of working. Psychotherapist and author Lisa Wake (2008), for example, argues that Neurolinguistic Psychotherapy is enriched when the practitioner has other perspectives such as those, for instance, of Object Relations.[12] With the benefit of hindsight, one might question the impact of extracting defined techniques from the context of the principles that motivated the people who most influenced its development. To what extent, when NLP became marketed as a product, did those techniques become stripped of their context? Haber (2002:32) notes that Virginia Satir 'was suspicious of the way NLP used her techniques to create change without attention to its higher purpose: "What got me is that my work was taken, without heart and soul, and then it was used as a manipulation thing ... Anything that's potent for change can be used negatively or positively".'

The rationale for complementarity is three fold. First, a complementary practice may provide its own ethical reasoning. Second, this usage of NLP is more in tune with the notion of NLP as a methodology, or meta-discipline, that exists to *enhance* people's practice, not as a method that is sufficient by itself. Thirdly, it reflects NLP's emphasis on the importance of being able to take multiple perceptual positions.

Fourth, and finally, we note a criterion generally considered to be part of the ethical duty of a profession, which is that of engaging 'in ongoing research to demonstrate how and when their work positively helps clients' (Jones, Shillito-Clarke, Syme, Hill, Casemore & Murdin 2000:5). Thus we reiterate our argument about the need for research and evaluation in NLP.

Conclusion

It is undeniable that NLP can be used appropriately as well as inappropriately. We resist and challenge the suggestion that NLP is somehow more amenable to unprofessional usage than other methods of working with people, yet the nub of the issue is that people want to know if its techniques and practitioners can be trusted.

NLP can offer a radical challenge to some 'common sense' assumptions about language, communication and behaviour. At best, NLP can raise people's awareness of how they may be influencing other people, educates them, and encourages them to be more responsible for the effects they have on other people. Arguably, it provides a public service through educating people about such language patterns, and the ability to recognise when others are influencing us.

This escalates, rather than diminishes the level of ethical responsibility on the trained practitioner. Once we accept the principle that we cannot *not* influence other people through our communication, it becomes more problematic to distinguish between appropriate and inappropriate influence. There is no simple answer to this; it requires moral development and ethical reasoning. We have emphasised the need for dialogue about ethics to be more in the foreground as NLP develops. Among our recommendations is that it may be time to review the standard designation of 'practitioner' for people who have only attended basic training courses.

13
NLP as a Movement – Values and Discourse

NLP is a set of ideas located in time, a particular story, in de Shazer's (1994) terms, about people development. As Mike Pedler wryly notes, in his foreword to Dave Molden's 'Managing with the Power of NLP', 'NLP is indeed from California but it has travelled well' (Molden 2003:xi). Since it is suggested in NLP that unconscious modelling is such a powerful learning process, perhaps there are features that might have become incorporated into NLP unawarely from its historical and cultural circumstances? There is little in NLP literature that attempts to be reflexive in this way, and which addresses the field as it might be seen from outside.

Drenched in the sudden freedoms of the 1960s, exploration of the limits of human experience and consciousness led to a torrent of new practices: Timothy Leary's experimentation with LSD; R. D. Laing's 'anti-psychiatry'; Arthur Janov's primal scream therapy; and many more. The leitmotiv of California in the late 1960s and early 1970s in particular was not country, family and achievements, but love, peace and personal happiness, together with the exploration of altered states of consciousness; Huxley's 'Doors of Perception' – the source of the name of LA rock band 'The Doors' – is cited in The Structure of Magic I (Bandler & Grinder 1975b:9–10).

As noted before, NLP can be seen as part of that era's 'growth movement'. This refers to diverse practices, loosely configured, many of them emerging from Abraham Maslow's advocacy of a 'third-force' in psychology (following Freud and behaviourism), which was called 'humanistic' psychology. Maslow, among others, was concerned about the reductionist nature of behaviourism, and the authoritarianism and pessimism of psychoanalysis. Along with figures like Carl Rogers,

161

Maslow developed an approach in which people were to be treated as human beings, not as rats in a laboratory. Maslow was also the chief influence behind the development of transpersonal psychology which began to explore the spiritual dimension of human experience.

Robbins (1988) reports that, according to sociological analyses, the growth movement gave rise to various 'new religious movements' of the 1970s, such as Werner Erhard's 'est'. Robbins suggests that these can be seen not as new creations but as mechanisms through which people sought to resolve the tensions between the expressiveness of the counterculture and traditional American values, essentially through enabling them to feel inwardly liberated.

While we do not develop this type of sociological perspective here,[1] this chapter attempts to make the familiar strange by asking what kinds of features may have become taken for granted within the community? For example, what values are apparent in NLP that may reflect its historical and cultural origins?

The features we explore here are:

- The ethos of self-help, with its pursuit of individual freedom, happiness, power, wealth and excellence;
- The 'Wild West': mavericks, pioneers, and outlaws who challenge orthodoxy and the establishment;
- NLP as a cult.

NLP as self-help

Among the *values* apparent in the discourse of NLP, notions of freedom, happiness, power, wealth and excellence are prominent. In tenor, these seem congruent with the idealism of 'the American Dream'. Some of these values, at least, appear self-evidently worthwhile, so can remain unexamined facets of the field.

Freedom

From the beginning, NLP publications have espoused the autonomy of the individual. Its motives have been described as 'sharing the resources of all those who are involved in finding ways to help people have better, fuller and richer lives' (Bandler & Grinder 1975b, from book jacket).

NLP is based on the idea that people can realise their potential for self-determination through overcoming their learnt self-limitations; for example, it can 'enable you to increase your own self-awareness in order to allow you to achieve self-empowerment' (Henwood & Lister 2007:3). In the 1980s Bandler emphasised the right of people to 'run their own brain' (Bandler 1985:21); in other words to be involved in the repair, maintenance and enhancement of their own minds, and not be dependent on professionals.

Bandler's own emphasis on 'freedom' is sometimes so strong that it seems more a drive than a mere value. For example 'Conversations' (Bandler & Fitzpatrick 2005) is subtitled 'Freedom is Everything, and Love is all the Rest'. Inside, Bandler emphasises 'a freedom from labels' (Bandler and Fitzpatrick 2005:118), where 'labels' refers to the orthodox psychological assumption that change is inevitably difficult.

This type of plea seems more charged than a simple espousal of the American value of 'liberty'. One possible interpretation, that this expresses a desire for freedom from *authority*, would be congruent with the frequent, sharp dismissal of various types of professionals. Hence we find psychotherapists parodied and condemned as 'the-rapists'; researchers are 'people who will *not associate* with the people who are practicing!' (Bandler & Grinder 1979:6); academics are serious and, according to Bandler 'being serious is a disease'.[2] It seems ironic that this desire for freedom from other people's labels involves so much labelling of other people.

The notion of 'freedom' in the discourse of NLP reflects an emphasis on individualism. Seeing the individual as self-creating can ignore the ways in which identity is socially constructed, and overplay the degree to which identity is a matter of individual psychology. It is rare, however, to find acknowledgement within NLP literature of the way our sense of identity emerges from participation in social contexts. Even the human potential movement, to which NLP broadly belongs, and which was characterised by a radical intent to liberate people from oppressive social roles and expectations (Rowan 2001:219), did not go so far as to suggest that 'identity' is within the conscious control of an individual.

This emphasis on the heroic potential for the person to change themselves seems to reflect more that aspect of the growth movement that became known as the 'me generation'. This also reflects the American ethos of self-improvement that can be traced back to

Dale Carnegie's 'How to Win Friends and Influence People'. Carnegie (2006), for example, prefigured NLP's emphasis on changing one's own response in order to influence other people.

The packaging and selling of NLP as a commercial product may lend weight to the view that NLP, at least in one of its guises, is part of this movement. Many of the products and artefacts of NLP tend to 'sell' solutions and appeal to individual desires for success and happiness (which are themselves values particular to Western cultures), more than to self-understanding, wisdom and the 'greater good'. Thus we are offered 'Instant Confidence' (McKenna 2006), a book that is subtitled 'the power to go for anything you want'; 'Managing with the power of NLP' for 'comparative advantage' (Molden 2003); and 'effortless and lasting change' (Bandler 2008).

This self-help ethos is now characterised as the 'makeover' culture that is the subject of critiques by authors such as McGee (2005). Included in McGee's analysis is a discussion of Tony Robbins (McGee 2005:60), a figure sometimes associated with NLP. Robbins, author of books like 'Unlimited Power', has a distinctive approach to motivation and success, using large group awareness training with audiences of thousands. Robbins readily acknowledges the influence of NLP on his approach and its contribution to his success, and he appears to use NLP in some aspects of his work – he attended NLP courses before branching out on his own – but he does not offer NLP trainings or certificates, nor does he associate himself directly with NLP.

As useful as self-improvement can be, it can also peddle the delusion that we can control every aspect of our lives. A related facet found in NLP is that of the extent of personal responsibility for one's experience. NLP, as a constructivist approach, assumes that we can influence the meaning we make of any events and how we respond to them; we can also influence the attitude with which we approach life.

We have heard accounts of practitioners extending this idea into glib assertions that suggest, for example, that each person is directly responsible for, and in effect has chosen, any misfortune that befalls them, even violent assault. While there are belief systems, and personal growth methods, that see the world in this way, there is nothing in NLP or its philosophical roots (e.g. in Bateson's work) that gives rise to this stance.

This type of belief may well reflect Fritz Perls' typical injunction to develop 'response-ability', by which he meant that we can choose how to *respond* to events in our lives; and thus we are responsible for our responses. In that sense, while events happen that are outside our personal control, nobody is compelled to behave as a 'victim'. A classic illustration of this is Victor Frankls's (1965) analysis of the beliefs that distinguished those who survived concentration camps. Did they choose to be in a concentration camp? Of course not. Where they exercised choice, where the characteristic features of their behaviour and demeanour appeared, and where Frankl suggests may lie some valuable insights into the capacity of the human spirit to endure and survive the most terrible of circumstances, was in the meaning they made of the experience.

Positive thinking

NLP also shows traces of another classic of the self-help movement, Norman Vincent Peale's emphasis on 'The Power of Positive Thinking' (1998). NLP can convey a seemingly relentless emphasis on the pursuit of individual happiness, as in Losada's characterisation of NLP as 'variations on feeling great' (Losada 2001). This links to current interest in positive psychology, with which NLP shares a broad interest in health and well-being, and a refusal to base its outlook on what is wrong with people. This was also characteristic of humanistic psychology's emphasis on realising potential.

There is, for example, the principle that a 'well-formed outcome' must be expressed as a positive, as something one wishes to move towards. If taken to an extreme, however, seemingly 'negative' emotions can become repressed. Outsiders sometimes remark on a drive in NLP to maintain a positive outlook, with so-called 'negative' emotions regarded as something to avoid, or to be altered with a quick 'state change', rather than as part of the full emotional spectrum of human experience.

NLP can, often does, and in fact must, work with emotions. Early NLP acknowledged the importance of emotions and there is regular reference to the role of feelings in NLP work in, for example, 'Frogs Into Princes' (e.g. Bandler & Grinder 1979:95, 118, 151). Indeed Bandler and Grinder stated in 'The Structure of Magic' that 'therapists may be sure that the reference structure is incomplete, or, in the terms we have developed in this book, not well formed, if the client's feelings are not represented in the reference structure. This is equivalent to saying that human emotions are a necessary component of human experience' (Bandler & Grinder 1975b:160).

Yet NLP did not develop the same type of emphasis on emotion that characterised the work of Perls and Satir. Unlike some modes of counselling and psychotherapy, NLP does not employ the principle that the release of distress produces insight. In therapeutic work using NLP, catharsis is much more likely to be a by-product, something experienced as a result of insight or change.

There is a positive intent to this, and it can make sense when we consider what NLP was reacting against. Bandler and Grinder noticed that some people would wallow in their feelings, seemingly more interested in doing that than in achieving the change they said they desired. They also noticed that some practitioners would be distracted by emotion and thus stop attending to process. One side-effect of this, however, is that it may have encouraged a somewhat robotic and non-empathetic approach to NLP.

A related question is why NLP practitioners appear to avoid 'negative' emotions. There are, again, sometimes very good reasons for this. Chief among these is that NLP has identified how a person can go into a disabling place, characterised (for example) by a slumped posture, downward gaze, shallow breathing, lifeless tone of voice and kinaesthetic predicates. In this case the practitioner knows how to facilitate a state that is more likely to be helpful to that person for their particular purpose (desired outcome). State changes, though, need to be appropriate to a particular context. For example, just before giving an important business presentation, it is probably useful not to be immersed in anxiety about everything that could go wrong. Knowing how to access feelings of confidence and to keep one's attention on the audience is likely to be helpful. At other times it may be entirely appropriate to experience and to acknowledge one's feelings.

From a cybernetic perspective, any emotion a person experiences is neither good nor bad. It provides information, and it has utility (or not) in relation to that person's desired outcome. NLP's view is that a practitioner needs the ability to notice the emotion, to register it as information, and to decide how to act in a way that is appropriate for the person. The appropriateness of a person's state is therefore context-dependent.

The insight that NLP offers is that many psychological therapies focus on problems not solutions. There is nothing to be gained, however, through promoting a 'happy clappy' culture that uses artifice to avoid anything apparently 'negative'. Authentic emotional states are invaluable information, 'feedback not failure'. To assume that 'negative' emotion should always be avoided is, obviously simplistic, as well as disrespectful to a client.

In this respect it is interesting that the pre-eminent European psychologists, Freud and Jung, are scarcely mentioned in NLP, apart from Dilts and DeLozier's surprising view that 'many of his (Freud's) principles constitute the foundations upon which NLP has been built' (Dilts & DeLozier 2000:430). Elsewhere Freud is regarded as epitomising the psycho-archaeological approach to change that NLP so firmly rejects; American psychology as a whole has tended to reject Freud's dark view of the unconscious. That Jung scarcely figures in NLP[3] may seem even more strange, given his emphasis on imagery, dreams and symbols. Jung, of course, was deeply concerned with the meaning of symbols, whereas NLP emphasises the form and structure of imagery, and its place in various 'programmes', over its content.

Excellence

Another term that appears frequently in NLP is that of 'excellence'.[4] This idea did not figure in the earliest NLP books, nor does it appear to have been defined. It may stem from its entry into popular consciousness in the 1980s through the publication of Peter's and Waterman's business book, 'In Search of Excellence' (1982).[5]

The idea of excellence may have worked a subtle shift from NLP's populist value of 'sharing the resources of all those who are involved in finding ways to help people have better, fuller and richer lives' (Bandler & Grinder 1975b), to one that is more elitist. Originally, while NLP certainly drew from *exemplars* – who were referred to as 'charismatic superstars' in The Structure of Magic (Bandler & Grinder 1975b:5) – it emphasised the purpose of developing effective skill or competence. The focus was on healthy human functioning, as a reaction against the pathology-focused psychological establishment.

The subsequent emphasis on *achieving* excellence probably resonated with the commercial potential of NLP. In the 1980s we also find an emerging focus on 'genius'. Robert Dilts, (Dilts 1994a; Dilts 1994b) studied 'strategies of genius' based on people such as Einstein, Jesus and Walt Disney. The sub-title to 'Turtles All The Way Down' is 'Prerequisites to Personal Genius' (DeLozier & Grinder 1987:vii). As Derren Brown comments, 'the shining stars of the field are tagged with another buzzword, "genius", and become the sum of their anecdotes' (Brown 2007:131).

The shift is from the usage of 'excellence' as a descriptive term, to one that is aspirational, to one that is normative. In other words we start by noticing that Satir (say) is an exemplar with excellent skills, and therefore is worth modelling; to offering the hope that other people can therefore become excellent; and eventually to implying that everyone *should* achieve excellence because it is within everyone's reach.

The problem this leaves is that, in a field that professes to believe that the acquisition of virtually any human achievement is open to any individual, and which claims to have identified the means by which excellence can be attained, how does one explain ordinariness? It appears that everyone can be a genius and everyone can be excellent; everyone can be powerful and happy. By implication, the ordinary individual must either lack the intelligence to recognise and use those tools, or lack the motivation or will to realise their full potential.

The Wild West: Mavericks and pioneers

If NLP reflects some of the values associated with the American Dream, it also seems to embody more than a hint of the culture of the 'Wild West'. Thus the founders are characterised as 'mavericks' (McNab 2005:19), prepared to act outrageously in order to achieve results. Grinder has quoted George Bernard Shaw several times as saying:

> Reasonable men adapt themselves to the world, unreasonable men attempt to adapt the world to themselves. That's why all progress depends on unreasonable men.
>
> (DeLozier & Grinder 1987:iv)

Like the 'ruthless opportunists' (Feyerabend 1993:10) who can innovate by disregarding convention, Bandler and Grinder offered a brave alternative that challenged the entrenched orthodoxy of another belief system. They criticised psychoanalysis for being a system which kept clients in their problems for years (whilst continuing to take their fees), and specifically for the assumptions that the roots of experience have to be uncovered; that insight has to come through conscious awareness; and that this process can only be managed by professional practitioners (Bostic St. Clair & Grinder 2001:2–3).

They have revelled in the notion of adventure; 'These two men... have set out to make a coherent story out of an outrageous adventure', states Grinder (O'Connor & Seymour 1990:15). They are pioneers opening up new territory; if NLP were a car, then it would be an off-road vehicle. Lewis and Pucelik (1990:i) call Bandler and Grinder 'two exciting and charismatic individuals'.

Grinder acknowledges that he and Bandler may have shared certain characteristics:[6] 'Arrogant; Curious; Unimpressed by authority or tradition; Strong personal boundaries – well-defined sense of personal responsibility for their own experiences and an insistence that others do likewise; Willingness to try nearly anything rather than be bored (or boring); Utterly lacking in self-doubt – egotistical; Playful; Full capability as players in the Acting As If game; Full behavioural appreciation of the difference between form and content' (Bostic St. Clair & Grinder 2001:121–122).

Grinder notes that 'such characterlogical (*sic*) adjectives leave much to be desired – namely the entire set of contexts in which they occur' (2001:122). Nevertheless the list is interesting, especially because it may help to differentiate between the influence of cybernetics and constructivism on NLP, and the particular spirit injected by its founders.

Let us be clear that we do not imply any judgement about this 'characterology'. Indeed we are concerned to point out the risk of the classic *ad hominem* argument, whereby a theory or practice is judged according to the characteristics or behaviours of the person who created them. The flaws of this type of argument are easily demonstrated. For example, a well-known figure was a smoker, gave up his first child for adoption, is alleged to have had numerous affairs, and his work encouraged the development of the atomic bomb. His name was Albert Einstein – one of the geniuses studied by Robert

Dilts. Yet scientists do not reject Einstein's theories of relativity because of his behaviour as a human being.

Fritz Perls' behavioural repertoire included a strong streak of outrageousness, which he would readily use if he felt it would be helpful. Bandler's deep immersion in Perls' work, to the extent that he began to mimic his behaviour, may have involved affinity as well as curiosity. Erickson was also unorthodox in many ways, and not regarded as mainstream in hypnotherapy circles. Bateson was a non-conformist in terms of any academic discipline, and would often challenge but did not seek to shock. Even cybernetics, which now may sound technical and unexciting, represented a profound challenge to established ways of thinking, based on linear notions of cause and effect.

A certain mischievousness is part of the culture, and part of the appeal, or one might say charm, of NLP. Its refreshing, invigorating quality attracted many people to it, thus; 'in our early studies of NLP we noticed and enjoyed the ways in which more traditional forms of therapy were held up to question on the grounds that they had replaced reference to processes with nominalizations' (McKergow & Clarke 1995:53). Without a readiness to break the rules and 'think outside the box', it is difficult to innovate. The experimental spirit of NLP, and its refusal to be constrained by established views about personal development, enabled it to be creative and mercurial.

Is NLP a cult?

Especially in the transient entries about NLP on the internet, the suggestion that NLP has cult-like characteristics sometimes appears. Dowlen refers to NLP's 'almost cult following' (Dowlen 1996:32). Seen by some as a pseudo-science, NLP is apparently perceived by others to be a pseudo-religion. Brown refers to his experience as 'highly evangelical in its tone' (Brown 2007:186), and Hayes notes that:

I have heard several people liken it to a modern secular religion... There are founding father figures of the Moses type...There is a version of the Ten Commandments (the NLP presuppositions). There is certainly something resembling a priesthood, and some of the more flamboyant trainers have begun to resemble prophets and gurus with cadres of 'disciples' in tow (Hayes 2006:12).

This religion, presumably, would have Bateson as its god.

To consider NLP as a movement could provide an interesting perspective. There is literature that compares human potential movements in general with religion (Fromm 1950), and sociological literature, such as that by Robbins (1988) and Westley (1983) that examines 'new religious movements'. Is there any basis for considering that NLP might be a cult, though?

One prominent body working in this field, The International Cultic Studies Association (ICSA),[7] acknowledges that the term 'cult' is highly problematic, difficult to define, and prone to be used to imply disrepute. Usage of the term in relation to NLP may be an attempt to discredit it, or to express disapproval of the field. Are there more specific concerns?

One is the suggestion (e.g. Drenth 1999) that NLP had links with Dianetics, which later developed into Scientology. These purported links (setting aside the question of what they would signify) are either non-existent, or tenuous, based mainly on contemporaneity. Drenth, who is one of the authors who accuses NLP of being a 'pseudoscience', alleges that NLP uses the concept of 'engrammes', a notion that is apparently used in Scientology. This notion does not, to our knowledge, appear anywhere in NLP; it certainly plays no part now in the technical vocabulary of the practice. There is some evidence of the cross-fertilisation of ideas in NLP with Landmark Education, which developed from Werner Erhard's 'est'. For example, presumably due to a shared interest in Korzybski's ideas, one finds the expression of being 'at cause' in both fields. There was some evidence of people being encouraged to use *Est*'s notion of 'personal editing' formats in NLP in the early 1990s. However, these overlaps represent no more than the type of cross-pollination one would find in contemporaneous fields.

Another concern is about the format of trainings. *Est* and Landmark Education are among the best known examples of what is often known as 'Large Group Awareness Training'. While NLP trainings do not routinely use this format, the four hundred or so people participating in the training experienced by Losada (2001:185) and Derren Brown clearly constitutes a large group setting. Despite concern expressed in the usual array of internet articles, research does not appear to suggest that the format itself has any harmful effects. For example, Fisher *et al* (1989) concluded that participants experienced no significant effects, either positive or negative.

Brown does say that: 'Both Bandler and Anthony Robbins[8] package their goods primarily as an attitude, and clearly use the evangelical hype to render us as emotional and suggestible as possible in order to make sure that a) the message hits home and b) we want to purchase further courses' (Brown 2007:187). The fact that NLP trainers can engender enthusiasm and an attitude of curiosity in their listeners, and make the practice appealing, is one of the attractions of the trainings. On the other hand, Hayes (2006:13) says:

> ... there is no doubt that on some of the large scale training events you experience manipulative techniques such as powerfully suggestive music used specifically to trigger certain planned types of responses. I also have concerns about the patent personal inauthenticity of some of these 'guru' trainers – there are times when they seem deeply incongruent in their behaviour... There is no doubt, however, that these large scale events represent a successful business model – some courses have hundreds of participants, each paying thousands of pounds. Sometimes it is hard not to think of parts of the NLP industry as get rich quick schemes.

Clearly, it is important for participants to remain discerning about what to buy into, be it new ideas or further courses. Anyone attending an NLP training course can enquire in advance about the proposed format, and can inform themselves about the psychological and educational advantages and disadvantages of that format, whether it is large group, small group, or distance.

Taking a slightly left-field approach to this, let us pretend for a moment that NLP actually aspired to becoming a 'cult'. What would have to happen? The central characteristics of cults, according to Lalich and Langone (2006), are concerned mainly with influence and control, and the extent to which members of a movement may be manipulated, exploited, or abused. It would seem, therefore, that NLP practitioners have far too much freedom to come and go as they please, and to determine how they spend their lives and with whom. There is no question of people who train in NLP being required to cut ties with family and friends, for example.

What needs to be recognised, however, is that NLP courses offer more than a training in skills; they also offer membership of a community of people identified as 'NLP practitioners', with its language, social networks, leaders, events, and potential for psychological support. It is important to acknowledge that NLP could fulfill some people's desires for belonging, belief and guidance. Even though NLP may not set out to be a pseudo-religion, some people may use it to meet equivalent needs. Ponting's findings (2006), that the main outcome reported by participants is that they gain confidence, might hint at this possibility.

One characteristic cited by Lalich and Langone (2006) that seems relevant to NLP is, 'The leader is not accountable to any authorities'. As noted in previous chapters, there is no formal system of accountability in the field unless within specified professions such as Neuro-linguistic Psychotherapy. There are also adherents who sometimes appear to display 'unquestioning commitment' to their leader and regard his or her 'belief system, ideology, and practices as the Truth, as law' (Lalich & Langone 2006). Some trainers insist that they alone follow the true party line; this makes NLP into an ideology rather than a set of practices and an attitude of curiosity. Illustrating one of the ways in which allegiance can be secured, Losada (2001:185) describes being given a 'contract' to sign when attending her training. This, which is not a universal practice in NLP, requires the signatory, among other things, not to teach NLP themselves unless they become a certified trainer.[9] As one example, we have heard people in the NLP community express fear of litigation over intellectual property rights, whether this prospect is real or perceived.

Any movement or organisation, however loosely knit, has norms to which people tend to conform. This is as true of academic and business communities as it is of the personal growth movement, and expecting any organisation or association to be benign and devoid of issues of power is naïve. Freud had difficulties with people questioning his authority, and his splits with Adler and Jung are well-documented. Walker (1996) recounts how Freud also rejected Perls, not even allowing him over the threshold of his study when Perls wanted to visit him. Perls was apparently heartbroken.

In relation to this last point, Bandler and Grinder's criticism of psychology, with its 'different religious belief systems with very powerful evangelists working from all these differing orientations' (1979:5–6) may now appear ironic. While we can reject the allegation that NLP resembles a cult, perhaps more pertinent are the ways in which it may have come to resemble the very 'theology' that the founders originally challenged.

Conclusion

NLP, like any other system of ideas, inevitably absorbs influences from its culture and circumstances, and develops its own patterns of power and discourse. Here we have discussed those of the ethos of self-help, the theme of freedom from authority, an emphasis on individualism, the search for excellence and empowerment, and an outrageous streak in pursuit of innovation. Concerns voiced about NLP as a 'cult' wither in the face of serious scrutiny. Yet it can also be seen as a system of belief in which guru-like figures hold out the promise of changing lives and the hope of acquiring wealth and happiness, and may expect allegiance to their authority and their own brand of truth. As such it is appropriate to consider the relevance of critiques of the self-help movement.

Part IV

14
Synthesis

What are the answers to our core questions?

In this chapter we summarise our conclusions about the questions we posed in the opening chapter. Those were:

- What is NLP?
- Where and for what can I best use it?
- What is it based on?
- Where did it come from?
- Why is it sometimes so hard to grasp what it's about?
- Is there any research behind it?
- How can the claims made by practitioners be assessed?
- Does it have any theory?
- Is it 'pseudoscience'?
- Why doesn't NLP seem to be interested in emotions?
- Is it manipulative?
- Is NLP a cult?
- What does it offer to HRD?

What is NLP?

NLP has been remarkably successful in promulgating itself from its psychotherapeutic origins; its use is now widespread in business, especially in coaching, as well as education, healthcare and other sectors. We regard NLP as concerned centrally with what Watzlawick *et al* (1967) called the *pragmatics* of human communication.

We have portrayed NLP as having six 'faces', any combination of which may be apparent, and between which tensions may exist. The six are a function of three underlying aspects of NLP, as a *practice*; as a *philosophy*; and as a *product*. These six faces are:

1. 'Practical magic', or naturally occurring patterns of excellent communication;
2. A methodology – as used in the original NLP studies, and reflected in the various approaches to 'modelling' that are used to reverse engineer human capabilities;
3. A living philosophy, or set of beliefs about the world, as represented by the NLP presuppositions;
4. A technology – behavioural techniques to enhance the way people communicate in practice, represented in a codified 'body of knowledge' comprising the frameworks and techniques described in NLP literature;
5. A commercial product, part of the 'self-help' industry, reflected in the many artefacts and events available to be consumed;
6. A range of services provided by professionals, including coaching, consulting, training, psychotherapy and more.

Our working description of NLP is:

> NLP is interested in how people communicate, perform skills and create experiences through patterns of thought and behaviour, mediated by language. NLP helps people create more preferable and useful (to them) experiences in the world, typically by attending to and modifying those patterns of thought and behaviour.

Where and for what can I best use it?

As a pragmatic form of knowledge, NLP offers a versatile toolkit that can help any person towards accomplishing the things they wish to achieve, whether it is chairing a meeting, writing a proposal, selling an idea, finding out what is really important to another person, and so on. These tools are 'heuristic', meaning that they may be used *as if* they were true, without commitment to belief in their validity.

Applications are, in that sense, without limit. NLP has been used in HRD for the following categories of need or development:

- Modelling 'excellence'; this is a way of 'reverse engineering' human capabilities, that can identify the keys to excellent practice and enable others to learn how to do it themselves;

- Designing and refining outcomes, ranging from broad visions to very specific goals, and understanding the resources needed to achieve them;
- Exploring and improving communication skills (verbal and non-verbal; spoken and written);
- Increasing self-awareness (e.g. of one's behaviour patterns, of one's internal world of imagery and self-talk, and so on);
- Coaching for performance, for example to improve specific behaviours and skills, and to increase confidence and flexibility;
- Overcoming limiting beliefs, perceptions and/or patterns of behaviour; as Derren Brown says, the value of methods like NLP is that they 'tend to undo the general feeling that we have to be "stuck" in unhelpful patterns of thought' (Brown 2007: 214–215).

According to this description, people who use NLP as practitioners have been introduced to both (a) a systematic approach to communication, and (b) methods through which it is possible to understand and influence the way people create their experience. Accordingly NLP practitioners, in whatever field they may operate, can be thought of as offering two generic services. The first is to identify how an existing outcome or effect is achieved through particular combinations of people's language, thought and behaviour. The second is to facilitate people who wish to enhance their existing behaviour and skills, or to change something they dislike about their experience, to learn relevant new combinations of thought and behaviour that will be both effective and respectful for the client and their environment. Practitioners achieve this by using language and communications skilfully and flexibly.

What is it based on?

The substantive contents of NLP are based on insights into observed human communication; initially, into the verbal interactions between psychotherapist and client as gleaned from Richard Bandler's familiarity with the practices of exemplar psychotherapists, Fritz Perls and Virginia Satir. Bandler found he could reproduce their behaviour and achieve similar results.

Bandler and Grinder went on to propose that there were certain patterns of communication that appeared to distinguish Perls and Satir from other, apparently less effective therapists. They challenged the belief that effective therapy relied upon the innate qualities of charismatic therapists, showing that the 'structure' of this apparent 'magic' could be mapped out and learnt by other people. Grinder linked these observed language patterns to his knowledge of contemporary ideas about transformational linguistics. This resulted in the original 'meta-model' of language patterns.

NLP then grew by applying the same principle of identifying and testing patterns in observed behaviour – in other words, by reverse engineering or 'modelling' – to other aspects of communication. Notably, at Gregory Bateson's suggestion, they studied a third influential exemplar, Milton H. Erickson.

Where did it come from?

NLP itself emerged from the Santa Cruz area of California in the early 1970s. Robert Spitzer, publisher of Science and Behavior Books, employed Bandler and encouraged his early explorations of Perls and Satir. This developed into a creative collaboration between Bandler, Grinder and others associated with the educational experiment that was taking place at Kresge College, University of Santa Cruz. At Kresge they also encountered Gregory Bateson who, from the summer of 1974, lived close to Bandler and Grinder and some of their friends and colleagues.

There is relatively little in NLP that is *wholly* original; we have shown, for example, that all its presuppositions can be traced back to prior sources. Indeed the extent of innovation in NLP may have been obscured by overemphasising its uniqueness and downplaying its place in a stream of ideas and traditions. As with many fields of emerging practice, it has built upon and added fresh insights to previous work. The ideas underlying NLP are influenced by intellectual developments and practices such as the work of the Mental Research Institute and the outcomes of the Macy Conferences. There are many other social, cultural and historical ingredients in the melting pot from which NLP emerged. We have suggested that the ethos of the self-help movement, the counter-culturalism of the 1960s and early 1970s, and the 1980s notion of the pursuit of 'excellence', have all shaped NLP as a movement.

Why is it sometimes so hard to grasp what it's about?

If it remains hard to grasp, in our view there are various possible reasons. Among these:

1. It has multiple 'faces' or identities, as described above;
2. It is often easier, and probably much more effective for clients, to experience how NLP can be used than it is to define it in words;
3. NLP is eclectic, drawing from many practices and cutting across academic disciplines. It can be hard to label, and sometimes it can be hard to reconcile its diverse contents;
4. Its theoretical roots (which we have suggested lies in cybernetics and the MRI form of constructivism) are seldom made clear or explained in detail;
5. The drive to sell NLP as a commodity can mean that information about it serves the purpose of promotion more than that of, say, education.

Is there any research behind it?

Three main types of research are relevant to NLP:

1. Research findings from relevant disciplines.
2. Direct, independent research into NLP's claims.
3. Evaluation from within NLP.

Of these, the first is the area that may offer most support to NLP's pragmatic knowledge. We have described for example the work of Lawrence Barsalou on the role of the senses in cognition, which supports NLP's ideas about the role and significance of internal representations, and that of Robert Goldstone on categorisation, which supports NLP's stance on the relationship between language and thinking. NLP authors such as Richard Bolstad (2002), Susie Linder-Pelz and Michael Hall (Linder-Pelz & Hall 2007) and Richard Churches and Roger Terry (2007), have identified relevant research findings from mainstream psychology and other disciplines. This work counters a tendency for NLP training courses and literature to rely on knowledge that was current in the 1970s, which needs to be updated.

There has been little *direct* research into NLP. The findings that do exist, whilst not favourable to NLP on the whole, were from a narrow vein of experimental research. They may be treated, in the terms Michael Heap used in 1988, as an interim verdict, which requires further studies. To date, few further studies have materialised.

The evidence base created from within NLP remains in need of development. Even acknowledging that NLP is by no means alone in this among practices found in HRD, the 'trail of techniques' left in the wake of the early developments in Santa Cruz has been over-sold and under-tested. In the final chapter we indicate eight types of research projects that would help to address this issue in relation to HRD. There is evidence of an emergent wave of NLP practitioners engaging in research, including some at doctoral level in universities.

How can the claims made by practitioners be assessed?

In response to any practitioner's claims about the effectiveness of NLP it is appropriate to ask the classic NLP question, 'how do you know that?' In other words, how do practitioners satisfy themselves about the validity of their claims? The response, 'I know it works, I've experienced it myself', is of very limited value, and for various reasons may be unreliable.

To become more widely accepted, as many practitioners seem to desire, and to give non-NLP people greater confidence of its efficacy, NLP needs an evidence base. To achieve this, NLP's procedures, principles and models may need to be held more open to doubt within the field, and tested so that they can be re-evaluated and modified. For all its emphasis on curiosity about the uniqueness of each individual's experience, the risk is that, *in the absence of openness to evaluation*, the contents of NLP become taken-for-granted perceptual filters through which practitioners create an essentially self-sealing system.

Does it have any theory?

No human endeavour that formulates 'if-then' propositions and proposes systematic relationships between actions and effects can avoid using theory. It is surely self-evident that a field that offers participants the opportunity to learn a way of practising that is claimed to be effective must have some kind of theory about what makes the difference between effective and ineffective practice.

Some practitioners seem, paradoxically, to believe that theory and NLP do not mix. Through unravelling this belief we have identified some supportable and worthwhile principles that can challenge conventional ideas about knowledge.

In other respects the nature of theory may have been stereotyped in NLP, and its value. We have argued that its central ideas are based in cybernetics, a pivotal intellectual development of the twentieth century that rejected explanations for human behaviour that relied on simple notions of cause-effect and 'forces', and developed an alternative theory in which circular causality and feedback play the central role.

We have also argued that it is important to take into account 'second-order cybernetics' (Von Foerster & Poerksen 2002), which regards a practitioner as a participant in the systems they are attempting to facilitate. This yields a quite different ethical view from that of 'first-order' cybernetics which, conceptually, treats people as equivalent to mechanisms, the paradigmatic example of which is the thermostat. The persistence of metaphors derived from computing in NLP may reflect a first-order cybernetic perspective.

NLP can also be understood as a form of constructivist theory, in the sense that it is interested in how people create their reality through communication. In its early days NLP was influenced, to varying degrees, by the work of the Palo Alto group, by Chomsky and other transformational linguists, and by psychologist George Miller. Today, it can potentially draw on knowledge about language, cognition and perception from disciplines such as cognitive linguistics, neuroscience, and cognitive psychology.

Is it 'pseudoscience'?

The charge of being a 'pseudoscience' can be used merely as a term of abuse. If we were to use 'pseudoscience' in its strict, original Popperian sense, we could expect NLP, along with many 'people development' practices in HRD and psychotherapies, to be regarded as unfalsifiable and therefore pseudoscientific.

NLP may attract this charge more than most practices because of its name, which suggests connotations of an academic discipline, and therefore may be thought misleading. As a movement primarily concerned with practical knowledge, it would make little sense for NLP to aspire to become a field of formal academic study.

More relevant is the risk that NLP could be considered as pseudo-scientific by virtue of rejecting the relevance of theory and research, relying on knowledge that is out of date, and neglecting the need to establish a credible evidence base. These features could be countered by linking to other research and practice communities, and by articulating NLP's theoretical links to cybernetics, which is an established discipline.

Why doesn't NLP work with emotions?

NLP can, often does, and in fact must, work with emotions. Yet NLP did not develop the same type of emphasis on emotion that characterises the work of Perls and Satir. NLP does not, for example, employ the principle that the release of distress produces insight. One side-effect of this, however, is that it may have encouraged a somewhat robotic and non-empathetic approach to the practice of NLP.

The appropriateness of a person's state is therefore context-dependent. NLP's view is that a practitioner needs the ability to notice emotion, and to decide how to act in a way that is appropriate for the person. To assume that 'negative' emotion should always be avoided is far too simplistic.

Is it manipulative?

In our view there is nothing inherently manipulative or unsafe about NLP; for example there is nothing in NLP that makes it impossible to apply standard principles found in professional codes of conduct. Furthermore, codes of ethical conduct exist within NLP that are comparable in their contents to those of helping professions generally. Ultimately, adherence to these codes is voluntary, hence the ethical stance and capability of the individual practitioner is significant.

We have argued that NLP literature refers to three main types of ethical judgements in the practice; that of the 'ecology' of the client's outcome, that of whether the end justifies the means (i.e. the intervention chosen by the practitioner); and that of the practitioner's integrity. More detailed exploration of these issues within NLP could promote debate about ethics, and could help to assuage the concerns of those who perceive the practice to be 'manipulative'.

NLP's understanding of the inevitability of communicating with the unconscious has implications for all forms of development. For example, any practitioner in any field is likely to influence other people through 'hypnotic language' because these language patterns are naturally occurring in everyday talk. Furthermore, normal everyday experience involves a range of what may be considered 'altered states' or trances.

Finally, we have raised the question of whether it is time to review the designation of people as 'practitioners' based on completion of a basic training alone.

Is NLP a cult?

There is no basis for regarding NLP as a 'cult'. There are, nevertheless, aspects of the field about which practitioners could usefully be more reflexive. For example, the extent to which NLP training offers membership of a community, with its social networks and the potential for psychological comfort, could be acknowledged. As a commercialised system of belief in which guru-like figures hold out the promise of changing lives and the hope of acquiring wealth and happiness, it merits critical review. It could also be useful to examine NLP as a social phenomenon, including ways in which it may have come to resemble the very 'theology' that the founders originally challenged.

What does it offer to HRD?

What NLP offers is an innovative synthesis of existing and newly discovered practical knowledge. It is characterised by insights into perception, cognition (including internal imagery), language, emotional state and behaviour that people can use in everyday life and professional practices. It is probably most distinctive in its insights into the practical relationships between language, thought and behaviour, and its understanding of how to utilise these insights to help people achieve their goals.

NLP is democratically inclined, in the sense that its tools are in principle available to everyone, not just to specialist professionals. It challenges orthodoxy and provides an alternative to professional monopolies over knowledge. It has generated a great variety of tools and techniques that may be helpful to people wanting to achieve improvements in their lives. In particular, NLP was originally conceived as a way for people to complement and enhance their existing knowledge and practice, whether it be in personal or professional domains. That remains, in our view, the most worthwhile and viable position for NLP to occupy.

We end this chapter by highlighting six 'landmarks', those aspects of NLP that we think are of the greatest value to people in HRD, and which can provide reference points when navigating the complex terrain of this field:

1. First, there is the enduring and detailed focus on language that runs through the major NLP literature, which has extended the research themes pursued by Bateson and the Palo Alto group. The meta-model patterns, sensory predicates, the Milton model patterns, reframing, and more can all be found in everyday language. Today, NLP developers like Christina Hall, Steve Andreas and Charles Faulkner are continuing to advance this type of work.

2. Second, there is its emphasis on the importance of a whole body-mind approach to performance and learning. This includes NLP's ideas about, for example, the significance of physiological state, the value of having fun, and the use of multiple senses, perceptual positions, imagery and stories. We have seen that mental rehearsal, for example, is an area of practice that receives support from the research literature.

3. The ways in which NLP frameworks can facilitate the exploration of inner worlds are significant. These include the ways in which 'modelling' can be used to map the structures, sequences and patterns involved in experience, using frameworks such as sub-modalities. Applications range from coaching and organisational consulting (e.g. mapping a process or skill) to formal research, as represented by Vermersch's 'psycho-phenomenology'.

4. The framework of metaprogrammes has been applied within coaching, recruitment, market research and more. The acceptance by the British Psychological Society of an instrument based on this framework demonstrates its potential.

5. The very fact that NLP provides managers and developers with immediate, pragmatic knowledge in the form of tools, techniques and models is itself significant – even if that knowledge must be held open to revision. We have cited Karl Weick to support the importance for managers of having maps and tools to precipitate action. The disadvantages of insisting on formal research evidence before making use of knowledge are, first, that this is typically a

long term process – people need to take action today – and second, that such knowledge can then become owned by, and only accessible through, specialised groups of people.

6. Finally, we value NLP especially for the extent to which it continues to put forward a cybernetic perspective on human communication. At a practical level this gives people a working appreciation of the systemic nature of human interaction, which still runs counter to the dominant paradigm of 'cause-effect' thinking. It is reflected, for example, in NLP's emphasis on attending to form, process and structures, rather than to content. At a more conceptual level, this maintains the legacy of Gregory Bateson's work, and his significant insights into epistemology and ecology.

In the final chapter we address one final question, what does the future hold for NLP?

15
Quo Vadis?

At a crossroads

We have acknowledged that NLP is a widespread and internationally-known field of practice. It can be regarded as a commercially successful, diverse, and eclectic system of practical knowledge. It has survived for more than 30 years, and has been an established form of psychotherapy in the UK for more than 15 years. There are copious NLP books on the market and more than 50 organisations offering NLP training in the UK. A Google search yields 1.5 million hits.[1] Many executive and life coaches cite NLP as a method they use, and managers identify NLP as part of their working knowledge. It is a practice that emphasises fun, healthy functioning and the achievement of potential. Organisations like the ANLP and the Professional Guild are seeking to support shared standards, and there are increasing signs of research activity in Europe, the USA and Australasia.

At the same time NLP has failed, so far, to become accepted as a 'mainstream' practice, which is the desire of many of its practitioners. We have elaborated on the issues throughout the book. NLP's six faces make it difficult to define. It has no significant presence in the academic world, and some people regard it as a 'pseudo-science'. It has yet to create an established, public evidence base, and it continues to rely heavily on practitioners' assertions that it is effective. Its models and frameworks, originally designed to enhance curiosity and sensory awareness, risk becoming a dogma handed down through training courses. As McKergow and Clarke (1995:48) have said, 'NLP has itself become a nominalization', an object rather than a process. Bateson's ideas are sometimes treated as almost biblical pronouncements. The principal attempt at a scholarly journal for NLP, 'NLP World', ceased publication in 2001 and neither of the two scholarly reviews of the field (Esser 2004; Walker 1996) is available in English. Its structure of training courses and ever increasing levels of certification appear to be driven by commercial needs. It has acquired an unfortunate reputation for potentially being 'manipulative' and its maverick quality is often regarded with suspicion. It remains an underground movement in the sense that, as we have heard from numerous fellow practitioners, in their work as coaches, managers, trainers and so on, they use many NLP insights and techniques, but do not reveal that what they do comes from NLP.

All this together makes sense of the ambivalence that characterises the attitudes of several commentators, including Anthony Grant, Isabel Losada, Charles Tart and ourselves, who perceive that there is value in NLP yet remain wary of other aspects. As another example, Hayes (2006:12) comments as follows:

> The picture I have of the NLP 'industry' is one of something dynamic and positive but also tainted in places by perceptions of factionalism, ego-driven conflict, legal disputes and commercial greed... Even as a fan and practitioner myself I would certainly caution anyone against swallowing NLP uncritically.

Given all this, we think NLP is at a crucial time in its development, and stands at a metaphorical crossroads. Which road will this knowledge system take? While many possible futures exist, the themes we have explored in this book suggest three possible scenarios.

Entropy?

Entropy, in general terms, refers to the way the energy in a system disperses over time, such that disorder increases. In this scenario, NLP is losing momentum.

Some of the things that fuelled the emergence of NLP, such as the rebellious, experimental counter-culture of the post-Vietnam years and the booming human potential movement, are long in the past.

The energy that attracted many people to the field seems to have disappeared, and its knowledge base is being recycled more than it is being extended. Several of NLP's key ideas are rooted in the 1970s. NLP's 'story' of human development was infused, and in some respects still is, with the metaphor of man-as-computer, for example with its notion of 'programming'. This seems anachronistic in the age of bio- and nano-technology.

Despite burgeoning electronic materials and discussion groups, NLP publications are dominated by secondary takes on the field. While books are not the be-all and end-all of the field, and while the founders of a field are of course perfectly entitled to publish or not, the appearance of a new volume by Bandler and Grinder used to engender a sense of excitement about their latest revelations and inventions. That creative stream of books, whether joint or separate, describing *new* models and applications, ended well before the 1990s.

Looking at NLP publications in recent years, Dilts and DeLozier's 'Encyclopedia of Systemic NLP and NLP New Coding' (Dilts & DeLozier 2000), was undoubtedly a major publication, if one that sometimes offers an idiosyncratic view of the field.[2] 'Richard Bandler's Guide to Trance-formation' (Bandler 2008a) updates and refreshes material that appeared in the first decade of NLP's existence (e.g. Grinder & Bandler 1981), and does so effectively. However, it also exemplifies the way that many new books in the field appear to be re-packaging material that has existed for twenty years or more.

John Grinder's major recent contribution has been 'Whispering in the Wind' (Bostic St. Clair & Grinder 2001). This is an important document, especially for researchers because of its expanded account of the ways in which NLP developed (a self-published volume, it could surely be improved through editing, indexing and comprehensive referencing). The main difficulty is that the book is effectively not in the public domain – for example, it is not available for purchase through Amazon,[3] unless occasionally as a second-hand item, or through the major UK distributors of NLP books, Anglo-American.[4] The apparent reluctance to distribute the book symbolises the inward focus of the NLP community.[5]

In this scenario, therefore, NLP's clock is running down. Feeding on itself, in effect, is not sustainable, so the energy of NLP dissipates. As the knowledge system cycles and recycles the same ideas, NLP resembles an established rock band that is past its creative peak and has come to concentrate more on income generation than on its initial energy and idealism. For the time being the fans continue to attend world tours and buy merchandise – but for how much longer?

The seeds of its own destruction?

NLP in its present form appears to contain within it not only the potential for further adaptation and survival, but also the seeds of its own destruction.

Any field inevitably has, and needs, diversity of opinion and dissent in order to grow. Is it undergoing a crisis of growth or decay? Could this simply be a sign of a maturing field, since it is not unusual for a new movement to experience crises and fractures as they develop, like an adolescent seeking an identity separate from that of its parents? Psychoanalysis was an example of this.

Even so, NLP's body sometimes seems so fractured that it is difficult to imagine it recovering from its self-inflicted injuries. Due especially, we suspect, to the effects of litigation about intellectual property rights in NLP (Hall 2001), something appears to have died. The legal matter may have been resolved but its impact persists. To use an English cricketing metaphor, NLP has been knocked for six.

We have referred to the divisions between those who believe in the 21 day training, and those who follow a more recent introduction of the accelerated 7 day practitioner course. Another fracture line is the division between the Bandler and Grinder camps, two different sources of a trainer's certification. Which one has the 'true message' about personal change and improvement? While there appear to be cordial relations between the founders, many practitioners identify with one or the other, and adhere to their individual approaches. We know of trainers with great generosity of spirit, and yet have also witnessed a culture of backbiting, and of belittling the efforts of other training establishments.

There is also the significant impending issue of state regulation in the USA, UK and Europe, which is likely to mean that people wanting to use NLP openly as an 'applied psychology' urgently need to advocate its legitimacy and demonstrate its efficacy. Whatever the specific challenges that regulation may bring, they are likely to need politically astute people in the field who are prepared to engage in patient dialogue with many external agencies.

However, in this scenario it persists with ostrich-like attitudes towards issues of theory and research, and with its capacity to create antagonisms. It could be too late already for NLP to mend the fractures with academic communities. If so, NLP will remain of interest to researchers only as a social phenomenon, an example of a 'movement' that was a child of the counter culture which petered out as the twenty-first century unfolded; not as a substantive contribution to human development. As unfortunate as it would be to lose the most valuable features of NLP, it could share the same fate as Phrenology, now dismissed as a quaint movement, led by eccentrics which came to an end as the nineteenth century drew to its close.

Developments in fields such as neuroscience increasingly seem to support many of the practices that have been used in NLP for decades. Those developments could prove double edged, however. They may lend support to NLP, but also raise the prospect that NLP could be overtaken by these fields, leaving NLP as a quaint but archaic conglomeration of knowledge and techniques. Even if NLP did arrive at some of these insights first, such historical fact will count for little if those fields are seen as legitimate and NLP is not. For example, NLP has contributed to the research method developed by Vermersch, as is acknowledged, but his approach has a new name, 'psycho-phenomenology' (Vermersch 1994). The relatively new, but already more widely recognised than NLP in academic circles, interdisciplinary field called Social Cognitive Neuroscience identifies its areas of research as;

> (a) understanding others, (b) understanding oneself, (c) controlling oneself, and (d) the processes that occur at the interface of self and others (Lieberman 2007:259).

In parallel with those developments, already we observe that related practices such as 'Clean Language' (Lawley & Tompkins 2000; Sullivan & Rees 2008) and Solution-Focused Work (Jackson & McKergow 2007) are attracting people because, among other things, they are less complicated, and simply not burdened with the various forms of baggage that NLP has accumulated (acknowledging that these new areas also need further research into their claimed efficacies).

In summary, in this scenario the inward tensions, combined with the inability to make more constructive external connections, lead to NLP being subsumed within, or overtaken by, more recent emergent fields. The vestiges of NLP may live on, but its identity and name are lost.

Renaissance?

Christina Hall wrote in 2001 that the splits in the field had been healed. Could that episode mark a rebirth such that NLP could rise, phoenix-like, from its own ashes? Are those court judgements a stepping stone on the path to a flourishing new phase in NLP's development?

In this scenario NLP rediscovers and reasserts its identity as essentially a pragmatic system of knowledge; one that is designed to be used, and one that is best suited to complementing other practices, particularly through the 'landmarks' identified in Chapter 14. It is then recognised for its contribution to enabling the application of knowledge from other fields, and potentially making interesting new discoveries from the field of practice. Far beyond the goal of NLP as personal liberation, which is redolent of its 1970s Californian aspirations, it is appreciated as a powerful tool for understanding the mysteries and limitations of our inner worlds and how they guide action, based on Bateson's thinking and assimilating contemporary ideas about complexity and emergence. Someone may synthesise NLP with work in other fields, so that it becomes less imbued with the 1970s metaphor of computer programmes, and reflects instead the new cybernetics of people like Humberto Maturana and Francisco Varela. The idea that by itself it constitutes a new paradigm of psychology would be abandoned.

Among NLP books that have fresh ideas and show where the field could be heading we would cite, perhaps, Steve Andreas' work elaborating and refining aspects of NLP's language models (Andreas 2006b; Andreas 2006c); and Lucas Derk's 'social panoramas', which shows how NLP can address the social and group dimension of experience (Derks 2005).

The relationship between NLP and formal research would play a central role in this scenario. One area for engagement that we have identified is cognitive linguistics, which has produced many new insights on the relationships between language structures and our particularly human ways of knowing and making sense. A glance at the bibliography of one of the latest authoritative text books (Evans & Green 2006) is fascinating, not only because of what is there, but also because of what is missing. There is, for instance, no reference to Bateson, or to anyone from the Palo Alto Group. What could happen if the fields of NLP, with its supremely practical approach, and cognitive linguistics, which is more academic and cerebral, began to cross-fertilise each other? Together they could make a vigorous hybrid.

As a first step towards this scenario, it is more important for NLP to be *talked about* and investigated in a community of inquiry than to be 'proved'. By opening up to inquiry, and by engaging in dialogue with the academic world, NLP can share its many gifts and insights. What are some ways in which this could happen?

One of our purposes in this book has been to indicate a research agenda for NLP. While some practitioners long for proof of its efficacy, in the hope that this will confer legitimacy and respectability on them and their practice, it is based on a narrow conception of the nature of research. Certainly there are fields of practice in which a formal evidence base is critical, such that if people want to use NLP openly it will have to be seen as efficacious and well researched. Some conventional research of this kind is already under way, especially in Europe and the USA. Obviously, research could also disconfirm aspects of NLP, and it is vital that NLP remains open to being disconfirmed otherwise it would become a closed system. But research has a wider function than the pursuit of proof. Another purpose, for example, is that of increasing understanding of the field and its approach for the benefit of both practitioners and users.

In our view, research into NLP as it relates to HRD is important regardless of one's beliefs about its validity, by virtue of the fact that it is a widespread practice. In addition to that conventional research into efficacy, therefore, we can identify at least eight areas of research that are likely to be fruitful:

1. Action research by practitioners, including both managers and developers, investigating the ways they have used NLP in their practice;
2. Case studies and evaluations (which may be qualitative) of NLP in (for example) coaching, consulting and training programmes and more, especially by taking into account users' experiences;
3. Modelling projects into individual and organisational capabilities (obviously with systematic evidence procedures);
4. Review and testing of specific NLP models and techniques, both empirically and conceptually in the light of developments in cognate fields;
5. Surveys of the incidence of NLP – how many people use it, where it is applied, and so on;
6. Elaboration and critique of the underpinning philosophy and epistemology of NLP – for example appraising and updating Bateson's ideas;
7. Sociological, historical and other studies of NLP as a social phenomenon, analysing and understanding its discourses and values;
8. Use of NLP to enhance existing research methods, as in Vermesch's psycho-phenomenology.

In conclusion, we set out in this book to explore the simplicity and the complexity of NLP by addressing numerous questions that are asked about this field of practice. Our aims were to inform readers in order to help them make their own choices about NLP, and to contribute to constructive dialogue about the field. We hope you feel you have been informed in this way.

Appendices

A timeline of NLP

Precursors
1890
Publication of William James' 'The Principles of Psychology'.

1893
Fritz Perls is born on 8th July in Berlin.

1901
Milton H. Erickson is born on 5th December in Aurum, Nevada.

1904
Gregory Bateson is born on 9th May in Grantchester, England, the son of geneticist William Bateson.

1916
Virginia Satir is born on 26th June on her parents' farm in Neville, Wisconsin.

1933
First publication of Alfred Korzybski's 'Science and Sanity'.

1940
John Thomas Grinder is born in Detroit, Michigan.
Gregory Bateson enters the USA as a resident.

1942
Milton Erickson addresses the precursor to the Macy Conferences, which Gregory Bateson attends.

1946
The inaugural Macy Conference (8th & 9th March 1946, New York), entitled 'Feedback Mechanisms and Circular Causal Systems in Biological and Social Systems'. Gregory Bateson is a member of the core group.

1950
Richard Wayne Bandler is born on 24th February in New Jersey, USA.

1956
Publication of Miller's 'The Magical Number Seven, Plus or Minus Two' (Miller 1956).

1959
The Palo Alto Mental Research Institute is founded.

1960
Publication of Miller, Galanter and Pribram's 'Plans and the Structure of Behaviour' (Miller, Galanter & Pribram 1960), source of the TOTE model.

1964
Fritz Perls, co-founder of Gestalt therapy, arrives at Esalen.

1966
The Brief Therapy Centre at Palo Alto is formed.

Origins
1967
Robert S. Spitzer meets Richard Bandler (Spitzer 1992:1).
Publication of 'Pragmatics of Human Communication' (Watzlawick, Beavin & Jackson 1967).

1968
Publication of 'The Teachings of Don Juan: A Yaqui Way of Knowledge' by Carlos Castaneda.
Grinder enrols at the University of California, San Diego, as a graduate student in the department of Linguistics.

1969
Grinder begins an academic year as a guest researcher in George Miller's lab at Rockefeller University.

1970
Grinder gains his PhD, titled 'On Deletion Phenomena' (Grinder 1971) from the University of California, San Diego.
Grinder takes up position as assistant professor at the University of California, Santa Cruz in the fall of 1970.
Kresge College (University of Santa Cruz) is founded.
Fritz Perls dies on 14th March.

1972
Bandler attends Satir's month-long workshop in Canada
Publication of Gregory Bateson's 'Steps to an Ecology of Mind'.
Bateson is appointed Visiting Professor, University of California at Santa Cruz.
Bandler starts to give workshops in Gestalt Therapy at Kresge College.

1973
Gregory Bateson joins Kresge College (at the end of 1973).
Spitzer publishes 'Eyewitness to Therapy' (Perls 1973).

1974

Gregory Bateson, his wife Lois, and their daughter Nora move into the community near Ben Lomond.

Bateson makes Bandler and Grinder aware of Milton Erickson's work.

1975

Publication of 'The Structure of Magic' (Bandler & Grinder 1975b), and 'Patterns of the Hypnotic Techniques of Milton H. Erickson, M.D. Volume I' (Bandler & Grinder 1975a).

1976

According to Robert Dilts, the title 'Neuro-linguistic Programming' first appears in print.

Publication of 'Structure of Magic II' (Grinder & Bandler 1976) and of 'Changing with Families' (Bandler, Grinder & Satir 1976).

1977

Publication of Bandura's seminal paper on self-efficacy (Bandura 1977a).

Publication of 'Patterns of the Hypnotic Techniques of Milton H. Erickson, M.D. Volume II' (Grinder, DeLozier & Bandler 1977).

Steve and Connirae Andreas are first introduced to NLP (Bandler & Andreas 1985b:2).

Development

1978

Bateson leaves Kresge College.

'Not Ltd.', run by Richard Bandler, Leslie Cameron-Bandler and associates, offering training and developments workshops (McLendon 1989:113).

Bandler and Grinder go their separate ways (McLendon 1989:117). Bandler buys Grinder out of the Society of NLP.

Grinder and DeLozier form Grinder, DeLozier & Associates.

1979

'Frogs into Princes' (Bandler & Grinder 1979) is published – the first time Bandler and Grinder use the term 'Neuro-linguistic Programming' in a book.

1980

Milton H. Erickson dies on 25th March.

Gregory Bateson dies on 4th July.

Publication of 'Neuro-Linguistic Programming: volume 1, the study of the structure of subjective experience' (Dilts, Grinder, Bandler & DeLozier 1980).

1981

Publication of 'Trance-formations' (Grinder & Bandler 1981).

'In October of 1981, John Grinder and Richard Bandler signed an Agreement governing the specific commercial use and rights involved in their joint creation – the technology of Neuro-Linguistic Programming.' (Hall 2001:16)

1982
Publication of 'ReFraming' (Bandler & Grinder 1982), Bandler and Grinder's last joint publication).

1983
Publication of 'Roots of NLP' (Dilts 1983).
NLP training begins in Vienna.

1985
Publication of 'Using Your Brain' (Bandler & Andreas 1985b).
John Seymour Associates is formed in the UK.
Association for NLP (now ANLP) is formed in the UK.
First issue of Rapport magazine is published.

1987
Publication of 'Turtles All The Way Down' (DeLozier & Grinder 1987), which marks the development of 'New Code' NLP.

1988
Virginia Satir dies on 10th September.
Publication of 'An Insider's Guide to Submodalities' (Bandler & MacDonald 1988).

1993
In the UK the first National Register of Psychotherapists is presented to the Government. It contains 'around 3000 names, of which 52 are NLP Psychotherapists' (Lawley 1994:43).

1994
The first issue of 'NLP World: the intercultural journal on the theory and practice of neuro-linguistic programming', appears in March 1994, created and edited by G. Peter Winnington.

At a crossroads
1996
Bandler files a suit against Grinder.

1997
Bandler and co-plaintiffs file their civil action.

1998
The UK Patent Office removes Richard Bandler's registered trademark on 10th September following a legal challenge by Tony Clarkson.

2000
The trial for Bandler's civil action takes place in the Superior Court of California, County of Santa Cruz, January 31st–February 10th.
Publication of the 'Encyclopedia of Systemic NLP and NLP New Coding' (Dilts & DeLozier 2000).

2001
Publication of 'Whispering in the Wind' (Bostic St. Clair & Grinder 2001).
'NLP World' journal is taken over and relaunched as a magazine (retaining the title).

2004
Gregory Bateson's centennial.

2007
Paul Watzlawick dies on 31st March.

2008
Publication of 'Richard Bandler's Guide to Trance-formation' (Bandler 2008a).

NLP training levels

While there are no unified standards for NLP training or its assessment, there is a broad consensus about the content and standards of NLP training. There is no universally accepted overarching body responsible for standards in the field of NLP.

The structure of NLP training and certification (there are exceptions) is as follows. Examples of the contents and criteria for these levels are sometimes posted on websites.[1]

Diploma or Foundation: despite what may be suggested by the title 'diploma', this is the most basic level of NLP training. It may involve an introductory course of a few days.

Practitioner: an NLP Practitioner training course covers the main principles, frameworks and techniques of NLP. Practitioner trainings offered in the UK mostly conform to one of two models, one of around 20 days and one of around 7 days. The relative merits of these models are contested within the field. In fact it is now possible to gain NLP certification online, by distance learning, meaning that face to face attendance at a training course may not be required.

Master Practitioner: this level is a more in-depth understanding of NLP, with advanced material. Many Master Practitioner trainings require participants to do an NLP 'modelling' project.

Some organisations also offer advanced Trainer Training and Master Trainer courses.

Trainer: a further level of training that is effectively a prerequisite for anyone wishing to offer public training course in NLP and to issue certificates for Practitioner and Master Practitioner levels.

Some organisations also offer advanced Trainer Training courses.
A recent development is in specific NLP training and certification for coaching. A course offered by UK NLP training organisation ITS, for example, is an accredited coach training programme under the International Coaching Federation.

Weblinks[2]

The American Society for Cybernetics: http://www.asc-cybernetics.org/
Anchor Point (including Anchor Point magazine): http://www.nlpanchorpoint.com/
The Association for NLP International: http://www.anlp.org/
The Bateson archive, University of California, Santa Cruz: http://www.oac.cdlib.org/findaid/ark:/13030/kt029029gz
Christina Hall (The NLP Connection): http://www.chris-nlp-hall.com/
Encyclopedia of Systemic NLP and NLP New Coding, by Robert Dilts and Judith DeLozier: http://nlpuniversitypress.com/
The Esalen Institute: http://www.esalen.org/
The European Association for NLP Therapy (EANLPt): http://www.eanlpt.org/
The Institute for Intercultural Studies (includes information about Gregory Bateson): http://www.interculturalstudies.org
The International NLP Trainers' Association (INLPTA): http://www.inlpta.com/
La Programmation Neuro Linguistique: http://www.pnl.fr/
The Mental Research Institute, Palo Alto: http://www.mri.org/
The Milton H. Erickson Foundation: http://www.erickson-foundation.org/
NLP Comprehensive: http://www.nlpco.com/
The Neuro Linguistic Psychotherapy and Counselling Association: http://www.nlptca.com/
The NLP Conference (includes listing of most UK NLP training organisations): http://www.nlpconference.co.uk/
The NLP Research and Recognition Project (USA): http://nlprandr.org/
The Neuro-Linguistic Programming Research Data Base, University of Bielefeld: http://www.nlp.de/cgi-bin/research/nlp-rdb.cgi
NLP Research (University of Surrey): http://www.nlpresearch.org
NLP World (Journal edited by G. Peter Winnington): http://theletterworth-press.com/nlpworld/
The Professional Guild of NLP: http://www.professionalguildofnlp.com/
The Society of Neuro-Linguistic Programming: http://www.purenlp.com/society.htm
Steve Andreas: http://www.steveandreas.com/
The Virginia Satir Collection, University of California, Santa Barbara: http://www.oac.cdlib.org/findaid/ark:/13030/ft6q2nb44m
The Virginia Satir Global Network: http://www.avanta.net/

Notes

Chapter 1

1 http://www.flyingwithoutfear.info/questions.htm, accessed 28th February 2009.
2 'This book is also the written record of a mystery story of sorts' (Bandler & Grinder 1979:1).
3 In the legal agreement reached between them in 2000, which is reproduced in full in 'Whispering in the Wind' (Bostic St. Clair and Grinder 2001: 376–381) Bandler and Grinder formally recognised each other as 'co creators and co-founders of the technology of Neurolinguistic Programming'.
4 NLP Comprehensive, www.nlpco.com/pages/about, accessed 28th February 2009.
5 Charles Faulkner, personal communication (September 2007). See also; http://en.wikipedia.org/wiki/Charles_Faulkner, accessed 28th February 2009.
6 http://www.guardian.co.uk/education/2008/feb/26/schools.teaching accessed 28th February 2009.
7 As Jane reads both French and German, we have been able to consult these sources.
8 Paul as Master Practitioner (1992) and ANLP member; Jane as a Master Practitioner (1990) and Trainer (1992).
9 This book is a project within our research investigating issues and practices of adult learning. The wider aim is to contribute to the theory and practice of 'transformative learning', which means learning that involves significant change or development for the learner (e.g. Mezirow 1991). Our recent research has three main aims:
 1. To support the emergence of an NLP research community, increasing dialogue between academic and practitioner communities.
 2. To developing a critical appraisal of the field (i.e. this book).
 3. To progress our work on transformative learning and teaching.

Chapter 2

1 Bostic St. Clair and Grinder (2001:50–52) identify three aspects, NLP modelling, NLP application, and NLP training.
2 Robert Dilts claims to have used the title in 1976. It does appear in the foreword to Dilts' 'Roots of Neuro-Linguistic Programming', which is dated 1976, although this volume was not published until 1983.
3 From Lankton (1980).
4 http://www.john-seymour-associates.co.uk/whatisnlp.htm, accessed 28th February 2009.

5   Reference to the study of subjective experience sounds, to researchers, like the long-established methodology (and philosophy), called 'phenomenology', which is also concerned with studying the way people experience the world. Apart from an isolated entry in Dilts and DeLozier (2000:951), who say that NLP is 'phenomenological in the sense that it considers a person's sensory experience, or primary experience, to be the basic material from which he or she builds their model of the world', there is little if any evidence in NLP publications of familiarity with phenomenology. It is unclear why NLP has not drawn more from that field. The potential for modelling as a formal research method is being explored in France, where Pierre Vermersch has drawn extensively on NLP as an investigative tool in his 'Psychophenomenology' (Vermersch 1994), and through our own research (e.g. Mathison & Tosey 2008).

6   While the authors do not describe their book as an NLP publication, their involvement in and contribution to the field of NLP is acknowledged (e.g. through their biographies on the book jacket).

7   This and other articles on modelling are available online at http://www. steveandreas.com/, accessed 28th February 2009. Andreas, who was formerly known as John O. Stevens, has worked in the NLP field since the late 1970s.

8   Sociologist David Silverman (1975) has pointed out that these books are of interest primarily because of the questions they raise about knowledge.

9   In this book, references are to the 2000 edition of Bateson's classic 'Steps to an Ecology of Mind'.

10 Details of a series of audio tapes by 'Grinder & Associates' appear at the back of Grinder, DeLozier & Bandler (1977).

11 'Rapport' magazine, issue 10 page 20 Winter 2007.

12 John Seymour Associates, founded in 1985 (O'Connor & Seymour 1990:239); PPD (formerly Pace Personal Development), founded by Julian Russell and Roy Johnson in 1987 and now owned by Judith Lowe; ITS (International Teaching Seminars), founded in 1998 and still run by Ian McDermott; and Sensory Systems, founded in 1987 and still run by John McWhirter.

13 According to the listing on the NLP conference website http://www. nlpconference.co.uk/organisation, accessed 11th January 2008.

14 The figure is based on an average of 500 practitioner trainees per year for the 10 years from 1987 until 1996 (5,000); plus 2,000 trainees per year for the 5 years from 1997 until 2001 (10,000); plus 3,000 trainees per year for the 5 years from 2002 until 2007 (15,000). Numbers of trainees are estimated based on claims from UK NLP training providers (e.g. John Seymour Associates; http://www.john-seymour-associates. co.uk/nlpcourseswelcome.php, accessed 9th March 2007; PPD Learning http://www.ppdlearning.co.uk/, accessed 9th March 2007), on known increases in the numbers of training providers (especially since the mid 1990s) and on increased capacity of some courses (as mentioned, for example, by Derren Brown and Isabel Losada).

15 http://www.thenlpgroup.ie/nlp_group_djg.htm, accessed 28th February 2009.
16 Jo Hogg's 'NLP Conference' website http://www.nlpconference.co.uk/, accessed 28th February 2009, includes a database that identifies the affiliations of all the current training organisations.
17 There are distinct bodies and accreditation arrangements for NLP psychotherapists. The Neuro Linguistic Psychotherapy Counselling Association (NLPtCA) is a member organisation of the UK Council for Psychotherapy (UKCP); http://www.psychotherapy.org.uk/index. html, accessed 28th February 2009. In mainland Europe there exists the European Association for NLP Therapy (EANLPt): http://www. eanlpt.org/, accessed 28th February 2009.
18 http://www.inlpta.com/, accessed 28th February 2009.
19 www.nlpco.com/pages/articles/nlp/GoodTraining.php accessed 28th February 2009.
20 http://www.anlp.org/: accessed 28th February 2009.
21 The initiator of the ANLP was Frank Kevlin, a trainer and psycho-therapist. It was formed so that NLP could become a member of the UK Council for Psychotherapy, and originally had charitable status. Subsequently the Neuro Linguistic Psychotherapy Association (NLPtCA) was developed as a separate association that could focus exclusively on psychotherapy. In 1999, ANLP changed its status and became a limited company, becoming a community interest company in 2008.
22 Naturally, copyright laws continue to apply to all published works.
23 A course offered by UK NLP training organisation ITS, for example, is an accredited coach training programme under the International Coaching Federation.
24 NLP community events include an NLP practitioner conference is held in London every November, organised by Jo Hogg, who has served the NLP community for many years. There are several other regular, smaller NLP conventions in the UK. In Europe, regular conferences and other events with a psychotherapeutic emphasis are organised by the European Association for Neurolinguistic Psychotherapy (EANLPt). The privately-sponsored Institute for the Advanced Studies of Health (IASH), based in the USA, runs a World Health Conference. In 2008 there was also an NLP practitioner conference in Brasil. The inaugural International NLP Research Conference was held at the University of Surrey, in the UK, in partnership with ANLP, on 5th July 2008.
25 The role of language is multi-faceted. It is difficult to mention in only one part of the description because language is treated as part of thought as well as part of behaviour (e.g. spoken and written behaviour). Language is also a principal medium used by practitioners when facilitating change.

Chapter 3

1 http://www.anlp.org/, accessed 11th April 2007.
2 September 5th 2001 p. 4, 'Boost your skills with emotional intelligence; learning curves'.
3 'Learning? It's All in the Mind', Times Educational Supplement, 21st May 2004.
4 http://www.cipd.co.uk/default.cipd, accessed 28th February 2009.
5 Personal communication, 1992.
6 The title 'cdaq' is used alone, not as an acronym.
7 http://www.cfbt.com/, accessed 28th February 2009.
8 An INLPTA accredited Diploma level course.
9 Also personal communication, Richard Churches, CfBT Educational Trust, December 2008.
10 http://www.cipd.co.uk/subjects/maneco/general/nlp.htm?IsSrchRes=1, accessed 28th February 2009.
11 Spechler explains that he used modelling for this study in an article in NLP World (Spechler 1995).
12 http://www.anlp.org/, accessed 28th February 2009.

Chapter 4

1 See for example the review by Steve Andreas (2003) available online at http://www.steveandreas.com/Articles/whispering.html, accessed 28th February 2009.
2 Personal communication, Dr John Martin, Open University, UK, 1st February 2009.
3 Esalen continues to be a leading centre for alternative and experiential education today.
4 The first three of these mirror the three stages of development described by Bostic St. Clair and Grinder (2001).
5 Not to be confused, however, with Dr Robert L. Spitzer, a Professor of Psychiatry at Columbia University, who chaired the task force producing the third edition of the Diagnostic and Statistical Manual of Mental and Psychiatric Disorders.
6 Foothill College website: http://www.foothill.fhda.edu/index.php accessed 28th February 2009.
7 Spitzer (1992:2) appears to suggest that this meeting took place about the time that Fritz Perls died (i.e. in 1970). However, Banmen (2002:4) refers to Satir spending three months in Manitoba, Canada in 1972. This date is supported by a listing in the Virginia Satir archive, University of California, Santa Barbara, of an item 'Claive Buckland's Notes to R. Bandler for Monthlong, 1972'; http://content.cdlib.org/view?docId=ft6q2nb44m& chunk. id= c02-1.7.6.7.5&brand=oac, accessed 28th February 2009. 1972 is the date given by Walker (1996:31).
8 'Alba Road' is identified on Google Earth.

9 'In 1975, Bandler, Grinder and Bateson all had their individual residences at 1000 Alba Road, Ben Lomand (*sic*), California' (Bostic St. Clair & Grinder 2001:173).

Chapter 5

1 From Watzlawick (1978).
2 Elgin went on to develop her own practical, language-based model of communication, which she called 'Syntonics' (Elgin 1989:v). In its emphasis on 'verbal self-defence' it has some similarities with a later model developed in NLP called 'sleight of mouth' (Dilts 1999).
3 Pucelik now works as a business consultant in the Ukraine: http://eng. frankpucelik.com, accessed 28th February 2009.
4 'Bill was the founding editor of the first NLP Newsletter (1978–1980) and did his master's thesis... on Bandler and Grinder's "Patterns of Communication and Change." (The term NLP had not yet been invented.) NLP had (and still has) a profound influence on him, his work and his life. Bill studied with Dr. Milton Erickson in the midst of his NLP studies (he was certified in NLP in 1978 in New Orleans, in the same graduating class as Steve and Connirae Andreas, by Richard Bandler, John Grinder, Leslie Cameron-Bandler and Judith de Lozier). http://www.anlp.org/index.asp?PageID=361, accessed 28th February 2009.
5 We are especially grateful to Judith Lowe, PPD Learning, for her views on this subject.
6 For example, no article in the Letterworth journal, *NLP World*, has addressed this theme. The term does not appear in the title of any article, nor is the topic addressed substantively in any contribution.
7 Others include Connirae Andreas, Lara Ewing and Charlotte Bretto.
8 Judith DeLozier, personal communication, 21st November 2007.
9 A footnote in 'Changing With Families' (Bandler, Grinder & Satir 1976:176) refers to the (presumably then forthcoming) title as 'The Magic of Patterns/Patterns of Magic'.
10 The painting was chosen by Bandler (Spitzer 1992:3).
11 See the Transport for London website, http://www.tfl.gov.uk/, accessed 28th February 2009.
12 See also 'Changing with Families' (Bandler, Grinder & Satir 1976:186). In both places Karttunen is misspelt as 'Kartunnen'.
13 See for example: http://www2.parc.com/istl/members/karttune/, accessed 28th February 2009.
14 The significance of mirror neurons for understanding of issues of learning was noted by Guy Claxton in his keynote speech to the British Educational Research Association in 2006 (Claxton 2006).
15 Most recently the hypnotic state, and its induction, has also been shown to have neurological correlates (Jamieson 2007). Even our understanding of time and its passage may be the result of certain processes

in our cortex (Mauk & Buonoman 2004). Sense making takes on yet another dimension; both skilful and unskilful communicators are producing neurological effects in others.

Chapter 6

1　This idea has been contested by empirical research, which we discuss in Chapter 11.
2　The original formulation of the 4-tuple, in Grinder *et al* (1976), was based on interest in notating a client's present-time experience. This comprised visual, kinaesthetic, auditory tonal, and olfactory elements, plus an indication of the source of that experience (the referential index) 'as a way of distinguishing hallucinated or projected experience from experience originating in the external world' (Grinder, DeLozier & Bandler 1977:12). The 4-tuple is of course a simplification of the sensory apparatus.
3　Personal communication, Christina Hall, April 22nd 2008. Jane is particularly indebted to Christina Hall, who collaborated with Richard Bandler for some years, for demonstrating the ways in which language and submodalities interacted.
4　We acknowledge Ranjit Sidhu for sharing her enquiries into this topic.
5　See for example the review by Dave Allaway at http://www.nlpand.co.uk/resources/review8.shtml, accessed 28th February 2009, which says they fall into the Cartesian trap and distinguish between First Access and the 'real' world.

Chapter 7

1　Surprisingly, therefore, Grinder comments that 'My... memory is that the only portion of the book... that Gregory was interested in discussing at any length was the syntactic processes underlying... nominalization' (Bostic St. Clair & Grinder 2001:193).
2　'Steps to an Ecology of Mind' documents communication between Erickson and Bateson in 1955 (Bateson 2000a:223), and Bateson refers to Erickson in a 1951 publication (Ruesch & Bateson 1951:237).
3　History of Cybernetics, American Society for Cybernetics, http://www.asc-cybernetics.org/foundations/history2.htm, accessed 1st March 2009.
4　McCue's critique appears in the same volume as the review of research into NLP (Heap 1988), which we discuss in Chapter 9.
5　Judith DeLozier, personal communication, 21st November 2007.
6　Bateson's usage of 'metalinguistics' dates back to 1954 (Bateson 2000a:178); Michael Hall's unpublished 'Bateson Report' also cites a lecture given by Bateson in 1959 (Bateson 2000a:248).
7　We acknowledge, but do not attempt to discuss here, that there are many and diverse versions of 'social constructionism', 'constructionism', and 'constructivism'.

8   Poerksen interviewed Von Foerster, and reports the following conversation (2002:43):
     Poerksen to Von Foerster: But you are a constructivist [...] you claim that every person constructs his or her reality, [...]
     Von Foerster: No no, I am Viennese. That is the only label I have come to accept.. [...] Of course you are correct when you say that there are a few people who claim that I am representative of a particular epistemology. But that just isn't right. I don't have any epistemology at all.
9   See papers at: http://cognitrn.psych.indiana.edu/, accessed 1st March 2009.
10   From Greenburg, D. (1964).
11   See Michael Hall's article, 'Not Quite Everything About Everything You Want to Know About the New Field', at http://www.neurosemantics. com/, accessed 1st March 2009.

Chapter 8

1   Kybernetes, Volume 34 no. 3–4.
2   Cybernetics and Human Knowing, Volume 12 no. 1–2.
3   Bateson's theory of learning is cited in literature in education, e.g. (Bloom 2004; Brockbank & McGill 1998; McWhinney & Markos 2003; Peterson 1999), psychotherapy and personal development, e.g. (Keeney 1983; Watzlawick, Weakland & Fisch 1974) and organisational learning, e.g. (Argyris & Schön 1978; Bartunek & Moch 1994; Engeström 2001b; Engeström 2001a; French & Bazalgette 1996; Roach & Bednar 1997; Tosey & Mathison 2008; Visser 2003; Wijnhoven 2001).
4   Lipset does not say whether this refers to the academic or calendar year.
5   From the Bateson Archive at the University of Santa Cruz. Three documents were identified and copies kindly supplied by the Archive administrator in response to our request for any information that pertained to NLP. The most useful of these is the letter discussed here.
6   We are grateful to Michael Hall for supplying us with a copy of this report.
7   As Bateson's daughter, Mary Catherine Bateson, comments: 'The processes with which Gregory was concerned were essentially processes of knowing: perception, communication, coding and translation...' (in Bateson 2000a:5).
8   At the time of their encounters in Santa Cruz Bateson was working on 'Mind and Nature', published in 1979.
9   Personal communication, Mary Catherine Bateson (by e-mail), 23rd March 2007.
10   Intriguingly, Karen Pryor, who directed the dolphin trainers in Hawaii, commented that Bateson 'hated the thought of bending creatures to one's will' yet 'goes around bending people to his will all the time' (Lipset 1980:248).
11   American Society for Cybernetics, http://www.asc-cybernetics.org/foundations/history/MacySummary.htm, accessed 1st March 2009. Although

Walker (1996:206) suggests that Milton Erickson participated in the later Macy conferences too, there is no evidence for this according to the American Society for Cybernetics website. It is possible that Walker is confusing Milton Erickson with the psychoanalysts Erik Erikson, who addressed the third conference in 1947.

12 It still exists today: http://www.josiahmacyfoundation.org/, accessed 1st March 2009.

13 The final conference was held in New Jersey.

14 Via: http://www-history.mcs.st-andrews.ac.uk/Mathematicians/Wiener_Norbert.html, accessed 1st March 2009.

15 http://www.asc-cybernetics.org/foundations/history2.htm, accessed 1st March 2009.

16 http://www.asc-cybernetics.org/foundations/history2.htm, accessed 1st March 2009.

17 http://www.asc-cybernetics.org/foundations/history2.htm#MacySum, accessed 1st March 2009. The middle section of this quotation notes that; 'The historical records for the field's birth have never been readily accessible, owing to an almost total lack of documentation for the first 5 conferences and the obscure status of the last 5 events' proceedings. This resulted in a reliance on personal recollections and anecdotal evidence in exploring how that process occurred'.

18 Bateson uses the term 'lineal' (Bateson 2000a:451) rather than 'linear'.

19 Some people have suggested that every system shares a basic goal, that of survival (Beer 1974). This view has been challenged and it may be more helpful to think of every human system as maintaining its own integrity (meaning its wholeness, not its honesty).

20 To which Keeney (1983:76) refers as 'cybernetics of cybernetics'. Some theorists nowadays are also discussing third-order cybernetics, which has some resonance with Dilts' notion of meta-position (Dilts & DeLozier 2000:754).

21 Von Foerster, a physicist, was also a magician, and was intrigued by the ways that perceptions of reality can be based on misdirection and illusion (Von Foerster & Poerksen 2002:124–127).

Chapter 9

1 The term 'presuppositions', as used to refer to axioms, may have entered NLP from Gregory Bateson. The statement that; 'Science, like art, religion, commerce, warfare, and even sleep, is based on presuppositions' (Bateson 1979:32) appears to predate the appearance in NLP literature of this term.

2 Dilts (http://www.nlpu.com/Articles/artic20.htm, accessed 1st March 2009) calls these 'epistemological presuppositions' in order to distinguish them from a 'linguistic presuppositions', which are described in The Structure of Magic I.

3 For example, 'if what you're doing isn't working...' (Bandler & Grinder 1979:13, 73) also p. 73; 'the map is not the territory' (Bandler & Grinder

1975b:7) ; 'the meaning of your communication...' (Bandler & Grinder 1979:61); 'you can treat every limitation that is presented to you as a unique accomplishment by a human being' (Bandler & Grinder 1979:67); the law of requisite variety (Bandler & Grinder 1979:74).

4   Translation by Jane Mathison.

5   Bostic St. Clair and Grinder have published an article (which makes no mention of NLP) in the academic journal 'Cybernetics and Human Knowing' (Malloy, Bostic St. Clair & Grinder 2005).

6   This principle has also been linked to the work of Feldenkrais (Cameron-Bandler, Gordon & Lebeau 1985:322).

7   http://www.univie.ac.at/constructivism/HvF.htm accessed 1st March 2009.

8   Gregory Bateson distilled his ideas down to four components in a 'sketch of an epistemology' (Brockman 1977:243):
   1. That message events are activated by difference.
   2. That information travels in pathways and systems that are collaterally energised...
   3. A special sort of holism is generated by feedback and recursiveness.
   4. That mind operates with hierarchies and networks of difference to create *gestalten*.

9   From the long-running UK TV series Dr. Who.

10 See Capra (1996:67).

11 It could reflect Virginia Satir's early (but later rejected) exposure to Christian Science, to which her mother was attached (Walker 1996:157).

12 See also DeLozier (1995).

13 For example, 'Style, Grace and Information in Primitive Art' (Bateson 2000a:128–152).

Chapter 10

1   This idea itself states a theory.

2   See for example Kahneman's Nobel prize-winning lecture at http://nobelprize.org/nobel_prizes/economics/laureates/2002/kahnemann-lecture.pdf, accessed 1st March 2009.

3   As defined by Heron.

4   Bateson archive, University of Santa Cruz, letter dated 10th January 1974.

5   A book published at this time called 'Paradigms and Fairy Tales' (Ford 1976) had a fairy-tale scene on the cover, and was a serious work on research methods.

6   This was the first of a series of books based on workshop transcripts that included 'Trance-formations' (Grinder & Bandler 1981) and 'Reframing' (Bandler & Grinder 1982), the latter being the last instance of co-authorship between Bandler and Grinder. Steve and Connirae Andreas, separately or jointly, edited all three. Steve Andreas, known at that time as John O. Stevens, had previously published Perls' transcript-based

'Gestalt Therapy Verbatim' (Perls 1969). 'Frogs Into Princes' used a similar format, being based on transcripts of workshops that took place at the Andreas' NLP Comprehensive.

7   'Frogs Into Princes' diverges interestingly from some other NLP books of this era, particularly those involving Robert Dilts (e.g. Dilts, Grinder, Bandler & DeLozier 1980; Dilts 1983), which retained a more conceptual approach.

8   As, for example, in the polemic by Beadle (2008a).

9   There is a potential paradox here in that, if NLP is a 'pseudoscience', as some allege, it cannot effectively manipulate anyone, which is one of the common concerns expressed about the practice.

10 As noted earlier, Brown levels the same charge at Ericksonian hypnotic techniques.

11 See also, for example, Lazarus' foreword in Henwood & Lister (2007:xiii).

12 NLP practitioners might like to analyse this claim as a 'convincer strategy'.

13 Nisbett and Ross (1980) have examined a wide range of beliefs, presuppositions and cognitive strategies that make inferences unreliable.

14 'What Other People Say May Change What You See', Sandra Blakeslee, The New York Times (Science), 28th June 2005 http://www.nytimes.com/2005/06/28/science/28brai.html?_r=2, accessed 1st March 2009.

Chapter 11

1   'Learning? It's All in the Mind', Fran Abrams, Times Educational Supplement , 21st May 2004.

2   One must also exercise some caution when citing research from other fields of study. It is easy to latch on to a finding from an unfamiliar field and interpret it as supporting something in which one believes, forgetting that one is treating this in isolation from the complexities and subtleties of work in the whole field.

3   See also studies cited on the EANLPt website's 'Research' page: http://www.eanlpt.org/, accessed 1st March 2009.

4   One example often cited in NLP trainings is the notion that communication is 7% verbal, 38% tone of voice, and 55% visual. This is based on the work of Albert Mehrabian, a psychologist who has specialised in the study of nonverbal communication (Mehrabian 1981). While the percentages cited are correct, Mehrabian stresses that they should not be generalised to all face-to-face communication; 'this and other equations regarding relative importance of verbal and nonverbal messages were derived from experiments dealing with communications of feelings and attitudes (i.e., like-dislike). Unless a communicator is talking about their feelings or attitudes, these equations are not applicable': http://www.kaaj.com/psych/smorder.html, accessed 2nd March 2009.

5   The same observation probably applies to many other practices found in HRD.

6   Personal communication, Judith DeLozier, 21st November 2007.

7   That quote is from the transcript of a workshop in the 1970s. It was part of an introduction through which the presenters, Bandler and Grinder, were setting a frame of relevance and interest for the participants. It was probably intended as a way to direct participants' attention towards their own sensory experience, and away from other people's espoused theories, not as a definitive statement of NLP's position on research. Nevertheless we would argue that statements like this have been influential in the latter way (remembering the NLP presupposition 'the meaning of your communication is the response that you get').

8   See Web links (appendix).

9   For example, Slater and Usoh (1994), of the University of London, used NLP in a study of Virtual Reality. Kauppi *et al* (1995) describe exactly the kind of empirical investigation of an aspect of NLP's language models (in this instance, modal operators) that could 'backfill' the NLP evidence base. Derks (1995) describes empirical work contributing to the development of his 'social panoramas' concept. Hancox and Bass (1995a) report a classic experimental study that supports the NLP principle that submodality changes can have physiological effects.

10 Of a total of 110 articles in NLP World, 40 are authored or co-authored by someone who cites a PhD as a qualification.

11 From an online article attributed to John Grinder: http://www.reperepnl.com/site/A_Review_of_an_interview_by_Robert_DILTS_par_John_GRINDER_29032006-234.html, accessed 1st March 2009.

12 See weblink in Resources section. This database is of considerable value to anyone researching NLP. For several years it appeared to be dormant; until early in 2008 it listed 180 publications. It was then updated by Dr Frans-Josef Huecker, who added more than 100 new publications.

13 Based on the observation that Heap's bibliography refers to these abstracts, not to the full studies.

14 Baddeley and Predebon could still be criticised for aspects of their question formats. For example, they designed the question, 'Imagine in detail looking at a painting you have never seen before' (Baddeley & Predebon 1991:21), as 'Visually Constructed'. What the question asks the respondent, to be precise, is to imagine the act or experience of looking. This could elicit a different response from a question that asks a person to imagine what the painting looks like.

15 As reviewed by Ehrlichman and Weinberger (1978).

16 On internet sites this study is widely attributed to an apparently non-existent researcher, one 'Dr Blaslotto'.

17 Including calibration and matching; internal representations and submodalities; the NLP phobia cure; and a technique known in NLP as the 'swish pattern'.

18 September 5th 2001 p. 4, 'Boost your skills with emotional intelligence; learning curves'.

19 We are grateful to Dr John Martin for bringing this example to our attention.

Chapter 12

1 'A Google search on 20th December 2008 produced 398,000 results for the terms Obama and NLP' (Richard Churches, unpublished paper, 12th January 2009).

2 It is ironic that in order to make this claim about the ethics of NLP, Megginson and Clutterbuck use, presumably unwittingly, a linguistic device called (in NLP) 'the verbal swish pattern', in which the sudden replacement of one image with another, more powerful one can result in a change in the listener's perception due to the new association that is suggested.

3 The same quote points out that they would, at the same time, purposely state the counterview that 'nothing is hypnosis, hypnosis doesn't exist'.

4 See for example Tettamanti *et al* (2005); Rizzolatti and Craighero (2004); Yokoyama *et al* (2006).

5 For example, the Professional Guild's commitment to a common standard, the ANLP's 'What Questions Could I Ask A Trainer?' feature, the Global Organisation of NLP's 'Guide to Trainings', and NLP Comprehensive's 'Good Training Guide'.

6 http://www.anlp.org/index.asp?PageID=79, accessed 1st March 2009.

7 For example, the NLPtCA code of ethics http://www.nlptca.com/ethics.php, accessed 1st March 2009.

8 NLP practitioners will recognise that this posits a 'complex equivalence' between compliance and ethical conduct.

9 The ANLP currently recommends 'a minimum of 50 attendance hours for Practitioner level and 90 attendance hours for Master Practitioner level'. These minimum hours form part of the ANLP Terms and Conditions of membership (section 2.1), which can be accessed via http://www.anlp.org/index.asp?CatName=Membership&CatID=8&PageID=253.

10 Isabel Losada's website includes the comment that; 'The course is expensive and to get the 'qualification' all you have to do is stay in the room'. http://www.isabellosada.com/, accessed 1st March 2009.

11 http://www.steveandreas.com/Articles/doingtherapy.html; accessed 1st March 2009.

12 The biography of Frank Pucelik (Lewis and Pucelik 1990:161), who participated in early NLP, refers to his 'extensive training in a variety of communication techniques and their scientific basis'.

Chapter 13

1 Such an analysis could make a valuable contribution to understandings of the field.

2 Heard by Jane Mathison at two different trainings at which she assisted.

3 There is substantial reference to Jung's psychological functions in James & Woodsmall (1988).

4 For example, http://www.nlpexcellence.com/, accessed 2nd March 2009.

5   An early, if isolated, appearance of 'excellence' in NLP appears in Cameron-Bandler *et al* (1985:3).
6   We note the clear statement in that source that these represent Grinder's personal view – there is no suggestion that Bandler would concur.
7   http://www.icsahome.com/, accessed 2nd March 2009.
8   As pointed out in Chapter 2, Robbins does not offer NLP practitioner training.
9   Jane can vouch from personal experience that practitioners and trainers licensed by Bandler sign a licensing agreement.

Chapter 15

1   A Google search on Neuro-Linguistic Programming yielded 1,490,000 hits; a search on NLP yielded 16,400,000 hits; scarches on 1st March 2009.
2   It is accessible via the internet: http://www.nlpuniversitypress.com/, accessed 27th February 2009.
3   Neither Amazon.co.uk nor Amazon.com, accessed 1st March 2009.
4   http://www.anglo-american.co.uk/, accessed 1st March 2009.
5   One of Bandler's most recent books, 'Conversations' (Bandler & Fitzpatrick 2005), also appears to be available only to trainees.

Appendices

1   For example the INLPTA website: http://www.inlpta.org/index.php?option=com_content&task=view&id=34&Itemid=84, accessed 28th February 2009.
2   All links active at the time of going to press.

Bibliography

Andreas, S. 2003, 'Whispering in the Wind (Book Review)', *Anchor Point*, vol. 17, no. 3, p. 3.

Andreas, S. 2006a, 'Modeling Modeling', *The Model*, vol. Spring.

Andreas, S. 2006b, *Six Blind Elephants: Understanding Ourselves and Each Other, Volume I, Fundamental Principles of Scope and Category* Real People Press, Moab, Utah.

Andreas, S. 2006c, *Six Blind Elephants: Understanding Ourselves and Each Other, Volume II, Applications and Explorations of Scope and Category* Real People Press, Moab, Utah.

Argyris, C. 1999, *On Organizational Learning*, 2nd edn, Blackwell, Oxford.

Argyris, C. & Schön, D. 1978, *Organizational Learning* Addison-Wesley, Reading, Mass.

Ashby, W. 1965, *An Introduction to Cybernetics* Methuen, London.

Baddeley, M. & Predebon, J. 1991, 'Do the Eyes Have It?: A Test of Neuro-linguistic Programming's Eye Movement Hypothesis', *Australian Journal of Clinical Hypnotherapy and Hypnosis*, vol. 12, no. 1, pp. 1–23.

Bandler, R. 2008, *Richard Bandler's Guide to Trance-formation* Health Communications Inc., Deerfield Beach, Florida.

Bandler, R. & Fitzpatrick, O. 2005, *Conversations: Freedom is Everything and Love is All the Rest* Mysterious Publications, Dublin.

Bandler, R. 1985, *Using Your Brain for a Change* Real People Press, Moab, Utah.

Bandler, R. & Grinder, J. 1979, *Frogs into Princes* Real People Press, Moab, Utah.

Bandler, R. & Grinder, J. 1975a, *Patterns of the Hypnotic Techniques of Milton H. Erickson, M.D. Vol. 1* Meta Publications, Cupertino, California.

Bandler, R. & Grinder, J. 1975b, *The Structure of Magic: A Book about Language and Therapy* Palo Alto: Science and Behavioural Books.

Bandler, R. & Grinder, J. 1982, *ReFraming: Neuro-Linguistic Programming and the Transformation of Meaning* Real People Press, Moab, Utah.

Bandler, R., Grinder, J. & Satir, V. 1976, *Changing with Families: A Book about Further Education for Being Human* Science & Behavior Books., Palo Alto, CA.

Bandler, R. & MacDonald, W. 1988, *An Insider's Guide to Sub-Modalities* Meta Publications, Capitola, CA.

Bandura, A. 1977, 'Self-efficacy: Toward a Unifying Theory of Behavioral Change', *Psychological Review*, vol. 84, pp. 191–215.

Bandura, A. 1986, *The Social Foundations of Thought and Action* Prentice Hall, New Jersey.

Banmen, J. 2002, 'Introduction: Virginia Satir Today', *Contemporary Family Therapy*, vol. 24, no. 1, pp. 3–5.

Barsalou, L. & Wiemer-Hastings, K. 2005, 'Situating Abstract Concepts', in *Grounding Cognition: The Role of Perception and Action in Memory, Language and Thought*, D. Pecher & R. Zwaan, eds, Cambridge University Press, Cambridge, pp. 129–136.

Barsalou, L. W. 1999, 'Perceptual Symbol Systems', *Behavioral and Brain Sciences*, vol. 22, pp. 577–660.

Barsalou, L. W. 2008, 'Grounded Cognition', *Annual Review of Psychology*, vol. 59, pp. 617–645.

Bartunek, J. M. & Moch, M. K. 1994, 'Third Order Organizational Change and the Western Mystical Tradition', *Journal of Organisational Change Management*, vol. 7, no. 1, pp. 24–41.

Bateson, G. 1979, *Mind and Nature* Fontana/Collins, Glasgow.

Bateson, G. 2000a, *Steps to an Ecology of Mind: Collected Essays in Anthropology, Psychiatry, Evolution and Epistemology*, Revised edn, University of Chicago Press, Chicago.

Bateson, G., Jackson, D. D., Haley, J. & Weakland, J. 1956, 'Toward a Theory of Schizophrenia', *Behavioral Science*, vol. 1, no. 4, pp. 251–264.

Bateson, M. C. 1994, *With a Daughter's Eye: A Memoir of Margaret Mead and Gregory Bateson* HarperPerennial, New York.

Bateson, M. C. 2000b, 'The Wisdom Of Recognition', *Cybernetics and Human Knowing*, vol. 8, no. 4, pp. 87–90.

Beadle, P. 'Who is the Fakest of Them All?' *Education Guardian*. 26-2-2008a. Ref Type: Magazine Article.

Beck, C. E. & Beck, E. A. 1984, 'Test of the Eye Movement Hypothesis of Neurolinguistic Programming: A Rebuttal of Conclusions', *Perceptual and Motor Skills*, vol. 58, no. 1, pp. 175–176.

Beddoes-Jones, F. & Miller, J. 2007, 'Using the Thinking Styles Instrument in Coaching', *Selection and Development Review, Special Edition: Psychological Models in Coaching*, vol. 23, no. 5, pp. 13–15.

Beer, M. & Nohria, N. 2000, 'Cracking the Code of Change', *Harvard Business Review*, vol. May–June, pp. 133–141.

Beer, S. 1974, *Designing Freedom* John Wiley & Sons, Chichester.

Berns, G. S., Chappelow, J., Zink, C. F., Pagnoni, G., Martin-Skurski, M. E. & Richards, J. 2005, 'Neurobiological Correlates of Social Conformity and Independence During Mental Rotation', *Biol Psychiatry*, vol. 58, pp. 245–253.

Beyerstein, B. L. 1990, 'Brainscams: Neuromythologies of the New Age', *International Journal of Mental Health*, vol. 19, no. 3, pp. 27–36.

Bloom, J. W. 2004, 'Patterns that Connect: Rethinking Our Approach to Learning, Teaching and Curriculum', *Curriculum and Teaching*, vol. 19, no. 1, pp. 5–26.

Bolstad, R. 2002, *Resolve: A New Model of Therapy* Crown House, Carmarthen.

Bostic St. Clair, C. & Grinder, J. 2001, *Whispering in the Wind* J & C Enterprises, Scotts Valley, CA.

Bretto, C., DeLozier, J., Grinder, J. & Topel, S. 1991, *Leaves Before the Wind* Grinder, DeLozier and Associates, Santa Cruz, California.

Brewerton, P. 2004, 'NLP and "Metaprogrammes"... Worthy of a Closer Look?', *Selection & Development Review*, vol. 20, no. 3, pp. 14–19.

Brion, M. 1995, 'The Supervision of NLP Therapists', *NLP World*, vol. 2, no. 2, pp. 41–55.

British Psychological Society 2007, *cdaq®: British Psychological Society Psychological Testing Centre Test Reviews*, British Psychological Society.

Brockbank, A. & McGill, I. 1998, *Facilitating Reflective Learning in Higher Education* Open University Press, Buckingham.

Brockman, J. 1977, *About Bateson* G. P. Dutton, New York.

Brown, D. 2007, *Tricks of the Mind* Channel 4 Books, London.

Brown, N. 2001, 'Meta Programme Patterns in Accounting Educators at a UK Business School', *Accounting Education*, vol. 11, no. 1, pp. 79–91.

Buckner, M. & Meara, N. M. 1987, 'Eye-movement as an Indicator of Sensory Components in Thought', *Journal of Counselling Psychology*, vol. 34, no. 3, pp. 283–287.

Cameron-Bandler, L., Gordon, D. & Lebeau, M. 1985, *The Emprint Method* Future Pace, San Rafael, CA.

Capra, F. 1996, *The Web of Life: A New Synthesis of Mind and Matter* Harper Collins, London.

Carnegie, D. 2006, *How to Win Friends and Influence People* Vermilion, London.

Castaneda, C. 1970, *The Teachings of Don Juan: A Yaqui Way of Knowledge* Penguin Books, Harmondsworth, Middlesex.

Cazden, C. B. 1988, *Classroom Discourse: The Language of Teaching and Learning* Heineman, Portsmouth, NH.

Chalmers, A. F. 1999, *What is this Thing Called Science?*, 3rd edn, Open University Press, Milton Keynes.

Charlton, N. G. 2008, *Understanding Gregory Bateson: Mind, Beauty, and the Sacred Earth* State University of New York Press, Albany, NY.

Charvet, S. R. 1997, *Words That Change Minds: Mastering the Language of Influence*, 2nd edn, Dubuque, Iowa, Kendall/Hunt.

Churches, R. & Terry, R. 2007, *NLP for Teachers* Crown House, Carmarthen.

Churches, R. & West-Burnham, J. 2008, *Leading Learning through Relationships: The Implications of Neuro-linguistic Programming for Personalisation and the Children's Agenda in England*, CfBT Educational Trust, Reading, Berkshire.

Clark, L. V. 1960, 'Effect of Mental Practice on the Development of a Certain Motor Skill', *Research Quarterly*, vol. 31, pp. 560–569.

Claxton, G. 2006, 'Expanding the Capacity to Learn: A New End for Education?', British Educational Research Association, Warwick University.

Covey, S. R. 1992, *The Seven Habits of Highly Effective People* Simon & Schuster, London.

Craft, A. 2001, 'Neuro-linguistic Programming and Learning Theory', *The Curriculum Journal*, vol. 12, no. 1, pp. 125–136.

Damasio, A. R. 2006, *Descartes' Error: Emotion, Reason and the Human Brain* Vintage Books, London.

Day, M. E. 1964, 'An Eye-movement Phenomenon Relating to Attention, Thought and Anxiety', *Perceptual and Motor Skills*, vol. 19, pp. 443–446.

Day, M. E. 1967, 'An Eye-movement Indicator of Type and Level of Anxiety', *Journal of Clinical Psychology*, vol. 5, pp. 146–149.

Day, T. R. 2008, *A Study of a Small-Scale Classroom Intervention That Uses an Adapted Neuro-Linguistic Programming (NLP) Modelling Approach*, PhD, Department of Education, University of Bath.

de Shazer, S. 1994, *Words were Originally Magic* W.W. Norton and Co., New York.

Deering, A., Dilts, R. & Russell, J. 2002, *Alpha Leadership: Tools for Business Leaders Who Want More from Life* John Wiley & Sons, Chichester.

DeLozier, J. 1995, 'Mastery, New Coding and Systemic NLP', *NLP World*, vol. 2, no. 1, pp. 5–19.

DeLozier, J. & Grinder, J. 1987, *Turtles All the Way Down: Prerequisites to Personal Genius* Grindler, DeLozier and Associates, Bonny Doon, CA.

Derks, L. 1995, 'Exploring the Social Panorama', *NLP World*, vol. 2, no. 3, pp. 28–42.

Derks, L. 2005, *Social Panoramas: Changing the Unconscious Landscape with NLP and Psychotherapy* Crown House, Carmarthen.

Dilts, R. 1983, *Roots of Neuro-Linguistic Programming* Meta Publications, Cupertino, California.

Dilts, R. & DeLozier, J. 2000, *Encyclopedia of Systemic NLP and NLP New Coding* Meta Publications, Capitola, California.

Dilts, R., Grinder, J., Bandler, R. & DeLozier, J. 1980, *Neuro-Linguistic Programming: Volume 1, the Study of the Structure of Subjective Experience* Meta Publications, California.

Dilts, R. B. 1994a, *Strategies of Genius: Volume I* Meta Publications, Capitola, California.

Dilts, R. B. 1994b, *Strategies of Genius: Volume II* Meta Publications, Capitola, CA.

Dilts, R. B. 1998, *Modeling with NLP* Meta Publications, Capitola, CA.

Dilts, R. B. 1999, *Sleight of Mouth: The Magic of Conversational Belief Change* Meta Publications, Capitola, CA.

Dilts, R. B. & Epstein, T. A. 1995, *Dynamic Learning* Meta Publications, California.

Dowlen, A. 1996, 'NLP – Help or Hype? Investigating the Use of Neuro-Linguistic Programming in Management Training', *Career Development International*, vol. 1, no. 1, pp. 27–34.

Drenth, P. J. 1999, 'Prometheus Chained: Social and Ethical Constraints on Psychology', *European Psychologist*, vol. 4, no. 4, pp. 233–239.

Driskell, J. E., Copper, C. & Moran, A. 1994, 'Does Mental Practice Enhance Performance?', *Journal of Applied Psychology*, vol. 79, no. 4, pp. 481–492.

Druckman, D. 2004, 'Be All That You Can Be: Enhancing Human Performance', *Journal of Applied Social Psychology*, vol. 34, no. 11, pp. 2234–2260.

Druckman, D. & Swets, J. A. 1988, *Enhancing Human Performance: Issues, Theories and Techniques* National Academy Press, Washington, DC.

Ehrlichman, H. & Weinberger, A. 1978, 'Lateral Eye Movements and Hemispheric Asymmetry: A Critical Review', *Psychological Bulletin*, vol. 85, pp. 1080–1101.

Einspruch, E. L. & Forman, B. D. 1985, 'Observations Concerning Research literature on Neuro-Linguistic Programming', *Journal of Counseling Psychology*, vol. 32, no. 4, pp. 589–596.

Eisner, D. A. 2000, *The Death of Psychotherapy: From Freud to Alien Abduction* Praeger, Westport, CT.

Elgin, S. H. 1989, *Success with the Gentle Art of Verbal Self-Defense* Prentice Hall, Englewood Cliffs, New Jersey.

Engeström, Y. 2001a, 'Expansive Learning at Work: Toward an Activity Theoretical Reconceptualization', *Journal of Education & Work*, vol. 14, no. 1, pp. 133–156.

Erickson, M. H. & Rossi, E. L. 1975, 'Varieties of Double Bind', *American Journal of Clinical Hypnosis*, vol. 17, pp. 143–157.

Esser, M. 2004, *La Programmation Neuro-Linguistique en Débat: Repères Cliniques, Scientifiques et Philosophiques* L'Harmattan, Paris.

Evans, J. S. 2008, 'Dual-Processing Accounts of Reasoning, Judgment, and Social Cognition', *Annual Review of Psychology*, vol. 59, no. 1, pp. 255–278.

Evans, V. & Green, M. 2006, *Cognitive Linguistics: An Introduction* Edinburgh University Press, Edinburgh.

Farrelly, F. & Brandsma, J. 1974, *Provocative Therapy* Meta Publications, Capitol, CA.

Fauconnier, G. 1997, *Mappings in Thought and Language* Cambridge University Press, Cambridge.

Faulkner, C. 1999, *Sub-modalities: An Inside View of Your Mind* NLP Comprehensive, Lakewood, Colorado.

Feltz, D. L. & Landers, D. M. 1983, 'The Effects of Mental Practice on Motor Skill Learning and Performance: A Meta-Analysis', *Journal of Sports Psychology*, vol. 5, no. 25, p. 57.

Feyerabend, P. 1993, *Against Method*, 3rd edn, Verso, London.

Fisher, J. D., Silver, R. C., Chinsky, J. M., Goff, B., Klar, Y. & Zagieboylo, C. 1989, 'Psychological Effects of Participation in a Large Group Awareness Training', *Journal of Consulting and Clinical Psychology*, vol. 57, no. 6, pp. 747–755.

Flemons, D. 1991, *Completing Distinctions* Shambhala, Boston.

Ford, J. 1976, *Paradigms and Fairy Tales: An Introduction to the Science of Meaning* Routledge & Kegan Paul, London.

Fox-Keller, E. 2000, *The Century of the Gene* Harvard University Press, Cambridge MA.

Frankl, V. 1965, *The Doctor of the Soul: From Psychotherapy to Logotherapy* Souvenir Press, London.

French, R. & Bazalgette, J. 1996, 'From "Learning Organization"' to '"Teaching-Learning Organization"?', *Management Learning*, vol. 27, no. 1, pp. 113–128.

Fromm, E. 1950, *Psychoanalysis and Religion* Yale University Press, New Haven, CT.

Fry, S. T. & Johnstone, M.-J. 2002, *Ethics in Nursing Practice*, Second edn, Blackwell, Oxford.

Gardner, M. 1957, *Fads and Fallacies: In the Name of Science* New York.

Glouberman, D. 1989, *Life Choices and Life Changes Through Imagework: The Art of Developing Personal Vision* Unwin Hyman, London.

Goldstone, R. L. & Barsalou, L. 1998, 'Reuniting Perception and Conception', *Cognition*, vol. 65, pp. 231–262.

Goldstone, R. L. & Kersten, A. 2003, 'Concepts and Categories', in *Comprehensive Handbook of Psychology Volume 4: Experimental Psychology*, A. Healy & R. W. Proctor, eds., John Wiley, New York, pp. 591–621.

Goleman, D. & Boyatzis, R. 2008, 'Social Intelligence and the Biology of Leadership', *Harvard Business Review*, vol. 86, no. 9, pp. 74–81.

Gordon, D. 1978, *Therapeutic Metaphors* Meta Publications, California.

Gordon, D. & Dawes, G. 2005, *Expanding Your World: Modelling the Structure of Experience* Desert Rain.

Grant, A. M. 2007, 'Reflections on Coaching Psychology', in *How Coaching Works: The Essential Guide to the History and Practice of Effective Coaching*, J. O'Connor & A. Lages, eds, A & C Black, London, pp. 209–214.

Grant, G. & Riesman, D. 1978, *The Perpetual Dream: Reform and Experiment in the American College* The University of Chicago Press, Chicago.

Greenburg, D. 1964, *How to be Jewish Mother* Price/Stern/Sloan, Los Angeles.

Gregory, J. 2008, *Facilitating Individual Change and Development*, University of Surrey, unpublished study guide.

Grimley, B. 2007, 'NLP Coaching', in *Handbook of Coaching Psychology: A Guide for Practitioners*, S. Palmer & A. Whybrow, eds., Routledge, London, pp. 193–210.

Grinder, J. & Bandler, R. 1976, *The Structure of Magic 2: A Book about Communication and Change* Science and Behaviour Books, Palo Alto.

Grinder, J. & Bandler, R. 1981, *Trance-formations: Neuro-Linguistic Programming and the Structure of Hypnosis* Real People Press, Moab, Utah.

Grinder, J., DeLozier, J. & Bandler, R. 1977, *Patterns of the Hypnotic Techniques of Milton H. Erickson, M.D. vol II* Meta Publications, Capitola, CA.

Grinder, J. & Elgin, S. 1973, *A Guide to Transformational Grammar* Holt, Rinehart and Winston, New York.

Grinder, J. T. 1971, *On Deletion Phenomena*, PhD, University of California, San Diego.

Grossman, M., Koenig, P., Kounios, J., McMillan, C., Work, M. & Moore, P. 2006, 'Category-specific Effects in Semantic Memory: Category-task Interactions Suggested by fMRI', *NeuroImage*, vol. 30, no. 3, pp. 1003–1009.

Haber, R. 2002, 'Virginia Satir: An Integrated Humanistic Approach', *Contemporary Family Therapy*, vol. 24, no. 1, pp. 23–34.

Haley, J. 1973, *Uncommon Therapy: The Psychiatric Techniques of Milton H. Erickson, M.D.* W.W. Norton & Co., New York.

Hall, C. 2001, 'In the Matter of Richard Bandler, Brahm von Hueme and Dominic Luzi, Plaintiffs, vs John Grinder and Carmen Bostic St. Clair, Christina Hall, Steve and Connirae Andreas, and Lara Ewing, Defendants', *NLP World*, vol. 8, no. 2, pp. 15–24.

Hall, L. M. 2000, *Meta-States: Self-reflexivity and the Higher States of Mind*, 2nd edn, Neuro-Semantics (E.T. Publications), Grand Junction, CO.

Hall, L. M. 2001, *The Bateson Report: Gregory Bateson's Foundational Contributions to NLP and Neuro-Semantics*, Neuro-Semantics Publications, Clifton, CO.

Halligan, D. & Oakley, D. A. 2000, 'Greatest Myth of All', *New Scientist*, vol. 168, pp. 35–49.

Hancox, J. & Bass, A. 1995a, 'Experimental Paradigms in Analysis of NLP', *NLP World*, vol. 2, no. 3, pp. 43–52.

Hancox, J. & Bass, A. 1995b, 'NLP and Academic Analysis', *Rapport* no. 29, pp. 38–40.

Harries-Jones, P. 1995, *A Recursive Vision: Ecological Understanding and Gregory Bateson* University of Toronto, Toronto.

Hawkins, P. 2004, 'A Centennial Tribute to Gregory Bateson 1904–1980 and His Influence on the Fields of Organizational Development and Action Research', *Action Research*, vol. 2, no. 4, pp. 409–423.

Hayes, P. 2006, *NLP Coaching* Open University Press, Maidenhead, Berkshire.

Heap, M. 1988, 'Neurolinguistic Programming – An Interim Verdict', in *Hypnosis: Current Clinical, Experimental and Forensic Practices*, M. Heap, ed., Croom Helm, London, pp. 268–280.

Helm, D. J. 1991, 'Neuro-Linguistic Programming: Gender and the Learning Modalities Create Inequalities in Learning: A Proposal to Reestablish Equality and Promote New Levels of Achievement in Education', *Journal of Instructional Psychology*, vol. 18, no. 3, pp. 167–169.

Henwood, S. & Lister, J. 2007, *NLP and Coaching for Healthcare Professionals* John Wiley & Sons, Chichester.

Heron, J. 1992, *Feeling and Personhood: Psychology in Another Key* Sage, London.

Hirst, W. 1988, *The Making of Cognitive Science: Essays in Honor of George A. Miller* Cambridge University Press, Cambridge.

Holl, H. G. 2007, 'Second Thoughts on Gregory Bateson and Alfred Korzybski', *Kybernetes*, vol. 36, no. 7/8, pp. 1047–1054.

Hollander, J. 1999, 'NLP and Science: Six Recommendations for a Better relationship', *NLP World*, vol. 6, no. 3, pp. 45–75.

Honey, P. & Mumford, A. 1992, *A Manual of Learning Styles* Peter Honey Publications, Maidenhead.

Hubbard, T. L. 2007, 'What is Mental Representation? And How Does It Relate to Consciousness?', *Journal of Consciousness Studies*, vol. 14, no. 1–2, pp. 37–61.

Hutchinson, G., Churches, R. & Vitae, D. 2007, *NCSL London Leadership Strategy, Consultant Leaders to Support Leadership Capacity in London's PRUs and EBD Schools: Impact Report*, CfBT Education Trust and the National College for School Leadership, Reading.

Ivanovas, G. 2007, 'Still Not Paradigmatic', *Kybernetes*, vol. 36, no. 7/8, pp. 847–851.

Jackson, P. Z. & McKergow, M. 2007, *The Solutions Focus: Making Coaching and Change Simple*, 2nd edn, Nicholas Brealey, London.

James, T. & Woodsmall, W. 1988, *Time Line Therapy and the Basis of Personality* Meta Publications, Cupertino, California.

Jamieson, G. 2007, *Hypnosis and Conscious States: The Cognitive Neuroscience Perspective* Oxford University Press, Oxford.

Jones, C., Shillito-Clarke, C., Syme, G., Hill, D., Casemore, R. & Murdin, L. 2000, *Questions of Ethics in Counselling and Therapy* Open University Press, Buckingham.

Jones, J. & Atfield, R. 2007, *Flying High: Some Leadership Lessons from the Fast Track Teaching Programme*, CfBT Education Trust, Reading.

Jung, C. G. 1985, *Dreams* Ark Paperbacks, London.

Karttunen, L. 1974, 'Presupposition and Linguistic Context', *Theoretical Linguistics*, vol. 1, pp. 181–194.

Kauppi, T., Toivonen, V.-M. & Murphey, T. 1995, 'You Don't Have To, But You Can: Observing Our Verbing', *NLP World*, vol. 2, no. 1, pp. 21–33.

Keeney, B. 1983, *Aesthetics of Change* Guilford Press, New York.

Kelly, G. 1991, *The Psychology of Personal Constructs, Volume One: Theory and Personality* Routledge, London.

Knight, S. 1995, 'NLP and the Learning Organization', *NLP World*, vol. 2, no. 2, pp. 5–9.

Knight, S. 2002, *NLP at Work: The Difference that Makes a Difference in Business* Nicholas Brealey Publishing, London.

Koppel, R. 1996, *The Intuitive Trader: Developing Your Inner Trading Wisdom* John Wiley & Sons, New York.

Korzybski, A. 1958, *Science and Sanity: An Introduction to Non-Aristotelian Systems and General Semantics*, 4th edn, The International Non-Aristotelian Library Publishing Company, the Institute of General Semantics (Distributors), Lakeville, Conn.

Laborde, G. Z. 1983, *Influencing with Integrity: Management Skills for Communication and Negotiation*, Syntony Publishing, Palo Alto, California.

Laborde, G. Z. 1988, *Fine Tune Your Brain: Next Steps to Influencing with Integrity* Syntony Publishing, Palo Alto, California.

Lakhani, D. 2008, *Subliminal Persuasion: Influencing and Marketing Secrets They Don't Want You to Know* John Wiley and Sons, Hoboken New Jersey.

Lakoff, G. 1987, *Women, Fire and Dangerous Things: What Categories Reveal About the Mind* University of Chicago Press, Chicago and London.

Lakoff, G. & Johnson, M. 1999, *Philosophy in the Flesh: The Embodied Mind and its Challenge to Western Thought* Basic Books, New York.

Lalich, J. & Langone, M. Characteristics Associated with Cultic Groups. The International Cultic Studies Association, 2006. Ref Type: Electronic Citation.

Lankton, S. 1980, *Practical Magic: A Translation of Basic Neuro-Linguistic Programming into Clinical Psychotherapy* Meta Publications, Capitola, CA.

Lawley, J. 1994, 'The Road to Recognition: NLP Psychotherapy and Counselling in Britain', *NLP World*, vol. 1, no. 2, pp. 43–48.

Lawley, J. & Tompkins, P. 2000, *Metaphors in Mind: Transformation Through Symbolic Modelling* The Developing Company Press, London.

Lee, M. 2003, 'On Codes of Ethics, The Individual and Performance', *Performance Improvement Quarterly*, vol. 16, no. 2, pp. 72–89.

Lewis, B. & Pucelik, F. 1990, *Magic of NLP Demystified* Metamorphous Press, Portland, Oregon.

Leynes, P. A., Grey, J. A. & Crawford, J. T. 2006, 'Event-Related Potential (ERP) Evidence for Sensory-based Action Memories', *International Journal of Psychophysiology*, vol. 62, no. 1, pp. 193–202.

Lieberman, M. D. 2007, 'Social Cognitive Neuroscience: A Review of Core Process', *Annual Review of Psychology*, vol. 58, pp. 259–289.

Lincoln, Y. & Guba, E. 1985, *Naturalistic Inquiry* Sage, Newbury Park, CA.

Linden, A. & Perutz, K. 2008, *Mindworks: An Introduction to NLP* Crown House, Carmarthen.

Linder-Pelz, S. & Hall, L. M. 2007, 'The Theoretical Roots of NLP-based Coaching', *The Coaching Psychologist*, vol. 3, no. 1, pp. 12–17.

Linder-Pelz, S. & Hall, L. M. 2008, 'Meta-coaching: A Methodology Grounded in Psychological Theory', *International Journal of Evidence Based Coaching and Mentoring*, vol. 6, no. 1, pp. 43–56.

Lipset, D. 1980, *Gregory Bateson: The Legacy of a Scientist* Prentice-Hall, London.

Logan, G. D., Taylor, S. E. & Etherton, J. L. 1996, 'Attention in the Acquisition and Expression of Automaticity', *Journal of Experimental Psychology, Learning, Memory and Cognition*, vol. 22, pp. 620–638.

Losada, I. 2001, *The Battersea Park Road to Enlightenment* Bloomsbury, London.

Malloy, T., Bostic St. Clair, C. & Grinder, J. 2005, 'Steps to an Ecology of Emergence', *Cybernetics and Human Knowing*, vol. 12, pp. 102–109.

Maslow, A. H. 1987, *Motivation and Personality* Harper & Row, New York.

Mathison, J. 2003, *The Inner Life of Words: An Investigation into Language in Learning and Teaching*, PhD Thesis, University of Surrey.

Mathison, J. & Tosey, P. 2008, 'Riding into Transformative Learning', *Journal of Consciousness Studies*, vol. 15, no. 2, pp. 67–88.

Maturana, H. R. & Poerkson, B. 2004, *From Being to Doing: The Origins of the Biology of Cognition* Carl Auer Verlag, Heidelberg.

Mauk, M. D. & Buonoman, D. V. 2004, 'The Neural Basis of Temporal Processing', *Annual Review of Neuroscience*, vol. 27, pp. 307–340.

McCue, P. A. 1988, 'Milton H. Erickson: A Critical Perspective', in *Hypnosis: Current Clinical, Experimental and Forensic Practices*, pp. 257–267.

McDermott, I. & Jago, W. 2001, *Brief NLP Therapy* Sage, London.

McDermott, I. & Jago, W. 2002, *The NLP Coach: A Comprehensive Guide to Personal Well-being and Professional Success* Piatkus, London.

McDermott, I. & O'Connor, J. 1996, 'On "The Prisoner's Dilemma"', *NLP World*, vol. 3, no. 1, pp. 54–59.

McGee, M. 2005, *Self-Help, Inc.: Makeover Culture in American Life* Oxford University Press, New York.

McGoldrick, J., Stewart, J. & Watson, S. 2002, *Understanding Human Resource Development: A Research-based Approach* Routledge, London.

McKenna, P. 2006, *Instant Confidence: The Power to Go for Anything You Want* Bantam Press, London.

McKergow, M. 2000, 'NLP, Science and Intersubjectivity', *NLP World*, vol. 7, no. 1, pp. 51–60.

McKergow, M. & Clarke, J. 1995, 'Occam's Razor in the NLP Toolbox', *NLP World*, vol. 3, no. 3, pp. 47–56.

McLendon, T. L. 1989, *The Wild Days: NLP 1972–1981* Meta Publications, Cupertino, CA.

McLeod, A. 2003, *Performance Coaching: The Handbook for Managers, HR Professionals and Coaches* Crown House, Carmarthen.

McMaster, M. & Grinder, J. 1980, *Precision: A New Approach to Communication* Precision Models, Bonny Doon, CA.

McNab, P. 2005, *Towards an Integral Vision: Using NLP and Ken Wilber's AQAL Model to Enhance Communication* Trafford, Victoria BC.

McWhinney, W. 1997, *Paths of Change: Strategic Choices for Organizations and Society*, Revised edn, Sage, Thousand Oaks, CA.

McWhinney, W. & Markos, L. 2003, 'Transformative Education: Across the Threshold', *Journal of Transformative Education*, vol. 1, no. 1, pp. 16–37.

Megginson, D. & Clutterbuck, D. 2005, *Techniques for Coaching and Mentoring* Elsevier Butterwoth-Heinemann, Oxford.

Mehrabian, A. 1981, *Silent Messages: Implicit Communication of Emotions and Attitudes* Wadsworth, Belmont, CA.

Merlevede, P. 2000, 'The Story of David', *NLP World*, vol. 7, no. 1, pp. 61–64.

Mezirow, J. 1991, *Transformative Dimensions of Adult Learning* Jossey-Bass, San Francisco.

Miller, C. 2005, 'Valid and Reliable: Reflections on NLP and Research', *Resource* no. Winter, pp. 19–23.

Miller, E. 1993, *From Dependency to Autonomy: Studies in Organisation and Change* Free Association Books, London.

Miller, G. A. 1956, 'The Magical Number Seven, Plus or Minus Two: Some Limits on Our Capacity for Processing Information', *The Psychological Review*, vol. 63, pp. 81–97.

Miller, G. A. 1970, *The Psychology of Communication: Seven Essays* Pelican, London.

Miller, G. A., Galanter, E. & Pribram, K. 1960, *Plans and the Structure of Behaviour* Holt, Rinehart and Winston, New York.

Molden, D. 2001, *NLP Business Masterclass* FT/Prentice Hall, London.

Molden, D. 2003, *Managing with the Power of NLP: Neuro-Linguistic Programming for Personal Competitive Advantage*, Revised edn, FT/Prentice Hall, Harlow.

Montagnini, L. 2007, 'Looking for "Scientific" Social Science', *Kybernetes*, vol. 36, no. 7/8, pp. 1012–1021.

Morgan, G. 2006, *Images of Organization*, 4th edn, Sage, London.

Nisbett, R. & Ross, L. 1980, *Human Inference: Strategies and Shortcomings of Social Judgement* Englewood Cliffs, NJ, Prentice-Hall.

Norman, D. A. & Shallice, T. 1986, 'Attention to Action: Willed and Automatic Control of Behaviour', in *Consciousness and Self-Regulation: advances in research and theory, 4*, R. J. Davidson, G. E. Swartz & D. Shapiro, eds, Plenum, New York, pp. 1–18.

O'Connor, J. & Lages, A. 2004, *Coaching with NLP* Element Books, London.

O'Connor, J. & McDermott, I. 1996, *Principles of NLP* Thorsons, London.

O'Connor, J. & McDermott, I. The Proof is in the Using. Rapport Winter [Special issue], 50–51. 2003. Ref Type: Magazine Article.

O'Connor, J. & Seymour, J. 1990, *Introducing Neuro-Linguistic Programming: The New Psychology of Excellence* Mandala, London.

O'Hanlon, W. & Wilk, J. 1987, *Shifting Contexts: The Generation of Effective psychotherapy* The Guilford Press, New York.

Peale, N. V. 1998, *The Power of Positive Thinking* Vermilion, London.

Pecher, D., Zeelenberg, R. & Barsalou, L. 2004, 'Sensorimotor Simulations Underlie Conceptual Representatioins: Modality-specific Effects of Prior Activation', *Psychonomic Bulletin and Review*, vol. 11, no. 1, pp. 164–167.

Perls, F. 1969, *Gestalt Therapy Verbatim* Real People Press, Moab, Utah.

Perls, F. 1973, *The Gestalt Approach & Eyewitness to Therapy* Science and Behavior Books, Palo Alto.

Peters, T. & Waterman, R. 1982, *In Search of Excellence* Harper & Row, New York.

Peterson, T. E. 1999, 'Whitehead, Bateson and Readings and the Predicates of Education', *Educational Philosophy and Theory*, vol. 31, no. 1, pp. 27–41.

Platt, G. NLP – No Longer Plausible? Training Journal, 2001. Ref Type: Magazine Article.

Ponting, C. 2006, *An Exploratory Study into the Use of NLP in Business,* MBA, University of Surrey.

Postle, D. 2007, *Regulating the Psychological Therapies: From Taxonomy to Taxidermy* PCCS Books, Ross-on-Wye.

Quinlan, P. & Dyson, B. 2008, *Cognitive Psychology* Pearson Education Ltd, London.

Ray, W. A. & Govener, M. R. 2007, 'Legacy: Lessons from the Bateson Team Meetings', *Kybernetes*, vol. 36, no. 7/8, pp. 1026–1036.

Richardson, D. C., Spivey, M. J., Barsalou, L. & McRae, K. 2003, 'Spatial Activation during Real Time Comprehension of Verbs', *Cognitive Science*, vol. 27, pp. 767–780.

Rieber, R. W. 1989, *The Individual, Communication and Society: Essays in Memory of Gregory Bateson* Cambridge University Press, Cambridge.

Rizzolatti, G. & Craighero, L. 2004, 'The Mirror Neuron System', *Annual Review of Neuroscience*, vol. 27, pp. 169–192.

Rizzolatti, G., Fogassi, L. & Gallese, V. 2001, 'Neurophysiological Mechanisms Underlying the Understanding and Imitation of Action', *Nature Reviews: Neuroscience*, vol. 2, pp. 661–670.

Roach, D. W. & Bednar, D. A. 1997, 'The Theory of Logical Types: A Tool for Understanding Levels and Types of Change in Organizations', *Human Relations*, vol. 50, pp. 671–699.

Robbins, T. 1988, *Cults, Converts and Charisma: The Sociology of New Religious Movements* Sage, London.

Robertson, J. E. 1989, *Sales, the Mind's Side: What They Didn't Teach You in Sales Training* Metamorphous Press, Portland, Oregon.

Rosen, S. 1982, *My Voice Will Go With You: The Teaching Tales of Milton H. Erickson* W.W. Norton & Co., New York.

Rowan, J. 2001, *Ordinary Ecstasy*, 3rd edn, Brunner-Routledge, London.

Rowan, J. 2008, 'NLP is Not Based on Constructivism', *The Coaching Psychologist*, vol. 4, no. 3, pp. 160–163.

Rowson, R. 2006, *Working Ethics: How to be Fair in a Culturally Complex World* Jessica Kingsley, London.

Ruesch, J. & Bateson, G. 1951, *Communication: The Social Matrix of Society* W.W. Norton & Co., New York.

Sandhu, D. S. 1994, 'Suggestopedia and Neurolinguistic Programming: Introduction to Whole Brain Teaching and Psychotherapy', *Journal of Accelerative Learning and Teaching*, vol. 19, no. 3, pp. 241–256.

Satir, V. 1978, *Peoplemaking* London, Souvenir Press.

Schütz, P. 1994, 'NLP Training in Austria', *NLP World*, vol. 1, no. 2, pp. 49–52.

Seligman, M. E. P. 1995, 'The Effectiveness of Psychotherapy: The Consumer Reports Study', *American Psychologist*, vol. 50, no. 12, pp. 965–974.

Sharpley, C. F. 1987, 'Research Findings on Neurolinguistic Programming: Nonsupportive Data or an Untestable Theory?', *Journal of Counseling Psychology*, vol. 34, no. 1, pp. 103–107.

Silverman, D. 1975, *Reading Castaneda: A Prologue to the Social Sciences* Routledge & Kegan Paul, London.

Slater, M. & Usoh, M. 1994, 'NLP and Virtual Reality', *NLP World*, vol. 1, no. 2, pp. 23–32.

Spechler, J. W. 1991, *When America Does It Right: Case Studies in Service Quality* Industrial Engineering and Management Press, Norcross, Georgia.

Spechler, J. W. 1995, 'The Process of Modelling Excellence in Business', *NLP World*, vol. 2, no. 2, pp. 17–22.

Spence, M. Expanding the Parameters of Possibility. Rapport Autumn [9], 14–16. 2007. Ref Type: Magazine Article.

Spitzer, R. 1992, 'Virginia Satir and the Origins of NLP', *Anchor Point*, vol. 6, no. 7.

Stanovich, K. E. & West, R. F. 2000, 'Individual Differences in Reasoning: Implications for the Rationality Debate', *Behavioral and Brain Sciences*, vol. 23, pp. 645–665.

Sullivan, W. & Rees, J. 2008, *Clean Language: Revealing Metaphors and Opening Minds* Crown House Publishing House, Carmarthen, Wales.

Tart, C. 1990, *Altered States of Consciousness*, 3rd edn, HarperCollins, New York.

Tettamanti, M., Buccino, M., Saccuman, M. C., Gallese, V., Danna, M., Scifo, P., Fazio, F., Rizzolatti, G., Cappa, S. & Perani, D. 2005, 'Listening to Action-related Sentences Activates Fronto-parietal Motor Circuits', *Journal of Cognitive Neuroscience*, vol. 17, no. 2, pp. 273–281.

Thompson, J. E., Courtney, L. & Dickson, D. 2002, 'The Effect of Neuro-Linguistic Programming on Organizational and Individual Performance: A Case Study', *Journal of European Industrial Training*, vol. 26, no. 6, pp. 292–298.

Tolman, E. C. 1948, 'Cognitive Maps in Mice and Men', *Psychological Review*, vol. 55, pp. 189–208.

Tosey, P. & Mathison, J. 2003, 'Neuro-linguistic Programming and Learning Theory: A Response', *The Curriculum Journal*, vol. 14, no. 3, pp. 361–378.

Tosey, P. & Mathison, J. 2007, 'Fabulous Creatures of HRD: A Critical Natural History of Neuro-Linguistic Programming', Eighth International Conference on HRD Research and Practice Across Europe, Oxford.

Tosey, P. & Mathison, J. 2008, 'Do Organisations Learn? Some Implications for HRD of Bateson's Levels of Learning', *Human Resource Development Review*, vol. 7, no. 1, pp. 13–31.

Varela, F. J., Thompson, E. & Rosch, E. 1993, *The Embodied Mind: Cognitive Science and Human Experience* The MIT Press, Cambridge, Massachusetts.

Vermersch, P. 1994, *L'entretien d'explicitation* EDF Editeur, Issy les-Moulineaux.

Visser, M. 2003, 'Gregory Bateson on Deutero-learning and Double Bind: A Brief Conceptual History', *Journal of History of the Behavioural Sciences*, vol. 39, no. 3, pp. 269–278.

von Bergen, C. W., Soper, B., Rosenthal, G. T. & Wilkinson, L. V. 1997, 'Selected Alternative Training Techniques in HRD', *Human Resource Development Quarterly*, vol. 8, no. 4, pp. 281–294.

Von Foerster, H. & Poerksen, B. 2002, *Understanding Systems, Conversation on Epistemology and Ethics* IFSR International Series on Systems Science and Engineering Volume 17, Kluwer Academic/Plenum Publishers, New York.

Wake, L. 2008, *Neurolinguistic Psychotherapy: A Postmodern Perspective* Routledge, London.

Walker, W. 1996, *Abenteuer Kommunikation: Bateson, Perls, Satir, Erickson und die Anfange des Neurolinguistischen Programmierens (NLP)*, 4th edn, Klett-Cotta, Stuttgart.

Wampold, B. E. 2001, *The Great Psychotherapy Debate: Models, Methods and Findings* Lawrence Erlbaum Associates, Mahwah, New Jersey.

Washburn, H. & Wallace, K. 1999, *Why People Don't Buy Things* Basic Books, New York.

Watzlawick, P. 1976, *How Real is Real? Confusion, Disinformation, Communication* Random House, New York.

Watzlawick, P. 1978, *The Language of Change* W.W. Norton & Co., New York.

Watzlawick, P. 1990, *Münchhausen's Pigtail: Or Psychotherapy and 'Reality'* W.W. Norton & Company, New York.

Watzlawick, P., Beavin, J. H. & Jackson, D. D. 1967, *Pragmatics of Human Communication* W.W. Norton & Co., New York.

Watzlawick, P., Weakland, J. & Fisch, R. 1974, *Change: Principles of Problem Formation and Problem Resolution* W.W. Norton & Co., New York.

Weick, K. E. 1994, 'Cartographic Myths in Organisations', in *New Thinking in Organisational Behaviour*, H. Tsoukas, ed., Butterworth-Heinemann, Oxford, pp. 211–220.

Weick, K. E. 2001, *Making Sense of the Organization* Blackwell, Malden, Mass.

Westley, F. 1983, *The Complex Forms of the Religious Life: A Durkheimian View of New Religious Movements* Scholars, Chico, CA.

Wiener, N. 1965, *Cybernetics, or Control and Communication in the Animal and the Machine*, 2nd edn, MIT Press, Cambridge, Massachusetts.

Wijnhoven, F. 2001, 'Acquiring Organizational Learning Norms: A Contingency Approach for Understanding Deutero Learning', *Management Learning*, vol. 32, no. 2, pp. 181–200.

Willig, C. 1999, *Applied Discourse Analysis* Open University Press, Buckingham.

Wilson, J. P. 2005, *Human Resource Development: Learning and Training for Individuals & Organizations*, 2nd edn, Kogan Page, London.

Yardley, G. 1995, *Business Confidence: Unleash the Power of Your Personal Space* Times Books International, Singapore.

Yates, F. 1992, *The Art of Memory*, 2nd edn, Pimlico, London.

Yemm, G. 2006, 'Can NLP Help or Harm Your Business?', *Industrial & Commercial Training*, vol. 38, no. 1, pp. 12–17.

Yokoyama, S., Miyamoto, T., Riera, J., Kim, J., Akitsuki, Y., Iwata, K., Yoshimoto, K., Horie, K., Sato, S. & Kawashima, R. 2006, 'Cortical Mechanisms Involved in the Processing of Verbs: An fMRI Study', *Journal of Cognitive Neuroscience*, vol. 18, no. 8, pp. 1304–1313.

Young, P. 2004, *Understanding NLP: Principles and Practice* Crown House Publishing, Carmarthen UK.

Zarro, R. & Blum, P. 1989, *The Phone Book: Breakthrough Neurolinguistic Phone Skills for Profit and Enlightenment* Metamorphous Press, Portland, Oregon.

Ziman, J. 2000, *Real Science: What It Is and What It Means* Cambridge University Press, Cambridge.

Index